The Dawn of
Guerrilla Warfare

The Dawn of Guerrilla Warfare

Why the Tactics of Insurgents against Napoleon Failed in the US-Mexican War

Benjamin J Swenson

Pen & Sword
MILITARY

First published in Great Britain in 2023 by
Pen & Sword Military
An imprint of Pen & Sword Books Limited
Yorkshire – Philadelphia

ISBN 978 1 39905 369 3

A CIP catalogue record for this book is
available from the British Library

Typeset by Mac Style
Printed in the UK by CPI Group (UK) Ltd, Croydon, CR0 4YY.

Pen & Sword Books Limited incorporates the imprints of After
the Battle, Atlas, Archaeology, Aviation, Discovery, Family History,
Fiction, History, Maritime, Military, Military Classics, Politics,
Select, Transport, True Crime, Air World, Frontline Publishing, Leo
Cooper, Remember When, Seaforth Publishing, The Praetorian Press,
Wharncliffe Local History, Wharncliffe Transport, Wharncliffe True
Crime and White Owl.

For a complete list of Pen & Sword titles please contact

PEN & SWORD BOOKS LIMITED
47 Church Street, Barnsley, South Yorkshire, S70 2AS, England
E-mail: enquiries@pen-and-sword.co.uk
Website: www.pen-and-sword.co.uk
or
PEN AND SWORD BOOKS
1950 Lawrence Rd, Havertown, PA 19083, USA
E-mail: Uspen-and-sword@casematepublishers.com
Website: www.penandswordbooks.com

*Dedicated to brothers Phillip and James Kaylor of
Costa Mesa (Goat Hill), California*

Contents

Acknowledgements

I would like to thank the following people for their help and support: Timothy Johnson of Lipscomb University for his inspiring work on Winfield Scott, Carlos Forcadell, at Zaragoza's Institución Fernando el Católico, John L. Tone at Georgia Tech, Linda Arnold, formerly at Virginia Tech, Geoffrey Jensen at the Virginia Military Institute, William Fowler at the University of St Andrews, Irving W. Levinson at the University of Texas Rio Grande Valley, the archivists at University of Texas Austin, Pedro Santoni at California State University, Anthony J. Gray, United States Armed Forces (Korea) Chief Service Division, and Timothy Dowling at *The Journal of Military History*. I am especially indebted to the *caballeros* at Pompeu Fabra University: Josep Maria Fradera, Jorge Luengo, Albert Garcia Balaña, and most importantly, my doctoral adviser Stephen Jacobson. Lastly, I wish to thank my dear wife for giving me the time.

Introduction

Before the System: Guerrilla Warfare Prior to 1808

In the summer of 1847 at the height of the Mexican-American War the *Sunbury Gazette* published an article, 'The Guerrilla System in Spain and Mexico'. The editors pointed out that US Army supply trains moving from Veracruz to Jalapa were suffering attacks like those that plagued the French Army during the Napoleonic War in Spain (1808–1814). The *Sunbury Gazette*, a Pennsylvanian newspaper for a town with a little more than a thousand people, commented that it hoped General Winfield Scott, the commander of the campaign to seize the Mexican capital, would 'resort to prompt and efficient means to arrest this inhuman warfare'. What exactly those means entailed was an open question, and that speculation prompted a comparison to the war in Spain and French general Jean-de-Dieu Soult's policy of executing captured Spanish guerrillas. 'When the system of guerrillas was resorted to in Spain,' the *Gazette* opined, 'it became for a while a source of great annoyance to the French, and was only arrested by the somewhat cruel but decisive retribution visited upon the assassinating foe by Soult.'[1] The article linking the Mexican War to the Spanish conflict shows the use of insurgent warfare was on the minds of Americans. In essence, the defeat of Napoleon Bonaparte in Spain by a formidable insurgency provided a contextual background against which both pro- and anti-war Americans viewed the conflict. For Mexicans, the guerrilla movement in Spain also served as an imitative model to adopt to defeat the American invaders.

Although it may be surprising to the contemporary reader that small-town Americans were familiar with the details of a war occurring a generation before on the opposite side of the Atlantic, the *Sunbury Gazette* article was one of thousands of such pieces in the late 1840s comparing the two wars. To the editors of the Sunbury town newspaper, Soult's actions against the guerrillas posed a comparable dilemma to the situation facing a US Army deep in the heart of Mexico. The article went on to explain that Soult 'resolved, in his proclamation dated the 9th of May 1810, to treat the members of the guerrillas not as regular soldiers, but as banditti ... and thus execute such of them as chanced to be made prisoners.' The information relayed to the people of Sunbury on the guerrilla war in Spain during a critical phase of the US invasion of Mexico was detailed. Not only were the *Sunbury Gazette*'s writers aware of French counter-insurgency efforts, but they knew of the ensuing escalation of violence when Spanish guerrilla leaders such as El Empecinado retaliated:

> The Spaniards replied that if this were done they would execute three Frenchmen for every one of their fellows who should suffer in consequence of Soult's proclamation. These threats were fulfilled on both sides; and when on one occasion a French gentleman took eight guerrillas of Empecinado, and crucified them by nailing their bodies to trees, the same number of Frenchmen were nailed to the same trees by the Spaniards, leaving them to fill the forest of Guadarama with their groans. Thus it soon became the interest of both parties to recur to the ordinary acts of war.[2]

The larger point of the 19 July 1847 article was to remind Pennsylvanians of the disaster that befell the French Army a generation earlier, and that the unrestrained executions of captured Spanish insurgents had resulted in more bloodletting – which contributed to the degeneration of the war from its 'ordinary acts'. At the height of the war in Mexico in 1847, similar pleas by war sceptics were common. 'It was, in truth, a kind of guerrilla struggle which exhausted the prodigious power and energies of the British in America', New York's *Evening Post* declared, 'and which in later times resisted Napoleon in Spain, and finally rid the peninsula of the French.' One defiant Mexican editorial commented that the 'system of guerrillas' was 'by no means new to Mexico', and that the Mexicans would adopt the same mode of warfare that exhausted the French during their retreat from Russia in 1812. The editorial added, 'Spain also adopted this system, and the war of the Spanish Americas was a war of guerrillas.' Pro-war newspapers invoked the Spanish war from an equally contentious but opposite perspective. Some were critical of the Mexican ability to resist, noting that that country's 'distant provinces are not organized' for guerrilla warfare. Many adopted the same position British historians used to detract from the efficacy of the Spanish insurgents and argued that the war in Mexico would be different: 'All of the guerrillas of Spain would not have driven the French out of that country had the central movement not been directed and *fought* by the Englishmen, under the Duke of Wellington.' In sum, pro-war Americans believed the Mexicans could never fight like the Spanish fought against the French and compared the intensity of the two wars to argue their points.[3]

Why did observers in the 1840s call guerrilla warfare a *system*? Although the term *guerrilla* derives from the Peninsular War, the usage of the word *system* associated with that form of warfare predates the Napoleonic Wars. The British were perhaps the first to refer to the irregular *system* of warfare the Americans employed to contest military occupation during the Revolutionary War (1775–1783), but the Americans did not use the term.[4] During the French Civil War in the Vendée (1793–1796) the term *military system* was used to describe the success of counter-insurgency operations and the tactical efficacy of forming troops '*en masse*' to stamp out insurrection – noting that this strategy had previously 'succeeded against the Piedmontese, and against the Spaniards'.[5] Likewise, during the period preceding the Napoleonic Wars the word *insurgent* more commonly entered the English lexicon – arising from both conflicts but gaining more currency after the Vendée from translations of French sources on that conflict. Other contexts in which *insurgent* was used in the late eighteenth century included the Haitian Revolution beginning in 1791, French-occupied Belgium in 1794, and the Irish republican rebellions beginning in 1798. Although *system* came into usage more abruptly during the war in Spain, the adoption and increasing use of new nomenclature to describe irregular warfare coincided with an increasing use of that mode of fighting among insurrectionist populations prior to 1808 – the year the Spanish War began.[6]

During the years between the Peninsular War in Spain and the Mexican-American War, the word *system* became more common. In 1816 Winfield Scott wrote to Secretary of State James Monroe from Liverpool that he was readying himself to escort to the United States a cadre of Spanish revolutionary 'patriots' who had fled Spain. Among them was Javier Mina, a prominent insurgent leader captured by the French in Spain in 1810. Scott wrote that the seasoned insurgent fighters, whose final destination was revolutionary Mexico, would 'constitute an important acquisition to the patriots, particularly Gen'l M. who was the author of the *guirrella* [*sic*] system in the peninsula war.'[7] In the later 1810s and early 1820s, the term 'guerrilla system' or 'system of guerrillas' was used in British and American newspapers to retrospectively describe the Peninsular War, the Latin American revolutions (particularly the Mexican Revolution), and the violence occurring in Spain during the Trienio Liberal (1820–1823).[8] In his Peninsular War memoirs published in 1829, French general Gabriel Suchet called it a 'lawless system of warfare'. The following year, the most acclaimed British general of that conflict, the Duke of Wellington, published his *Military Memoirs* and used the term 'The Guerilla System' (with one 'r'), which furthered the association of the word *system* with guerrilla warfare in the early decades of the nineteenth century.[9]

Changes in warfare prompted the shift in language. The arrival of Spanish-guerrilla warfare was a catalyst for change because it forced military tacticians to accommodate a new strategic reality and adjust the laws governing the conduct of invading armies. In other words, guerrilla warfare upended both the established tactical and legal precepts of war. This sweeping change in conducting warfare and mitigating insurgency during military invasion is best illustrated by examining the connections between Napoleon's failed war in Spain, the tactics used by guerrillas in that conflict, and American success in the Mexican-American War. In the 1840s, the Mexicans tried to duplicate what the Spanish did to the French. However, due to infighting, and because the Americans learned from the French mistake of seizing too much territory, the US Army was able to avoid a prolonged guerrilla war. As a result of minimizing the conflict and effecting a treaty, the Americans were able to annex large portions of northern Mexico that include present-day California, Arizona, New Mexico, Utah, Colorado and Nevada. However, the United States did not annex the entirety of Mexico, or its heavily populated regions as pro-war proponents advocated. The debate over that decision, abruptly stymied by the unexpected arrival of a treaty of peace in Washington DC in early 1848, was informed to a great degree by the strategic mistakes made by Napoleon and the perils of imperial overreach. The Mexican War therefore marks a crucial shift in conventional ways of war – an adaptation to the emergence of guerrilla warfare as a viable option for resisting invasion. This arc of tactical and legal evolution in military strategy stretches from the late eighteenth century and culminates in the mid-nineteenth. To understand how the unveiling of modern guerrilla warfare took place, we must first look to eighteenth-century revolutionary America.

The 'Irregular' American Revolution and Laws of War

On 4 December 1778, at the height of the American Revolution, Sir Grey Cooper rose in the British House of Commons and declared that 'Americans were no longer to be treated as Americans – but as Frenchmen'. His point was that Americans, who were considered insurrectionary rebels by the British government, should be deemed enemies in the same way as the French who were actively supporting their cause. Cooper quoted the sixteenth- and seventeenth-century legal scholar Hugo Grotius 'to prove that burning of towns that were nurturies of soldiers or arsenals, or magazines of military stores, was perfectly consistent with the principles of civilized war'.[10] Cooper's speech not only touched on the legal distinction drawn by the British in waging war against insurgents, it justified a harsh counter-insurgency campaign against a colonial population supporting independence by using the precepts of a scholar of the laws of war. The 'new system of war,' as Mr Cooke pointed out moments before Sir Grey Cooper spoke, exasperated the British:

> Mr Cooke expressed his indignation at finding that a new system of war was likely to be pursued in America … He could not think that the planners of such a system could have attended for a moment to the rules of policy and self-preservation. If a new mode of war was to be introduced, reprisals and retaliation ought naturally to be expected.[11]

While the Continental Army periodically engaged the British in pitched battles, many of the colonial fighters believed attrition was a more effective long-term strategy. Because of this, much of the revolutionary army, including members of state militias, engaged in guerrilla warfare. As early as 1775, Anglo-Irish parliamentarian Temple Luttrell could see the direction the war was heading when he spoke in the House of Commons about the 'social war' unfolding in the American colonies. 'I therefore presume your colonies are no longer treated as rebels,' Cooper jested, and 'will be entitled to the fame of military honours, to the same clemency and of grace that are usually practised, according to the modern system of war, by every civilized nation in the world.'[12]

Clemency was often not extended to American prisoners because the British considered them traitors and rebels. At the time the word *guerrilla* did not exist, but the issue of what to do with captured insurgents employing an illegal form of warfare confronted the British just as it later frustrated the French in Spain. Nor did the British recognize the legitimacy of the Continental Congress, which put captured regular colonial soldiers in legal limbo. In 1781, the Duke of Richmond submitted a petition to the House of Lords on behalf of American prisoners of war at Forton Prison near the English port and naval base of Portsmouth, to ask 'whether those unhappy sufferers were detained and treated as rebels, or as prisoners of war. If they were detained as rebels, then they were entitled to be treated as prisoners of state.' On the other hand, 'if they were detained as prisoners of war, their pretensions to just and generous treatment were settled and established by the laws of nations.'[13]

Ultimately the combination of attrition and conventional battles wore down the occupiers, just as Spain's royalist forces in Latin America succumbed to the grinding effect of guerrilla warfare. Unlike the revolts in Spanish America, for a long time the American Revolutionary War was not considered a guerrilla war. In retrospect, the majority of wars of independence in the Americas – including the American Revolutionary War – employed elements of guerrilla warfare.[14] Most of these conflicts, including the later success of US forces in

Mexico, rested on the ability of the invading army to support itself along a vital logistics corridor. As will be examined, logistics also proved important to the outcome of the Peninsular War. In the waning days of the Revolutionary War, Prime Minister Lord Shelburne was not only forced to sue for peace, but reluctantly recognized the tactical efficacy of insurgent methods. 'Enough mischief has been done already by the fatal system of war in America,' he told the House of Lords in 1782, and he 'hoped never to see the day when that system should again be pursued.'[15] However, the system was coming of age.

Ten years after the end of the American Revolution, the *Evening Mail* of London was still citing Grotius and Vattel to navigate the complicated legal questions that arose during the war concerning British treatment of American subjects declaring themselves citizens of a new republic. 'Vattel, in his Treatise on the Laws of Nations, lays it down …' the article declared, while speculating that 'whether the Americans will submit to disquisitions on the Laws of Nations, is yet in the womb of time.'[16] The question posed by the *Evening Mail* was rhetorical. Astute British statesmen knew that American colonial jurisprudence had modelled itself on English law long before independence, and most of the same conventions and rules for proper conduct during wartime had been assumed by the Second Continental Congress in 1775. One of the reasons Vattel and Grotius were considered authorities during the Napoleonic Wars was that both scholars addressed the law of the sea – essential to Europeans (and the British particularly) given that Napoleon was focused on restricting British trade with the continent. Both scholars addressed the rights of neutral states, which played a large role in diplomatic and commercial activity. Other standards and norms of conduct relating to war, including basic assumptions of decorum, etiquette and humanity, were commonly held among officers, statesmen and monarchies, and simply passed down from one generation to the next. Many of those standards and norms were unwritten, but the Americans generally adopted long-held English conventions of warfare.

Nevertheless, international law in the late eighteenth century was a work in progress. Vattel's deliberations in his 1758 *The Law of Nations* were far from specific, limited to those areas deemed *civilized* and contingent on mutual recognition by states. Vattel wrote that if 'a custom or usage is generally established, either between all the civilized nations of the world, or only between those of a certain continent, as of Europe', then those states 'are considered as having given their consent to it, and are bound to observe it towards each other.' The language Vattel used to outline binding international law was far from absolute. Nor did he address guerrilla warfare, because it did not officially exist. In the absence of the *system*, as guerrilla warfare was initially called in its gradual unveiling, *regular war* was the term most often used to address the subject of *irregular* warfare. By examining existing conventions prior to the conflict in Spain, it is easier to understand how Europeans within the civilized (rules-based) domain considered irregular warfare. One important example in which Vattel built on Grotius's ideas was the principle of *just war* – a theory of international law governing warfare commonly invoked by the Spanish guerrillas after the war began in 1808. 'The end of a just war is to avenge or prevent injury,' Vattel claimed, while drawing the limits of whatever action that entailed to the 'tribunal of conscience'. The theory was malleable enough for any state to justify acting in self-defence, and Vattel wrote that when 'we have declared war we have a right to do against our enemy whatever we find necessary for the attainment of that end.' Some conventions existed within that vague definition. For example, in times of regular war executing prisoners was considered forbidden. Vattel asserted there were 'limits of that right. On an enemy's submitting and laying down his arms, we cannot with justice take away his life.' From a legal standpoint the issue appeared simple. 'Thus, in battle, quarter is to be given to those who lay down their arms; and, in a siege, a garrison offering to capitulate are never to be refused their lives.'[17]

Akin to Vattel's suggestion of avoiding unnecessary violence against civilians was a plea for 'moderation' when pillaging and ravaging enemy country. If an unnecessary military action was directed towards the property of the enemy, then that action would usually result in 'increasing animosity' – which ultimately made peace more difficult to achieve. According to Vattel, this 'detestable' approach – often deemed 'scorched-earth' warfare – although not ideal, was nonetheless legal if the aggressor had some military justification for it beyond simply punishing the enemy population or reducing their ability to fight by destroying resources. Vattel wrote, 'The pillaging of a country, or ravaging of it, is not, in a general view of the matter, a violation of the laws of war.' However, he issued a caveat to that rule by explaining that 'pillage and destruction of towns, the devastation of the open country, ravaging, setting fire to houses, are measures no less odious and detestable ... without absolute necessity, or at least very cogent reasons.'[18]

A guiding principle accompanying scorched-earth warfare was the ancient right of an invading army to live off the resources and supplies of the conquered as it moved through enemy territory. What an invading army could not devour in one location or carry off, it would often destroy. This concept – first articulated in Latin as *bellum se ipsum alet*, or 'war feeds itself' – was chronicled by the Roman historian Titus Livy in his work *History of Rome* and attributed to Cato the Elder, when his army set out to conquer Iberia after landing in 195 BC at the Greek merchant port of Emporiae – located in present-day Catalonia. Cato's army arrived at the 'time of year when the Spaniards had the grain on their threshing-floors', and he deemed it unnecessary to consume Roman supplies. He 'therefore forbade the contractors to purchase any and sent them back to Rome, saying, "This war will support itself".' Leaving Emporiae, 'he burned and laid waste the fields of the enemy and filled everything with flight and terror.'[19]

From Roman times until the establishment of the Geneva Conventions in the mid-nineteenth century there were no laws of war relating to the rights of non-combatants, but only ethical considerations among enlightened and benevolent conquerors. Military expediency was the single consideration for generals, and Vattel's deliberations on violence against civilians were contingent on whether that violence was justifiable. If an enemy engaged in irregular warfare, consideration of protection within the 'universal society of nations' engaging in the 'voluntary' laws of war was moot. In other words, engaging in irregular warfare nullified the mutual agreement between belligerents. 'The first rule of that law,' Vattel commented, 'respecting the subject under consideration, is that regular war, as to its effects, is to be accounted just on both sides.' Taken in totality, Vattel's 'just war' theory of defensive warfare first articulated by Grotius contradicted his legal argument against the use of irregular war.[20]

Counter-insurgency in the Vendée

The French played an active role in aiding the colonists in the American Revolutionary War and were informed of British debates on the laws of war. That situation was later reversed when open revolt broke out on French soil in the Vendée in 1793 and the French Army turned to unmitigated violence to suppress it. In the French National Convention, Joseph François Laignelot called the war in the western half of France 'deplorable' and testified to the 'shocking' counter-insurgency methods employed there – 'that the grain, cattle, sheep, and other means of subsistence had been destroyed ... by design.'[21] Ultimately, tens of thousands of were killed in this civil war.

While British politicians wrestled with the legal implications of the American Revolution, the large-scale violence in the Vendée forced the French military to confront the tactical efficacy of a novel system of warfare. For the republican army – the predecessor of Napoleon's *Grande Armée* – formal counter-insurgency began in the Vendée. Despite this experience, the foundations of French anti-insurrectionist military doctrine employed traditional enemy-centric methods, which contrasted with the population-centric approach later developed by the US Army – and became a prelude to the violence later inflicted on the Spanish. In 1793, prior to the implementation of counter-insurgency strategies by General Louis Lazare Hoche in the Vendée, General François Westermann wrote, 'The Vendée no longer exists ... Following the orders I have received, I have crushed children beneath hooves, and massacred women so that they won't spawn any more brigands.' His report to Paris finished with a bold but chilling claim: 'You can't reproach me with having taken any prisoners, the roads are littered with corpses.'[22]

As the British learned, and as the French came to learn, extremely harsh measures against populations only fuelled rebellion. One historian has recently noted that the conflict in western France 'strained the republic's ability to undertake pacification without persecution and to transform coercion into reconciliation'. Because the uprising tested the resolve of both revolutionaries (republicans) and traditionalists, the outcome moved to the extreme and 'contributed disproportionately to the Revolution's authoritarian outcome'. Estimates of deaths in that ideological confrontation range between 170,000 and 200,000. The Spanish confrontation, which was also characterized by extreme ideological and religious differences, would prove far bloodier.[23]

In the wake of the brutality in the Vendée new rules of engagement were put into effect by General Hoche. These rules represented one of the earliest efforts to systematically adapt to guerrilla warfare and armed rebellion. Implemented by the military, Hoche's rules helped to pacify the population until the exhausted rebels sued for peace and the government reciprocated with amnesty. Napoleon lauded the state's military success and was quoted as saying Hoche 'was one of the finest generals that France ever produced'.[24] While Hoche began his *Instruction* with ideological republican platitudes, he also advocated a benign military approach to 'respect the peaceful habitants of the region'. The concept was simple: treating citizens benignly enabled French soldiers 'to distinguish between Republicans doing their duty and those detestable individuals who have chosen to follow the despicable career of robbers and murderers'.[25]

Hoche was thorough in his tactical recommendations. In addition to iterating basic maxims regarding troop strength, he offered instructions for escorts, detachments operating against brigands, reconnaissance by day and night, night marches, patrols and billeting. In revolutionary (republican) language, Hoche proclaimed that 'ill-disciplined and disorderly robbers' were no match for the brave republican-inspired soldiers 'fighting for their country and for liberty'. Counter-insurgency prescriptions were also detailed. For escorts, an officer was required to inspect weapons before beginning operations and to ensure vigilance with 'a vanguard, a rearguard and scouts on each flank'. Hoche stressed that 'caution should be maintained whilst passing through villages ... and troops should not proceed down sunken roads' – but use embankments. To prevent ambushes, he recommended 'a quarter of the detachment's strength' be used to protect the flanks. If a group marched through rough terrain, the distance from the main column to the flankers could be adjusted to prevent them being cut off in case of attack. Appropriate distances for vanguards and rearguards to maintain from the main column were advised, as well as their sizes depending on the weather. Other imperatives for escorts included silence, 'frequent halts' and attention to stragglers. Even the proper way of escorting wagons was addressed, with a stern warning that fleeing an attack would result in the offender being 'tried as a traitor to the Republic and as one who has needlessly sacrificed the lives of his brothers in arms'.[26]

Most of Hoche's rules were designed to prevent a marching column from being ambushed – the principal tactic of guerrilla warfare. He elaborated on the need for someone to signal during an attack: 'At this signal, or at the very first shot, the vanguard, rearguard and flankers should rejoin the main body.'[27] Although these instructions seem logical, it is easy to imagine how such basic rules could be ignored by inexperienced officers. The instructions were designed to give a column a trained response, suppressing the instinctive urge to flee which would cause panic and scattering. If the rules were implemented effectively, an ambushed group could repel and resist an initial assault. In contrast, a group that panicked and fled would cede momentum to the enemy.

Other counter-insurgency rules listed by Hoche included the use of vegetation and natural contours in the landscape as cover, sealing off the exits of villages where guerrillas were known to be operating before launching an attack, and using stealth to approach targets. Conducting ambushes in anticipation of a guerrilla band's moves was 'best done in a ravine or wood'. Hoche noted that insurgents 'frequently make use of women and children to spy for them', and they often 'warn of [an enemy's] approach … by pretending to whoop and shout at their livestock'. Despite the use of civilians in insurgent warfare, he reiterated that 'no harm should come to them'.[28]

In addition to French counter-insurgency experience in the Vendée, Napoleonic War historian Jonathan North has recently written on the French experience of guerrilla warfare in eighteenth-century colonial North America: 'French officers witnessed irregular tactics in the forests of North America some forty years before the French Revolution.' The New World experiences of Europeans with Native American-style warfare 'sparked a debate and generated books such as Grandmaison's *La Petite Guerre* and de la Croix's *Traité de la Petite Guerre.*' Those conflicts, unlike the Vendée, were fought on foreign soil against an enemy whose tactics were novel to Europeans. During the Seven Years War in North America (1754–63), which began two years before a wider conflict broke out in Europe in 1756, both the British and French employed Native American tribes as proxies in their struggle for continental supremacy, and despite these experiences, the French later had difficulty adjusting to the style of warfare that effectively manifested itself in Spain. North argues that theoretically and practically, 'French officers were as yet ill-prepared to fight national uprisings or wage counter-insurgency warfare.'[29] While some French soldiers may have been familiar with Native American tactics, like the Americans they were not accustomed to occupying Native American settlements or policing villages – which represented a major change from the enemy-centric to population-centric forms of counter-insurgency. Tactically, Indian warfare and Spanish guerrilla warfare were similar, but there did not exist a military doctrine from which to draw previous knowledge or experience other than the Vendée – a civil war that went through an extremely violent period before peace was achieved.

When examined retrospectively, it can be seen that a pattern of guerrilla wars had unfolded before the French invasion of Spain: the Seven Years War and the American Revolutionary War in North America between 1754 and 1783, the Vendée and western France in the early 1790s, and Egypt at the turn of the century. Yet none of these conflicts inspired the French to codify a permanent military doctrine designed to prevent a population from supporting insurgency. Decisions in theatre were left exclusively to the generals, and it was the hard lessons learned by the French in Spain that changed military thinking.

Fighting 'various tribes'

One reason the French did not adapt to the new military situation in Spain was that the tactics employed in either the Seven Years' War in North America or the American Revolutionary War had not been widely disseminated. Viewed through the conventional perspective, the New World conflicts did not utilize guerrilla warfare enough to warrant its consideration by an army accustomed to winning conventional battles in Europe. In essence, the French were unable to shift from their successful, established methods. Writing during the Cold War, Walter Laqueur deliberated on why the French failed to incorporate this knowledge, and he cited as one of the earliest works on guerrilla warfare the 1789 work by Prussian Colonel Andreas Emmerich, *The Partisan War or the Use of a Corps of Light Troops to an Army*, in which Emmerich used many examples of 'partisan' (i.e. guerrilla) tactics from the American Revolutionary War. Laqueur noted that pre-Peninsular War literature dealt mainly with 'highly mobile' smaller units, and while the American Revolution was rife with examples, 'the literature published approximately before 1810 did not accord these units an independent role and it was exclusively concerned with the operations of professional soldiers acting in close cooperation with the main body of the army.'[30] Laqueur's argument is supported by the facts. While the French engaged in counter-insurgency efforts in the Vendée, that conflict was viewed as more of an aberration than a reflection of an ongoing and revolutionary shift in military methods throughout the western world. Yet, given the presence of pre-Peninsular guerrilla warfare, conventional counter-insurgency tactics and basic rules to sustain an invading army did exist – as they had for centuries.

If modern counter-insurgency means the application of both violence and persuasion (the sword and the olive branch) to achieve strategic objectives, the military aspect of that application is indeed ancient. John Elting wrote in his 1989 work on the *Grande Armée* that militarily the 'French counter-guerrilla strategy and tactics followed the general rules employed at least since the days of Alexander the Great.'Those rules required the army to control the 'major communications centers and main roads'. In hostile territory, an army was required to ensure safe transit for couriers, convoys or small detachments by maintaining fortified posts a day's march from each other along critical routes.[31]The basic tenet of fortifying posts at manageable distances has been a military maxim for centuries – as small armies, logisticians and couriers have always required safe areas to re-supply and rest. In Spain, French insistence on these general rules became an Achilles' heel, because Napoleon demanded secondary roads and routes be maintained to blanket the country. This policy was diametrically opposed to his own rules and scattered his army considerably. The same case could be made when looking at the defeat of the British during the American Revolutionary War.

Not surprisingly, most of the military memoirs written by French officers (usually generals or marshals) after the Peninsular War were intended to bolster their respective legacies while avoiding discussion of the disastrous policy of trying to control the entire country. This pattern is consistent throughout – save for the writings of Albert-Jean Michel de Rocca, a French lieutenant who recorded many insightful observations on the counter-insurgency strategy but believed the national nature of the war made traditional tactics ineffective. In his 1815 work, *Memoirs of the War of the French in Spain*, Rocca wrote honestly about the conflict's unconventional side, noting that 'garrisons which they had left on the military roads to keep the country in check, were constantly attacked' by insurgents. Securing posts in population centres where food supplies were more abundant also became problematic due to pervasive hostility from locals. Since living in towns or villages was dangerous, the solution mimicked strategies employed by Spain's previous invaders. According to Rocca, the French constructed 'little citadels for their safety by repairing old ruined castles which they found on the heights, and these castles were frequently Roman or Moorish remains which, many centuries before, had served the same purpose'. The problem became ensuring a stable supply of victuals in rural posts, an issue which rarely warranted attention in military memoirs written by generals. In areas with fewer heights, isolated French units were forced to be creative:

> In the plains, the posts of communications fortified one or two of the homes at the entrance of each village, for safety during the night, or as a place to treat to when attacked. The sentinels dared not remain without the fortified enclosures for fear of being carried off; they therefore stationed themselves on a tower, or on a wooden scaffolding built on the roof near the chimney to observe what passed in the surrounding country.[32]

Was the French military situation in Spain any different from that of the Roman or Moorish invaders centuries earlier. The answer is complicated but it is easily discerned from reading military memoirs. The French believed the Spanish were illegally employing tactics similar to those used by North African and Arab fighters, and (according to them) the difficult military situation was not due to French inability to adapt, but to a combination of geography and long-held stereotypes among the French of the Spaniards, embodied in an old myth known as the 'Black Legend.' Rocca agreed with French generals in this regard, and – despite obvious differences between military technology and weaponry – he perceived similarities between the Spanish mode of fighting and Arab warfare. These anti-Spanish sentiments eventually crossed the Atlantic and remained so persistent that they informed American views of the Mexicans in the 1840s.[33]

French prejudice about Spanish ability permeated the military structure, percolating from Napoleon down to the lowest ranks. Informing this pejorative and dismissive perspective was the French army's first-hand experience of cavalry-centric and ambush-oriented warfare after they invaded Ottoman Egypt in 1798. 'There is, even in our days, so striking an analogy between the mode of warfare in many parts of Spain,' Rocca recalled, 'and that of various tribes the French had to fight on the banks of the Nile.' According to Rocca, the parallels were so striking 'that, if we were to substitute Spanish for Arab names in many pages of the history of the campaign in Egypt, it might pass for a description of the events of the Spanish war'. Not only were the tactics similar, the social environment was too:

> In Spain as in Egypt our soldiers could not remain behind their companies without being murdered; in short, the inhabitants of the south of Spain

possess the same perseverance in hatred, and the same liveliness of imagination which distinguishes the nations of the east ... The Spaniards, like the Arabs, often treated their prisoners with the excess of barbarity; but they also sometimes exercised towards them the noblest and most generous hospitality.[34]

French writer Vivant Denon, who spent time in Egypt chronicling the French campaign at Napoleon's behest, may have influenced Rocca's assessment. In his book, *Travels in Upper and Lower Egypt*, Denon observed that caravans travelling at night needed detachments of soldiers at the front and rear 'to protect the convoy from the Bedouin Arabs, who, when they are not in sufficient force to attack the front, sometimes carry off the stragglers of the rear'. Denon's descriptions did not end with Egyptians. After the French routed the Ottoman army, its commander Murad Bey 'took from us the opportunity of putting an end to the campaign by decisive blows' by avoiding direct confrontation. As a result of his use of guerrilla-style tactics, the French 'were reduced to pursue an active and rapid enemy, who ... left us neither rest nor security'. From Denon's perspective, Egypt was the French Army's first taste of a nameless non-European style of horse warfare best described in an ancient analogy, one which would recur continually in descriptions of guerrilla warfare:

Our mode of warfare was now, to resemble that of Antony against the Parthians: the Roman legions, invincible in the field ... found no other obstacle than the space of the country which their foes left behind them; but exhausted with daily losses, the victors thought themselves fortunate to be able to quit the territory of a people who, always beaten but never subdued, would, even the day after a defeat, return with invincible perseverance to harass those with whom they just left masters of an unprofitable field of battle.[35]

Denon described the desert-dwellers as living in 'exalted independence and a state of warfare', leading them to commit regular depredations. The same sentiments were echoed by the French *Institut d'Égypte*, which published *Memoirs Relative to Egypt* during the same period. To avoid being attacked, Egyptians 'are obliged to receive them in their camps, and furnish them with provisions and barley for their horses.' Neither the French Egyptian Institute's writers nor Denon showed any respect for the nomads' predatory way of life. 'The Arabs never attack in line,' he complained, 'but always like foragers, uttering at the same time loud cries and invectives; their style of fighting being merely that of light troops.'[36] Although Spanish guerrillas worked with the population in Spain, their raiding tactics and cavalry-centric mode of warfare were similar.

W.S. Hendrix, an historian who wrote in the early twentieth century, believed that remnants of guerrilla-style tactics could be discerned in the medieval Spanish legend of El Cid – a hero celebrated for his cunning during the Reconquest of Iberia from the Moors and still the focus of an important cultural legend in Spain. In the epic twelfth-century poem, 'The Song of My Cid' (*El Cantar de Mio Cid*), ambush and surprise play prominent roles in the narrative. The tactics used during the medieval period by El Cid were not codified, as Hendrix noted in his 1922 article, but the poem contains 'elements of what later come to be a recognized system of military tactics and strategy'.[37]

One example of these tactics was the attack on the Navarrese town of Castejón. It was too heavily fortified to assault directly, but El Cid diverted the attention of its garrison by using foragers as decoys in the town's environs. When the Moors came out to attack the foragers, El Cid entered and seized the now lightly guarded town. In another instance, El Cid tricked his enemies at Alcocer by pretending to withdraw from a siege, ordering his men to flee in haste when the Moors came out to attack. As they pursued him, El Cid 'wheeled his forces' around and 'made for the gate, which they held until the main force came up'. In examining these and other battles, Hendrix concluded that 'the element of surprise in some form' is apparent and 'is of course an important factor in battle; that this fact was recognized by the Spaniards of the time of the Cid is clear.' Like all guerrilla fighters, Hendrix noted that El Cid devoted considerable attention to studying the terrain before battle. In essence, El Cid's style of warfare was anything but Napoleonic, and was more akin to the guerrilla tactics which re-emerged during the Peninsular War.[38]

One observer who made a tentative connection between the Reconquest and the guerrilla insurgency was British author Thomas Bourke. In 1811, while guerrilla warfare was breaking out in Spain, Bourke published *A Concise History of the Moors in Spain*. Rather than disparage guerrilla tactics, Burke saw in the war romantic echoes of an older form of combat. Again, like Rocca, the comparisons (while valid) are rooted more in preconceived stereotypes than in the idea of a geographic and cavalry-centric orientation informing a shift in tactics to confront a more powerful force:

> What ideas of tenderness as well as courage does not the illustrious Cid alone awaken us? … we know, that long after the expulsion of the Moors, the Spaniard bore away the palm of gallantry from the French, and that the manners of the chivalrous ages, though lost to the rest of Europe, are still, to a certain degree, perceptible in various parts of Spain.[39]

The story of El Cid was not well known in the English-speaking world in 1811, and Bourke drew attention to 'Moorish Tactics' because they contrasted with the military system most of Europe had adopted. He used the Almohad defeat at the Battle of Tolosa in 1212 to make his point. The Moors 'had seized all the defiles … hoping thus either to compel them to fall back by cutting off their supplies, or to crush them in the passage if they wanted to advance.'[40] Essentially, these were the same tactics the guerrillas used against the French after 1808.

Although the leaders of the Spanish insurgency did not publish tactical manuals on guerrilla warfare, surprising the enemy and employing psychological warfare against entrenched forces were implied methods. Even modern-day Spanish historians have subscribed to the belief that Spanish guerrillas were the inheritors of some military-cultural traditions passed down from Spain's historic conflict with non-European invaders, and that they 'resuscitated an ancient mode of fighting' out of military necessity.[41] The same can be said of the Cossacks who hounded Napoleon's army during its retreat from Russia. Geographically, Spain has been a crossroads between Europe and Africa, which like the land of the Cossacks, puts it on the periphery of Vattel's geographic definition of civilized Europe. Nevertheless, most of the French comparisons between the Spaniards and other non-Europeans apparent in military memoirs from the war are laden with bias. Apart from Rocca, these prejudices do little to accurately paint a picture of the desperate counter-insurgency tactics used by French garrisons.

Although guerrilla warfare was coming of age it arrived too quickly for the French to adapt. The Seven Years War in North America, the American Revolutionary War, the Vendée and the campaign in Egypt all preceded the 1808 invasion of Spain. Despite the evidence of a coming sea-change, the French felt they did not need to learn from previous wars because their mode of warfare had so far proved successful. They were not prepared for how to deal with the Spanish people, how to effectively treat captured guerrillas, or how to fortify their communications and logistics networks. When these issues began to exhaust them, they turned to terror – a 'detestable' but legal form of confronting irregular warfare. To make matters worse, when supplies and money began to run out Napoleon invoked the ancient military maxim first attributed to Cato's ancient war in Iberia: *bellum se ipsum alet* – 'the war will feed itself'.[42] The larger question Napoleon failed to ask was whether warfare waged to put down insurrection while taking resources from the people would contribute to victory. As will be examined, this is the very question the Americans asked themselves before invading the heart of Mexico.

Part I

The War in Spain

The management of his troops was the great art of [Simon] Bolivar; his partisans in their enthusiasm have compared him to Caesar, but he much more resembles Sertorius. Like him he had to reduce a savage people to obedience, and to combat a powerful and experienced nation. The places of contest were nearly alike; for there were, in this portion of America, the same difficulties to surmount, in the badness of the roads and the height of the mountains, as existed in the time of Sertorius. Like him Bolivar disconcerted his enemies by the rapidity of his marches, by the suddenness of his attacks, and by the celerity of his flights, which rendered it easy for him to repair his defeats at a distance … If his military tactics were different from those of Spaniards, his conduct was still more so.[1]

Vermont Aurora, Vergennes, 24 March 1825

Chapter 1

Mounting Insurgency and Counter-insurgency

The initial revolt against the French in Madrid on 2 May 1808, has been thoroughly addressed by historians. The summary of events leading to a general uprising (*levantamiento*) throughout Spain is best summarized as an escalation of violence as a result of popular resistance to Napoleon naming his elder brother Joseph as King of Spain after forcing the Spanish royal family to abdicate. The Peninsular War veteran William Napier, who was neither an admirer of the Spanish nor credited their contribution to ending the conflict, believed that 'the abstraction of the royal family, and the unexpected pretension to the crown, so insultingly put forth by Napoleon, aroused the Spanish pride.' Spanish resistance involved violence not only against French soldiers but also against fellow Spaniards deemed to be collaborating with the occupiers. News of the forced abdication and revolt in Madrid shocked Spain. Faustino Casamayor, one of the principal chroniclers of the brutal siege of Zaragoza, observed that 'the disorder and what occurred created a sensation'. It was the prelude to a war marked by unprecedented atrocities, and violence broke out in every corner of the country.[2]

Napoleon had grand plans for Joseph. One month prior to the revolt, he informed his brother that 'the Spanish army is not formidable', before summoning him from his kingdom of Naples. The Spanish crown was an unwelcome gift for a timid man who had been content to rule a quiet realm. Napoleon, however, told him of the 'good insurrection in Madrid' of 30,000 to 40,000 people who had taken part in riots, and informed him that 2,000 had lost their lives: 'I had 60,000 men in Madrid who could do nothing … We have taken advantage of this situation to disarm the town.' A few days later, Napoleon ordered Joseph to the French border city of Bayonne, writing, 'I destine this crown for you.' He also attempted to reassure him by saying, 'At Madrid you are in France; Naples is the end of the world.'[3]

But Spain was not in France, nor were the Spaniards like the French. Geographically, Spain has been described as closer to Africa than Europe. This fact returned to haunt French war planners, who never anticipated insurgents utilizing tactics more common among North African fighters. Napoleon's most highly regarded general, Louis-Gabriel Suchet, drew on precedents from insurgent wars in ancient Roman times when he wrote, 'The geographical form of Spain … is borne out by her history from the time of Sertorius to the present day.' Suchet understood that the Sertorian War (80–72 BC) had been an insurgent conflict that tore at the unity of the Roman Empire. Unlike his emperor, he also knew that Madrid was closer to Africa than Paris. From 'a geographical and physical point of view,' he wrote in his 1829 memoirs, 'Spain is in many respects as much connected with Africa as with Europe.'[4]

Similarities between the regions abound. Among them is the lack of water in large areas of Spain, which made it difficult to sustain large armies in scorching territory during the summer. Even in ancient times this factor had made campaigning during the hotter months particularly difficult. Suchet commented that the 'plains, and frequently the valleys, are visited with droughts'. Aridity is especially severe in the plains and in the south, where are found 'immense deserts, or else *desplobados*, the extent of which the eye vainly attempts … at the aspect of a space equally barren and dreary in every direction'.[5]

Although Madrid is the geographical centre of the peninsula, it is also isolated and faces south, away from France and flanked on the east and west respectively by the Sierra de Guadarrama and Serranía de Guadalajara. The southern side of the bowl-like plateau cradling Madrid ends at the Tagus River, which has cut itself into the earth over millennia, offering only a limited number of passable fords as it snakes its way into Portugal and the Atlantic. The mountains separating Madrid from the north of the country make up a major part of the watershed between the Ebro River and the Tagus. Even though Madrid is the strategic centre of Spain, its distinct geography, much like the rest of the country, results in great differences from other provinces. Ultimately, Madrid was not in France, even if Napoleon wanted to believe it was.

Accompanying the *dos de mayo* national uprising was a major Spanish victory at Bailén on 19 July 1808. After three days of fighting, more than 17,000 French soldiers surrendered. Despite attempts by the authorities to minimize its importance, the loss marked the first time Napoleon's army had ever been defeated in open battle, and the victory added fuel to Spanish resistance.[6] Louis-François Lejeune, the 12-year aide-de-camp of Napoleon's chief of staff Marshal Berthier, wrote that the 'catastrophe of Bailén' energized the Spanish: 'Everywhere the revolt against the armies of France was declared. The clergy of the main churches of Seville, Valencia, Valladolid and Zaragoza sought to excite the patriotic exaltation of the people … In Zaragoza, it revived the courage of the defenders of the city.'[7]

The defeat forced Joseph to flee Madrid, and Napoleon urged increasingly brutal treatment of the Spanish population. He also set about micromanaging affairs in preparation for a renewed invasion, informing Joseph that 100,000 soldiers were being sent, 'and in the autumn Spain will be conquered'. From that point the war escalated, and the popular uprising took on added significance in Navarre and the Basque country, the gateway for the French military offensive. In early September of 1808 Joseph implored his brother to end the war quickly by giving Galicia to Portugal and annexing the provinces north of the Ebro River to France, demands which Napoleon stubbornly resisted. Instead, the emperor encouraged his brother to become more ruthless, recommending further executions in Bilbao. 'If you do not perform some acts of rigour,' he wrote to Joseph, 'these disturbances will never end … It is strange that Navarre is so spared.' Napoleon insisted harsher methods be used to 'make a severe example of the insurgents … and to send hostages to France'. He also alluded to an impending shortage of food, supplies and money due to the war's unexpected escalation: 'You should make the inhabitants grind for you, and not always draw your flour from France. The provinces which you occupy can and must furnish you with provisions.' This factor later played an important role in the outcome of the war.[8]

Napoleon surveyed the political and military landscape after Bailén and formulated a new military strategy. In the *Plan for the Reorganization of the Army of Spain*, he outlined his belief that maintaining the flow of troops and supplies through the Navarre and Basque corridor remained critical to controlling the peninsula. The basic strategy followed a long-held maxim of war: the fewer the lines of operation into a country, the easier they are to defend and control. Napoleon ordered Marshal Ney to protect Joseph, giving the new king the courage to hatch an ambitious plan involving an assault on Madrid with 50,000 soldiers. He informed Napoleon, 'I could disperse the enemy and reach Madrid, where the government which they are trying to create would disperse.' Napoleon rejected this idea:

> The art of war is founded on principles which must not be violated. To change one's line of operation is an operation which only a man of genius ought to attempt. To lose one's line of operations is an operation so dangerous that to be guilty of it is a crime … But at this instance to rush into the interior of Spain, without any organized center or magazines, with hostile armies on one's flanks and in one's rear, would be an attempt without precedent in the history of the world … This scheme, opposed as it is to all the rules of war, must be given up.

After invoking Alexander and Caesar and lecturing Joseph on his lack of strategic vision, Napoleon demonstrated the hubris that would undo his army in Spain, underestimating the coalescing guerrilla insurgency and popular resistance:

> The line of communication is not lost because it is disturbed by guerrillas, by insurgent peasants, and in general by that which is called a war of partisans. A few detached men will always force their way, whatever course this takes; such enemies may stop couriers, but are not capable of making a stand against a van or rear guard.[9]

Similarly, and epitomizing his misunderstanding of the unfolding insurgency, Napoleon mistakenly believed he could win the war with one decisive victory. By taking his fight to the people, he exacerbated a conflict already changing into a people's war against an occupier. In November, Napoleon launched a successful counter-offensive with more than 250,000 men, and after a path of destruction had been cleared to Madrid, Joseph returned. For the remainder of the war the French occupation was marked by brutality and coercion. Once a network of collaborators was established in the major cities, Spain was effectively under foreign occupation and ruled from Paris.[10]

Zaragoza and the Church

Zaragoza, the defiant capital of Aragon in north-eastern Spain, witnessed the depths of French brutality towards civilians. The *dos de mayo* revolt and crackdown on the citizens of Madrid may have sparked the resistance, but the example French leadership made of Zaragoza was a catalyst which ensured that the occupation would be long drawn-out and marked by violence. Zaragoza became a symbol of the Spanish cause, and its historic defiance was later invoked by the Mexicans when confronting an invading US army. In sum, the war mythologized the city's name in siege history while cementing Spanish hatred of the French.

Napoleon believed taking Zaragoza was necessary for 'completing the pacification of the country'. One of the largest Spanish cities between Paris and Madrid, the capital of Aragon was essential to securing the Pyrenean frontier between Spain and France. On 4 August the French breached the city walls, and General Jean Verdier felt confident enough to ask Spanish general José Palafox to surrender. Palafox and the citizenry refused, but the expected renewed assault was postponed after news of the French defeat at Bailén. On 14 August, Verdier withdrew his forces to support the withdrawal of Joseph north of the Ebro and confirm control of Madrid, and Zaragoza briefly held firm as a symbol of Spanish resistance. 'The enemies who … threatened our ruin, have left us free,' the *Gazeta de Zaragoza* rejoiced.[11]

News of the siege of Zaragoza rallied Spain as the *dos de mayo* uprising had, and new national heroes emerged such as Agustina of Aragón and Palafox. In the contemporary account by Charles Richard Vaughan, Agustina became a legend 'to which history scarcely affords a parallel'. This young woman 'rushed forward over the wounded and slain, snatched a match from the hand of a dead artilleryman, and fired a 22-pounder, then jumped upon the gun' and began firing at the French. Nor was Agustina the only heroine in Zaragoza. Ramón Cadena, an employee of the cathedral distributing rations, noted that 'women occupied themselves with all zeal and vigour in bringing bread, wine, water, shrapnel, cartridges and all that was necessary for the subsistence of the defenders of the faith and country.'[12]

The second siege of Zaragoza lasted from 20 December to 20 February 1809. Before the French assault, the city garrison was bolstered by 10,000 soldiers and its walls reinforced. Despite extensive preparations, the outlook for the defenders was grim. In a city packed with soldiers, citizens and refugees, a typhus epidemic broke out killing hundreds daily. Faustino Casamayor noted that 'the sick continued to die every day', and their bodies were transported to the vacated houses of residents who had wisely evacuated

Qué valor!

the city. In a short time, the typhus affected the city's younger citizens, and those not struck by French projectiles were found 'falling dead through the streets'. Inside the city's walls, daily prayers were offered to Zaragoza's patron saint for deliverance from the bombardment. By mid-February, people were huddled within the cathedral's thick walls to avoid the projectiles which easily penetrated surrounding residences, but on 10 February the shelling broke through. Casamayor lamented 'the infinite dead people who were all on the streets, most of all to see the temple of Our Patron full of rubble by the ravages of so many bombs that fell on it.' The city held on for ten more days.[13]

The historian David Bell stated recently that once the walls and major defences were penetrated, 'then began the worst urban combat ever seen in Europe before the twentieth century'. The massacre of civilians at Zaragoza following weeks of bombardment was depicted in Goya's *Disasters of War*, showing siege victims being crushed beneath its shattered remnants. Many lucky enough to survive the bombardment were killed by soldiers moving from house to house blowing up partition walls or shooting through them. The city was defiled religiously as well, with interned bodies in churches being 'blown from their tombs'. One of the last redoubts of the remaining defenders was the convent of San Augustin, where soldiers exchanged fire from opposite sides of the chapel turning the house of worship into a bloody scene of urban combat. Prior to the house-to-house assault, as many as 42,000 explosive shells had hit the city, reducing much of it to rubble.[14]

The result was gruesome. All told, some 54,000 people died. Suchet noted the municipal 'burying grounds were too small for the dead carried thither; the corpses sewed up in cloth bags were lying in hundreds at the doors of several churches.' The fall of Zaragoza brought a false sense of accomplishment to the victors, leading many commanders to believe the opposition had been crushed. 'Aragon, in fact, appeared to be subdued by the fall of its capital,' Suchet boasted, 'under the ruins of which lie buried its choicest troops and inhabitants.'[15]

The destruction, in fact, had the opposite effect. The religious community in Spain reacted to the city's devastation with defiant hostility. The usurpation of their throne was one thing, intolerable as it had been, but the annihilation of a religious centre dear to Spanish identity was completely unacceptable. In the eyes of the Spanish the French were godless – enemies of religion and of the Roman Catholic church. Historian Adam Knobler recently wrote that the Spanish 'press made the historical parallel even more striking, casting the war against the French as a cause that was as holy as the war against the Prophet Muhammed'. Rallying the resistance was more easily accomplished after Zaragoza by conservative writers, who recast 'Napoleon and his humanistic and liberal allies as akin to Muslims', an accusation which 'tapped directly into part of Spanish collective historical memory. Those who defended Spain were thus the spiritual descendants of the *Reconquistadores* of the Middle Ages.'[16] The message that the invaders were 'former Christians and modern heretics' was promulgated by an incensed clergy. Since many viewed the conflict as a holy war, the ecclesiastical influence on Spanish society and insurgents should not be underestimated.[17]

Both the 2 May revolt and the massacre at Zaragoza confirmed the anti-French sentiment brewing in Spain. Foreign observers saw the destruction of Zaragoza and the war against the Spanish nation in similar terms. British literature and newspaper coverage painted the conflict with a romantic and nationalistic brush by frequently employing the term 'crusade'. Many of the pro-Spanish themes included romantic images of a nation reborn in war and recovering the 'virile heroism of its forefathers and empire-builders'. British writers utilized Zaragoza's misfortune in depictions of a country defiled like the female victims of war in Goya's pictures. A parallel theme in this regard was the destruction of family as a metaphor for the plight of the Spanish nation – a nation torn apart by an aggressive usurper. Ultimately, Napoleon could not have conceived of a worse public relations disaster.[18]

New Rules of Warfare: Reglamentos and Corso Terrestre

Routed by Napoleon's massive reinvasion in late 1808, the Spanish looked to non-conventional ways of fighting. Examples were found in Aragon, Catalonia and Galicia, where resistance in the form of small bands operating on familiar territory proved effective at keeping French forces bogged down, separated and tormented.[19] After 1808, insurgents refused to engage French forces in large decisive battles. This same strategy, later employed by revolutionary groups in Latin America during their independence movements, completely changed the tactical rules of modern warfare.

However, the insurgency needed to coalesce. In the final days of 1808, the Supreme Central Junta in Seville – acting as the de facto government of Spain while awaiting the restoration of King Ferdinand – issued a decree addressing irregular units operating outside traditional command structures. The regulations, or *Reglamento de Partidas y Cuadrillas*, were designed to legitimize and foster a nascent guerrilla insurgency by establishing procedures for its organization and operations. The opening of the *Reglamento* promised the Spanish would channel their hatred of Napoleon and take 'advantage of the great opportunities provided by the knowledge of the country' to defeat him. 'To facilitate the way to obtain such a noble object,' the *Reglamento* read, '[we] create a new kind of militia, with the denominations of parties or gangs, under the following rules.' A new type of war was launched.[20]

On the first day of 1809 the Junta published a 'Manifesto of the Spanish Nation to Europe' justifying the mobilization of civilians. The decree was essentially a declaration of national war against the French. Over the subsequent months various declarations were issued outlining the legitimization, regularization and incentivization of irregular warfare in Spain. The most famous decree promulgated by the Central Junta appeared on 17 April 1809 and is known as the 'Corso Terrestre'.[21]

The term Corso Terrestre is often translated as 'land corsairs' – the implication often being that these fighters were outside the law, since 'corsaire' is the French word for 'pirate'. This assumption is incorrect. David Bell correctly translates Corso Terrestre to mean 'Privateering on Land'.[22] There is an important difference. For those tackling the enemy army by engaging in ambushes, surprise attacks or stealing provisions designed to aid military occupation, there is a legal distinction between 'privateer' and 'pirate'. Other historians critical of the Reglamentos and Corso Terrestre dismiss them as simply legitimizing theft and link them with the opportunistic bands that robbed fellow Spaniards during the initial chaos of the war.[23] The irony with which the Spanish used the term, however, is apparent in the origin of the term itself, since naval corsairs had been employed during wartime for generations by French kings to attack enemy shipping. Officially, if a privateer operating under a letter of marque (lettres de course) was captured, he was entitled to be held as a prisoner rather than be executed out of hand – as was done to pirates.[24] The use of corsairs by the French, and the legal foundations associated with the system, would have been well known to Sevillian officials (where the Corso was written) because Seville's merchants vessels were among the targets of French corsairs operating in the Atlantic.

In this context, it is apparent that the Spanish were using established maritime practices to create a legal framework within which their (until then) unnamed mode of warfare would be validated. Just like belligerents during war who recognize neither pirates nor guerrillas, the name 'Corso Terrestre' is proof that the Spanish – although using a novel form of irregular warfare – were attempting to build upon legal precedent designed to protect insurgents abiding by Spanish dictates. That the French did not recognize the Corso as legitimate is not surprising, given that this would undermine long-held conventions and tactics. Nevertheless, to call it 'land piracy' is to ignore what the Spanish were doing and to take the French position that Spanish partisans were nothing more than opportunists and thieves. In an historical context, the 'land corsairs' were aptly named and quite appropriate to the early nineteenth-century context from which the term came. The name could easily have become as common as its etymological progenitor but was usurped shortly after the war began by the shorter and legally nebulous term *guerrilla*.[25]

The legal recognition of corsairs in an Atlantic context predates the early nineteenth century by hundreds of years. Historian Thomas Heebøll-Holm notes as far back as the thirteenth and fourteenth centuries that conventions surrounding corsairs and state-sanctioned use of them for reprisals were 'neither arbitrary nor anarchic but rather followed a sort of regulated custom or convention of conflict and dispute settlement'. Later, both Grotius and Vattel recognized the concept within maritime law. Vattel specifically stressed that 'formal warfare' should be 'distinguished from those illegitimate and informal wars, or rather predatory expeditions, undertaken either without lawful authority'. In this regard the jurist commented that the North African Barbary corsairs, 'though authorized by a sovereign', were considered pirates because they attacked 'without any apparent cause, and from no other motive than the lust of plunder'.[26]

Regardless of its translation, the *Corso Terrestre* of April 1809 allowed for the seizure of enemy property – an incentive for soldiers. The *Corso* read: 'The carts, horses, clothes or any other effects that belong to the French apprehended will be part of the prize or booty.'[27] News of the *Corso Terrestre* was published throughout Spain, calling for 'a novel system of war' in which large French armies would be countered with 'war on a small scale, with guerrillas and more guerrillas'. In occupied Catalonia, the Junta obliged every man to wage war to 'show profound hatred' for an enemy in pronouncements that 'eerily echoed the French declaration of the *levée en masse* of 1793'.[28]

Important discrepancies between the *Reglamentos* and *Corso Terrestre* offer an insight into the thinking, practicality and power of the juntas. Since the *Reglamentos* were created first, they provide a window into the original vision of how a guerrilla war could best be managed. For example, in the earliest cited *Reglamentos*, eight of the first ten regulations constituted by the Central Junta in Aranjuez in September, and later disseminated from Seville in December of 1808, specifically mention 'horses'. The first five regulations set the tone for the nature of the *partidas* and are a reflection not only of the vision for the guerrilla war in Spain but also of the equine culture existing in Iberia.[29] In Spain horses were essential for waging war. These lessons were not forgotten, and prescriptions for organizing small mounted units became so effective that Mexicans later tried to mimic the Spanish approach during the war with the United States. In essence, the organizational efficacy of the junta's novel approach to waging war became so renowned internationally that Mexican leaders were trying to copy it thirty-eight years after its inception.

Article One of the *Reglamentos* read, 'Each *partida* will consist more or less of fifty horsemen, with others on foot that will ride on the rump if necessary.' If the number fifty was maintained as the standard for small bands, it would effectively force the French to exceed the standard numbers for detachments accompanying couriers or other small units – requiring them to expend more money and resources. The focus on horses continued in Article Two, which stipulated, 'The horses must be useful for the service to which they are destined, in the event that size and defects deem it unfit for the cavalry.' This implied what the third article outlined, that 'anyone who comes to serve the homeland with his own horse without asking for its value, will have it replaced with another whenever he loses it in battle.' Article Three was critical, because horses were expensive and crucial to the livelihoods of small farmers. With a guarantee that his source of income would be replaced if it were killed (or maimed beyond utility) in battle, an insurgent was assured of receiving compensation. For those who wished to serve with expensive horses, Article Four addressed the issue: 'For those who ask for the value of the horse with which he presents himself to serve, he will be paid ... and he will be given another for service by the Royal Treasury, whenever he loses it in a war action, or inculpably for his illness or another accident.' Although it was difficult to replace expensive horses, Article Four implied an effort would be made to compensate for the loss. This article also seemingly reassured horse owners (and various ranks of the nobility) who borrowed tenants' or farmers' horses to use in the service of an insurgent cavalry unit.[30]

The early *Reglamentos* created opportunities for individual hussars to plunder the enemy. Many guerrillas bent on revenge did not need this incentive, but for those otherwise inclined to avoid the war, the *Reglamentos* combined a compelling incentive to fight for the homeland with the assurance that the authorities would attempt to compensate them for their initial investment. It did not matter to the defender what title his enemy gave him, 'bandit' or 'pirate'; what mattered was that he was given the opportunity to take a risk with honour and a modicum of insurance. This was the original intent of the *Reglamentos*.

However, by examining the subsequent *Corso Terrestre* it becomes apparent that the Junta backed away from its earlier explicit promise to compensate for lost horses, especially those with an assessed value. For example, Article One in the *Corso* of April 1809 gave a general order to 'assault and despoil' the enemy, but Article Two then stated that for those who enlisted with their horse (rather than on foot) 'the Government will attend in all times the merit that these [horses] contract in such useful and risky service'. This statement was vaguer than the promise in the original *Reglamentos*, which perhaps prompted the Junta to compensate hussars by creating a new incentive in Article Three of the April 1809 *Corso*:

> The Generals in Chief of the Spanish armies will of course reward any warnings of important news given to them by the mounted soldiers of these bands, or any of their individuals, regarding marches of the French troops, their strengths and positions, and their views or projects.[31]

The *Corso* expanded on the inducements to fight in the subsequent article (Article Four) by stating that important military action against the French would be 'accredited' by the Generals in Chief, who would then provide an 'account to the Supreme Board, so that they are taken into consideration and their services rewarded'. In other words, rather than issue a blanket declaration compensating horse owners for lost or damaged property, the updated *Corso* was designed to create individual *and* group incentives for action. With the issuing of Article Four, the Junta created a type of credit system accounting for the successes of individual *partidas* known to the authorities. Put another way, not only could the individual guerrilla groups keep what they plundered from the enemy, their accounts would be maintained by the government and theoretically evaluated on a monetary basis. The *Corso* thus rewarded bold action and the achievements of the most successful insurgent groups. This was another reason why guerrilla leaders, or *cabecillas*, used *noms de guerre* – these would avoid the confusion potentially caused by the use of common names. Eventually, the most effective guerrilla leaders were subsumed into the official military structure.[32]

Ramón Guirao Larrañaga, an historian of the Napoleonic War in Spain, outlines another discrepancy between the *Reglamentos* and the April *Corso*. The earlier *Reglamentos* stated in Article Twenty-One that 'enlisted men or draftees could not serve in the *partidas*'. This policy was originally implemented to prevent soldiers deserting the Spanish Army and joining the ranks of the guerrillas. The Spanish authorities did not want to lose much-needed soldiers, who – following a major defeat – often defected to insurgent groups.[33] However, in subsequent decrees the reference was eliminated.

Article Eleven was another important aspect of the *Corso*. Most historians tend to focus on the Junta's legitimization of plundering the French but miss the important military value of targeting the enemy's communications. The *Corso Terrestre* turned the precedent of respecting communications between sovereigns on its head and applied the same rules (and incentives) towards 'intercepting the mail of the enemy' in order to disrupt their ability to communicate. The value of captured correspondence was set at between a half *real* and four *reales*, depending on its importance.[34]

The targeting of French communications and couriers carrying vital information was a brilliant move. It forced the invaders to increase the protection afforded to couriers, using mounted soldiers who would otherwise have been used in offensive operations, and ultimately resulted in longer intervals between dispatches. By changing the conventional rules of war, the Spanish fostered an organic insurgency that – although initially chaotic – eventually coalesced to challenge and wear down Napoleon's army of occupation.

Despite efforts by the Spanish authorities to organize insurgent groups, in early 1809 Napoleon still dismissed them as '*banditti*' – the Italian term he used after his experiences with brigands in that country. He could not envisage unconventional forces in Spain becoming strong enough to challenge his authority – especially an army of 'bandits' who had little regard for the rules of war. Writing from Valladolid before his departure to France, the emperor requested Joseph not to 'think of Valencia till Saragossa is taken'. On 22 January Joseph entered Madrid for the second time. Napoleon never returned to Spain.[35]

The battlefield victories of the French in the summer of 1809 changed the military nature of the war but not the Spanish determination to continue the fight. According to the Peninsular War historian Don Alexander, after the summer of 1809 guerrilla 'divisions' began their assault against the occupiers.[36] The Duke of Wellington wrote that the 'inefficiency in regular warfare drove the patriots to adopt a new mode of hostilities, which harassed and distressed the French to an incredible degree'. He wrote admiringly of the conflict's transition:

> They collected in small bands; they chose leaders of a ready intelligence and a daring courage; and they commenced a system of war in detail, which granted their thirst for the invaders' blood, and suited well with their melancholy fortunes … To lead these guerrilla bands, the priest girded up his black robe, and stuck pistols in his belt – the student threw aside his books, and grasped a sword.[37]

The guerrilla insurgency's genesis in the summer of 1809 was the result of conventional setbacks. Following the Battle of Talavera in late July, General Wellington and his forces retreated into Portugal, where they remained for many months. The Spanish Army was in disarray, having failed to recapture Madrid. The conventional armies of the north-east were equally scattered. Food in the peninsula was growing scarce, especially in the dryer areas. Despite

Napoleon's successful retaking of Spain, these factors, along with a desire for immediate action, led to the emergence of the insurgency. Counter-intuitively, it was the emperor's successes which resulted in the French being vulnerable to insurgent warfare.

Guerrilla Icons and the War's Provincialization

Of the many *guerrilleros* to emerge during the war, one of the most prominent was Juan Martín Díez – *El Empecinado* ('The Undaunted'). Like other well-known guerrilla leaders such as Espoz y Mina and *El Charro*, he came from humble origins. Originally a farmer from the Valladolid area, El Empecinado had previously fought French republicans in his teenage years during the War of Roussillon, or War of the Pyrenees (1793–1795). With this combat experience shaping his opinion of the French, he willingly answered the exiled government's call for partisan war.[38]

El Empecinado's reputation for military effectiveness spread quickly. When early efforts to capture him failed, French officers led by General Joseph Léopold Hugo arrested his mother, Lucia Díez, in the family's home town of Castrillo de Duero. Their plan was to use her to lure El Empecinado to where she was being held in Aranda de Duero – a fortified town on the road from France to Madrid – and then capture him. According to one of the chieftain's biographers, the arrest was designed to 'serve as an example' to other insurgents, but it had the opposite effect. When El Empecinado learned of the news, he threatened to execute dozens of French prisoners. For the French it was another public relations disaster that only led to greater acclaim for the guerrilla leader. Wellington wrote of him: 'The famous Juan Martin El Empecinado was constantly descending from the Guadalajara mountains and spreading terror and alarms among the French garrisons ... The intrusive king dared not to sleep beyond the gates of Madrid.'[39]

That El Empecinado was able to operate freely in the heart of Spain is telling. Despite controlling the capital, the French were never able to dislodge the insurgents from the mountainous region surrounding Madrid. This fact quickly made El Empecinado a legend both at home and overseas. Nineteenth-century Spanish author and playwright Benito Pérez Galdós made an icon out of El Empecinado and portrayed guerrillas like him as chivalrous predators with 'the look of the eagle that, going back in broad daylight to immense height, sees a thousand accidents hidden from the vulgar eyes'. Although a playwright, Galdós showed military insight in describing the defensive advantages enjoyed by the insurgents and invoking the landscape as a weapon against the invaders. 'Imagine ... that the hills, the streams, the rocks, the gorges, the grottoes are deadly machines that go out to meet the ordered troops, and up, down, fall, crush, separate and destroy ... the geography itself attacking them.' Outmanoeuvring the enemy through intimate knowledge of the terrain, along with the low-level nature of guerrilla warfare, were the key advantages exploited by the Spaniards. More importantly to the insurgents, the novel tactics and methods they employed were not dishonourable:

> Among the guerrillas there are no real battles; that is to say, there is no planned and deliberate duel between armies that look for each other, meet, choose terrain and beat each other ... The first quality of a guerrilla, even before bravery, is good walking, because he almost always wins running. The guerrillas do not retreat, they flee, and fleeing is not shameful to them. The basis of their strategy is the art of meeting and dispersing. They condense to fall like rain, and they scatter to escape pursuit, so that the efforts of the army can be fought with the clouds. Their main weapon is ... the terrain.[40]

Another well-known guerrilla chieftain to ply his trade in central Spain was Julián Sánchez – or *El Charro* ('The Horseman'). Sánchez came from a farming family near Salamanca. Like El Empecinado, he had fought the French in the Pyrenees at the age of nineteen and harboured serious animosity towards them. When the war broke out in 1808, El Charro enlisted in a cavalry regiment in Ciudad Rodrigo. Because of his various skills – which included great ability on horseback – El Charro become a second lieutenant in early 1809 and went on to captain a group he forged called the 'Lancers of Castillo', which operated on the periphery of Salamanca. His popularity increased when the group became a regiment and later a much-feared brigade preying on units transiting to Portugal. Wellington wrote that he 'gave the Frenchmen of Old Castile no repose; he was always in the saddle, and continuously surprising detachments and making prisoners'.[41]

El Charro was known for his bravery but the chief factor behind his success was his mount. Known as the Spanish Pure Horse (*pura raza española*), the Andalusian was exceptionally suited to warfare and was likely El Charro's preferred mode of transport. Its closely related cousin, the Lusitano of Portugal, is also native to Iberia. For hundreds of years, the Andalusians' abilities had been respected across Europe, and these were the mounts used by the Conquistadores in the Americas. Known for their intelligence, stamina and compact build, their ability to cover long distances and keep their footing on rugged terrain made them a valuable weapon for mounted guerrillas.

The French, too, admired a horse that was also perfectly suited to the tumult of the battlefield. Rocca wrote that it was a breed 'proud, spirited and gentle; the sound of the trumpet pleases and animates him; and the noise and smoke of powder do not frighten him; he is sensible of caresses, and docile to the voice of his master.' Sensitivity to its rider but not to noise was a much sought-after quality for mounted warriors. Rocca added that when the Andalusian was 'overcome with fatigue, his master, instead of beating him, flatters and encourages him; the horse seems to recover his strength, and sometimes does from mere emulations what blows could never have extorted from him.'[42]

The seventeenth-century equestrian polymath William Cavendish, Duke of Newcastle, a consummate horseman both intellectually and physically, called Andalusians the 'princes' of the horse world. After riding one he commented that it 'was the readiest in the world. He went in corvets forward, backward, sideways, on both hands ... and did change upon his voltoes so just, without breaking time, that a musician could not keep time better; and went terra a terra perfectly.' The second Andalusian he rode made him a true believer, as it was 'the finest-shaped horse' he had ever seen 'and the neatest ... no horse ever went *terra a terra* like him ... so swift that the standers-by could hardly see the rider's face when he went.'[43]

When the Duke referred to 'terra a terra' he meant the gait of a charge in which rider and horse maintain their ability to manoeuvre, in order to strike or avoid being struck by an enemy. El Charro, one of thousands of Spanish guerrillas born riding horses, was known for his skills in this respect. Although insurgents stole French horses, Spanish hussars preferred native horses more accustomed to the scorching Iberian summers. French horses, on the other hand, no matter how swift they may have been, were more prone to heat exhaustion than their Iberian counterparts if not acclimatized properly. Horses also played a considerable role in guerrilla actions during the Mexican War – itself a cavalry-centric conflict.

Espoz y Mina, the guerrilla chieftain who later replaced his nephew Javier after the latter's capture, mentioned horses frequently in his memoirs. They were an essential part of warfare throughout the nineteenth century, as they had been since ancient times, and the terrain often dictated their importance. Along with general statistics concerning enemy deaths during battles and engagements, Mina recorded the number of horses captured, wounded or killed, and always mentioned if the division 'lost some horses' after a battle. Horses were valuable weapons, and their specific character was also important. There were 'fiery horses,' 'fresh horses' and 'useful horses', since many captured horses were not suitable for operations. Animals captured from couriers were referred to as 'mail horses', since they were faster and usually more valuable.[44]

The role horses played in the war is a critical aspect of the larger military picture. Although in a place like Florida horses may not have been effective due to the terrain, in Spain, Mexico and the American West horses were essential. Importantly, as the Peninsular War dragged on, the French loss of horsepower hampered their offensive and counter-insurgency capabilities.[45]

Funding Shortage and Reorganization

Coinciding with the breakdown of the French relationship with the church in Spain was a rupture between the Bonaparte brothers and a growing shortage of money to fuel the conflict. The shortage of funds was especially troublesome because it forced Napoleon to change the military structure of the occupation and the general dynamics of the war. 'Let the King know that my troops in Spain have no power over the provinces,' he wrote in August of 1809, 'and the feebleness of the Spanish authorities enables the junta to obtain money through its agents; that therefore the administration of the country must be put in the hands of the military commanders.' The change to military administration divided Spain into several regional theatres under the control of respective governors-general – a move exacerbating the provincial nature of the war. With each governor-general operating independently, Napoleon undermined the cross-provincial coordination needed to fight an insurgency operating without a centralized authority and heedless of boundaries.[46]

To make matters worse, Rocca commented that 'King Joseph had no regular means of levying his taxes' and therefore had to send 'moveable columns to scour the country' surrounding Madrid. Those forays were hated by a population that either 'fled to the mountains or defended themselves in their dwellings'. As insurgents became aware of the tax-collectors' problems, they often made things more difficult for the French by punishing those who contributed or did not flee. 'The inhabitants of La Mancha as well as those of the neighbouring provinces were exasperated by such violent measures,' Rocca commented, 'and the number of our enemies daily increased.'[47]

Forced to go home in 1810 after an injury, Rocca painted a grim portrait of an occupied country 'soon filled with partisans and guerrillas, some of them regular soldiers from the broken armies, and others the inhabitants both of mountain and valley'. Like Wellington, Rocca recognized the resistance was flourishing: 'Clergy, husbandmen, students, shepherds even had become active and enterprising leaders.' Moreover, he travelled the length of Spain from France to Andalusia and understood the role that provincialization, or *patria chica*, played in the national insurgency:

Every province, every town, every individual felt more strongly every day the necessity of resisting the common enemy. The national hatred which existed against the French had produced a sort of unity in the undirected efforts of the people, and to regular warfare had succeeded a system of war in detail; a species of organized disorder which suited the fierce spirit of the Spanish nation exactly.[48]

Napoleon, on the other hand, simply regarded the guerrillas as 'banditti'. Responding to reports from Astorga in late 1809, he wrote Berthier, 'Let General Loison know that I am sorry that he has taken no measures for getting rid of the gangs of banditti which are there.' The following day, he sent a similar message to General Suchet, who was dealing with similar problems in the north-east: 'Write to General Suchet that he does not pay sufficient attention to the banditti of Navarre.' Suchet had other plans which Napoleon encouraged, involving the emperor's reorganization of the occupation army and governor-general system, thereby undermining Joseph's authority. Joseph's biographer Michael Ross notes that the elder Bonaparte 'was marred by the fact that Napoleon refused to contribute to the maintenance of his armies in any way to the Spanish Exchequer.' In such a state of disorganization it became 'impossible to raise money for taxation'.[49]

By early 1810 the lack of funds for the war had reached a critical juncture. 'Spain swallows up a prodigious amount of specie,' Napoleon informed Berthier in February. The French treasury was 'exhausted by the immense sums which it is constantly obliged to send out'. By late spring the treasury was dry. As a result, the army was reorganized regionally, with each general ruling his respective province and directly taxing the population. Six separate military governments were created in northern Spain: Catalonia, Aragon, Navarre, Biscay, Burgos and Valladolid. This strategy played into the hands of the developing inter-provincial insurgency. Since reorganization meant the generals could not rely on funding from Paris, it inhibited cooperation. Each governor-general, operating with limited funds, was thereafter reluctant to spend his own appropriations in assisting counter-insurgency efforts in other territories. In future, the war would have to support itself.[50]

Formalization of *Partidas* and French Morale

In April of 1810 El Empecinado's insurgent group was officially formalized within the Spanish Army. Formalization was the fruitful harvest of the Junta's initial fostering of the insurgency through the *Corso Terrestre*. The Regency (Cortes) organized his *partidas* into two battalion groups: one named

Tiradores de Sigüenza (Sharpshooters of Sigüenza) and the other *Voluntarios de Guadalajara*. These battalions were subdivided into cavalry squadrons of around 250 men each – one of which El Empecinado led personally. The units maintained the ability to expand as they acquired more horses and soldiers during their operations – thus accommodating the successful original nature of an insurgent unit that survived, benefited and grew from sound leadership.[51]

A debate about the effectiveness of formalizing the *partidas* ensued and has persisted among historians to this day. Wellington, a product of conventional military thinking, asserted that 'desultory warfare had its peculiar advantage, was eminently suited to the genius and habits of the Spanish peasantry, and should have been watched and encouraged by the government, or left to grow up into a wide and wild spirit of resistance to the invader.' Despite supporting the guerrilla war, Wellington believed, counter-intuitively, that insurgent incorporation into the army reduced its effectiveness because 'the government began to regulate these irregulars; or rather, they clumsily attempted that which was not possible.' Furthermore, he believed giving guerrilla chieftains a formal rank simultaneously 'destroyed their independence, shackled their movements and froze up that fountain of zeal which had fed the torrent of their rage'. Wellington added that as a result 'once enterprising guerillas became bad, tame, indolent regulars, or they dispersed to their scattered homes. Thus many lesser bands disappeared and melted away.'[52]

Others view Wellington's observations that 'lesser bands disappeared or melted away' in a positive light. During the initial year of the war, many ad hoc bands were simply opportunist bandits, who preferred to avoid the enemy rather than fight. By 1810, then, many of the informal bands who in the absence of a central authority had been plundering fellow Spaniards were eliminated, marginalized or dispersed, as the insurgency's informal structure was slowly brought under the auspices of the exiled government in Cadiz.[53]

Whether or not insurgent groups were brought under the umbrella of the Cadiz Regency is not crucial, for as the war progressed, all groups engaging the enemy (officially and unofficially) were experiencing increasing success at the expense of the invader. In short, attrition was wearing down the French. Wellington understood the psychological advantage held by guerrillas. The French 'were engaged with the nation' and thus opposed by people who 'stood side by side in the marketplaces with men who were marking them as prey'. Although he himself did not employ guerrilla warfare, he admired its contribution to defeating his enemy:

The peasant was seen ploughing peaceably in his field; but in one of the furrows lay his long Spanish gun, ready to give aid in any chance contest between the *partidas*, or guerrillas, and the passing detachments of the enemy. Not a mountain pass in the romantic land but there lay among the rocks and bushes a group of these fierce and formidable men, awaiting the expected convoy or the feeble company. Even in the plains the posts of correspondence were compelled to fortify the belfry, or tower, or house; and the sentinel kept his vigilant look-out from a scaffolding of planks, that he might see all that passed in the fields around; nor could any of them venture beyond the enclosure thus fortified, for fear of assassination.[54]

Rocca addressed the question of how the insurgency – in which every Spaniard was a potential threat – took a toll on French morale. 'This sort of warfare, where there was no fixed object upon which the imagination could dwell, dampened the ardour of the soldier, and wore out his patience.' The combination of low morale, shortage of supplies and lack of clear mission created a perfect storm of desperation. Rocca commented that French generals and soldiers 'could only maintain themselves in Spain by terror; they were constantly under necessity of punishing the innocent with the guilty; and of taking revenge on the weak for the offences of the powerful'. In addition to the terrorizing of the people, forced contributions

had become necessary for existence, and such atrocities as were occasioned by the enmity of the people, and the injustice of the cause for which the French were fighting, injured the moral feeling of the army, and sapped the very foundations of military discipline, without which regular troops have neither strength nor power.[55]

In 1810 Rocca was granted leave by a Board of Health due to a leg injury and forced to hobble back to France. 'I was glad, at any price, to quit an unjust and inglorious war, where the sentiments of my heart continually disavowed the evil my arm was condemned to do.' Unlike the memoirs of generals, Rocca's sober testimonial is an accurate depiction of French desperation in 1810. He left Madrid with a caravan of other wounded officers under escort of seventy-five soldiers. The group travelled north on roads once alive with commercial activity and travellers, but now the contrast was stark. 'On the long and silent road no single traveller ever met our sight: every two or three days a convoy of ammunition or an escort met and joined us, to lodge in the ruins of deserted dwellings, whose doors and windows had been carried off to furnish firewood for the French army.' The battered veterans made their way north on the road between Bayonne and Madrid – the most dangerous route in Spain. Villages were abandoned. There was no usual 'crowd of children and idle spectators' nor 'strangers at the entrance of a country village', he wrote, but 'only a small French outpost, which, behind the palisade, would cry Halt! in order to reconnoitre us.' At other times, when entering 'a deserted village, a sentry would suddenly appear placed in an old tower, like a solitary owl among ruins'.[56]

As Rocca's group limped closer to France, the effects of the second year of war were apparent. He passed beyond the unmarked borders of El Empecinado's reach in central Spain, only to arrive in Espoz y Mina's guerrilla kingdom of Navarre. 'The nearer we approached France, the more danger we were in of being carried off by the partisans; at every station we halted we found detachments from different parts of the peninsula, waiting to march with us.' Detachments waited, because only large groups could avoid being attacked by the guerrillas, whose opportunistic maxim was to never confront numerically superior forces. At the gates of France, Rocca witnessed first-hand how the insurgency had worn down the occupiers. 'Battalions, and even whole regiments reduced to skeletons, that is, to two or three men only, were sadly bringing back their eagles and their banners' to their homeland. Rocca made it out of Spain at the end of July and never returned.[57]

Fears of being attacked on the road between Madrid and France were well founded, despite the regime's constant efforts to secure it. The *Observer* in London reported on a project through 'private letters of the Madrid state', citing 'interception of couriers with dispatches by peasantry' – a euphemism for insurgents. The *Observer* noted that 'orders have been issued by King Joseph for the erection of a number of forts, at stated distances, on the great road leading from Madrid to Bayonne'. The plan to create secure waystations in the heart of guerrilla country was an attempt at 'overawing the inhabitants, and securing the communication between the principal places'. The effort failed.[58]

Throughout the summer of 1810 Napoleon micromanaged the war from France. The 'banditti' needed to be pursued 'vigorously' whenever they were found in Navarre or elsewhere. In addition, the emperor ordered escorts in La Mancha reinforced to prevent captures by guerrillas, and demanded that Italian soldiers fighting for France no longer be sent to Catalonia – the emperor had 'no wish to crowd Catalonia with bad soldiers, or to increase the troops of banditti'. This was ordered because Italians were switching sides and joining the Catalans.[59] Taken as a whole, the growing efficacy of the *partidas* contrasted with the dismissive sentiments of French officials in the first year of the war:

In reality, without derogating from the bravery of our soldiers, we must say that worse troops than the Spanish soldiers do not exist. Like the

Arabs, they make a stand behind houses, but they have no discipline, no knowledge of tactics, and it is impossible for them to make any resistance on the field of battle. Even their mountains have afforded them but a feeble protection.[60]

Rise of the Guerrilla Kingdoms

The Supreme Junta never wrote a manual on how to conduct insurgent warfare. Instead, they created a blueprint via the *Reglamentos* and *Corso Terrestre* for its organization and left the tactical decisions to more experienced chieftains in the field such as Espoz y Mina and El Empecinado. The system itself, although chaotic in its initial stage, was driven and supported by flexible rules that offered incentives to the most successful and disciplined leaders. In essence, the rules were written by the leaders, but the insurgency organized itself. Later, it coalesced into something more formal as guerrilla units achieved parity. Tactically, the insurgent strategy amounted to pestering and exasperating a more powerful foe. Once the insurgency's organization took shape, the strongest and most effective *partidas* were brought into the official structure of the army.

In late March of 1810, Francisco Espoz Ilundáin took control of the insurgency in the north-east. Being the uncle of Javier Mina (his father's name was Juan Esteban Espoz y Mina) gave the elder insurgent the option to replace 'Ilundáin' with the *nom de guerre* 'Espoz y Mina'. This was done for continuity, name recognition and as a salute to his nephew's efforts. Espoz y Mina, like Javier Mina, was from a farming background. Born in Idocin in the Navarrese hills, he knew the territory, language and people who lived in the region straddling the French logistics lifeline. The emergence of another formidable Mina alarmed the French authorities – especially Henri Dufour, the newly appointed governor-general of Navarre. Dufour at first tried to employ his experience from the Vendée by offering an amnesty to those willing to lay down their arms and worked to recruit collaborators. He even, to the consternation of Suchet, spared the younger Mina's life. When these strategies failed, he turned to terror.[61] Espoz y Mina's rise to power in Navarre was directly related to Suchet's successes in Aragon – the provincial nature of the war again playing a key role. The more successful Suchet's counter-insurgency efforts became in Aragon, the more Espoz y Mina solidified his power base in Navarre. Suchet's successes only enabled the Navarrese guerrillas to strike harder against convoys entering Spain via Bayonne – convoys attempting to re-supply Suchet's forces and siege efforts in Aragon and Catalonia.

In 1811 things were going no better for the French in the heart of Spain, as unchecked incursions by El Empecinado forced them to implement exhaustive counter-insurgency operations there. General Augustin Daniel Belliard was given this task, along with four separate columns consisting of 2,000 soldiers each. Including supporting units from Madrid, more than 10,000 men were deployed to eliminate El Empecinado. Columns were ordered to Guadalajara, Tarancón, Sierra de Molina, Soria, Aranda and other sites in central Spain to surround the insurgent group and prevent their escape. The size of the units tasked with capturing or killing El Empecinado and his 'undaunted' soldiers meant that this operation was the largest counter-insurgency effort of the war.[62]

According to El Empecinado's biographer Andrés Pérez, the spring of 1811 also marked a change in the war: 'the deployments of the enemy were no longer those of the first years' or what they needed. This assertion was confirmed by historian Don Alexander, who adds that the deployments were complicated by Napoleon's failed 'schemes' to compensate for supply losses in Spain. Those schemes included reorganizing artillery units, creating new units 'from cadres already in the Peninsula', reducing infantry replacements to one-half and stripping regiments of 'elite infantry personnel to expand his imperial guard'. These moves were 'bitterly resented' by commanders already experiencing major difficulties due to shortages of men and supplies.[63]

The French Army and Spanish citizens paid dearly for Napoleon's stubborn refusal to see the war for the national struggle it was. The insurgency's use of an 'illegitimate' form of warfare only hardened the emperor's resolve to fight. Counter-insurgency campaigns were not the only costly forms of expenditure. Spain was pitted with fortresses and castles that held out behind ancient walls built to withstand long sieges. The French sieges were a throwback to an older form of warfare not fitted to Napoleon's penchant for strategic operations and the rapid movement of armies. The invaders expended countless lives, time and treasure in taking such important positions throughout Spain. This was especially true in the north-east under Suchet's command. In the end, these became pyrrhic victories over islands in a sea of hostility.

Chapter 2

Pyrrhic Victories: Costly Sieges and Attrition

The old system of intrenched camps and lines of contravallation is unsuited to the spirit of modern warfare. In ancient times, and more particularly in the middle ages, too much importance was attached to tactical positions, and not enough to strategic points and lines. This gave fortifications a character that never properly belonged to them. From the middle ages down to the period of the French Revolution, wars carried on mainly by the system of positions – one party confining their operations to the security of certain important places. Both Carnot and Napoleon changed this system, at the same time with the system of tactics, or rather, returned from it to the old and true system of strategic operations.[1]

Henry W. Halleck, *Military Art and Science* (1846)

Siege warfare has always presented an ethical dilemma to attackers due to the inevitable loss of civilian life. In ancient times, prudent conquerors avoided causing unnecessary death and destruction, not only because it was unethical, but because rulers understood the value of captured cities and the material support they offered to their armies. For example, Talmudic law prescribed laying siege to cities on three sides to give civilians the opportunity to flee – a corollary to the ancient requirement of allowing non-combatants the choice to leave a city under siege.[2] In 1839 the American anti-war journal the *Advocate of Peace* published an article on the Austrian siege of Genoa in 1800 – an undertaking which drew much-needed soldiers away from the Alps and resulted in Napoleon's surprise victory at Marengo. The siege was not only memorable because it helped launch Napoleon's career, but also because it caused starvation to French soldiers and civilians inside the city, who 'worn down by fatigue, and attenuated by famine, after having consumed all the horses in the city, were reduced to the necessity of feeding on dogs, cats, and vermin'.[3]

Because sieges usually target population centres they were often considered an option of last resort. Vattel commented in the *Law of Nations* that the 'maxims of war require' laying siege to somewhere if this meant capturing an 'important post', but also cautioned that such measures, which lead to civilian deaths, should be undertaken 'only in cases of the last extremity, and with reluctance'. Rather than starve or bombard a town into submission, Vattel believed that 'humanity obliges us to prefer the gentlest methods' to take important or strategic positions. To become 'masters of a strong place, surprise the enemy, and overcome him, it is much better, it is really more commendable … than by a bloody siege or the carnage of battle'. Although Vattel sanctioned seizing important strongholds in time of war, he noted that the ancients scorned the tactic of surprise in favour of pre-planned pitched battles:

> The contempt of artifice, stratagem and surprise proceeds often, as in the case of Achilles, from a noble confidence in personal valour over strength; and it must be owned that when we defeat an enemy by open force, in a pitched battle, we may entertain a better grounded belief that we have compelled him to sue for peace, than if we had gained the advantage over him by surprise.[4]

While the arrival of systematized guerrilla warfare was beginning to make the concept of pitched battles obsolete, sieges and the defence of entrenched positions continued to be important facets of nineteenth-century warfare. Henry Wager Halleck, a West Point graduate and one of the principal architects of US strategy in the Mexican War, lauded Napoleon's battlefield victories because the Corsican's foes were unable to adapt to his revolutionary tactics which favoured operations incorporating surprise manoeuvres. On the other hand, Halleck disagreed with Napoleon's strategy of spending critical time and effort in reducing entrenched positions in Spain – a strategy antithetical to the very system Napoleon himself had fostered. Entrenched positions in that country were usually cities like Zaragoza that had built massive fortifications over hundreds of years. Many of the sieges lasted for months, and each required a considerable amount of logistical support: horses and draught animals to carry heavy cannons and equipment, supplies of food and forage, and specialized personnel like engineers and artillerymen who ran entrenching and bombarding operations. In effect, the sieges required the French to erect military bases on the outskirts of cities where none had existed.

Halleck calculated that the logistical requirements of sieges reduced the overall success of the French campaign. Taking cities like Zaragoza wore down the invading army by forcing them to expend critical amounts of time, energy, supplies and specialized personnel. 'For those who wish to know the exact organization of the French engineering train, we give it as it existed in 1811,' Halleck wrote in 1846 before the US invasion of central Mexico. The numbers for supporting engineers are telling. While they are often passed over by historians, they are never overlooked by military logisticians:

> Seven troops, each troop consisting of three officers, one hundred and forty-one non-commissioned officers and privates, two hundred and fifty horses, and fifty wagons, conveying five thousand two hundred and seventy entrenching tools, one thousand seven hundred cutting tools, one thousand eight hundred and two artificer's tools, two hundred and fifty-three miners' tools, and eight thousand three hundred and eighteen kilograms' weight of machinery and stores.[5]

This is not to say that Halleck neglected the importance of fortifications in modern warfare, but only that when examining the outcome of the war in Spain there appeared to be an over-reliance by the French on besieging and capturing fortified cities as a strategy to win the war. Instead, Halleck advocated both fortifications *and* strategic operations, and believed that 'to follow exclusively either of these systems would be equally absurd'. He also wrote that the Napoleonic Wars 'demonstrated the great truth, that distance can protect no country from invasion, but that a state, to be secure, must have a good system of fortresses, and a good system of military reserves and institutions'.[6]

Suchet's Sieges

Many of the sieges in Spain took place in the north-east under General Suchet's command. After Zaragoza, Valencia became the main objective because it was a major sanctuary for guerrillas and a supply hub for the insurgency. However, to take this coastal stronghold, the north-eastern cities of Lerida, Mequinenza, Tortosa and Tarragona needed to be reduced first. Lerida was the largest city between Zaragoza and Barcelona and possessing it would allow French forces to coordinate with each other across the Catalonia-Aragon border. It was also a major base of guerrilla activity in the area, and it was discovered that Felipe Perena – a guerrilla leader and enemy of Suchet – was held up within the city's besieged walls. Thus, taking the city would achieve both strategic and personal goals. However, the occupying force was strong, and Suchet believed that Lerida's defender, General García Conde, 'indulged the hope of making the siege of Lerida last as long as that of Gerona'.[7]

The siege of the heavily fortified citadel provoked in Suchet a romantic sense of history more suited to his conventional nature than the counter-insurgency campaign he left behind in Aragon and Navarre. In his *Memoirs* he cited 'recollections which the history of ancient and modern wars has stamped with celebrity' and recalled that Lerida had featured 'during the campaigns of the Scipios, in the Second Punic War'. Suchet even assigned Perena and Conde symbolic roles in the drama, writing that 'Caesar besieged or rather kept in check, within the walls of this town, Afranius and Petreius, the two lieutenants of Pompey.' Within a month, Suchet became frustrated with his inability to force a surrender and had his soldiers drive the people by bayonet inside the fortress walls, where they were fired upon by artillery. As a result, after hundreds of civilians died in the shelling, the white flag of surrender was raised. As at Zaragoza, the siege of Lerida demonstrated the French ruthlessness toward civilians to achieve strategic ends. After Lerida was taken, other cities fell, and by the beginning of 1811 Suchet was ostensibly in control of much of western Catalonia.[8]

The strategy of taking towns located along logistic networks was not without a rationale, since it followed a well-known military maxim. The history of the war shows that the French, with the help of collaborators, had little difficulty holding major cities like Madrid, Barcelona or Seville, which the Spanish rarely contested once the invaders were ensconced within their defensive fortifications. What became more problematic was holding the smaller towns and outposts essential to communications and the coordination of armies scattered over long distances. To do this, the French used small detachments and generally requisitioned sturdy and defensible buildings such as convents or monasteries. Suchet wrote that 'churches and convents are, generally speaking, vast and solid edifices … which offer great resources for defensive warfare'. These buildings were ideal for housing men and storing grain and supplies, and were more resistant to insurgent artillery if attacked. Blockhouses also sheltered wounded soldiers and supported mobile units that could more readily secure the immediate surroundings of a town or village – a much safer approach to counter-insurgency than conducting far-flung sweeps which could result in detachments becoming isolated and vulnerable.[9]

For these reasons, garrisoned posts were fairly effective against guerrillas *if* they were properly manned. Unfortunately for the invaders, the lack of troops made implementing this strategy virtually impossible. In a comparative analysis of French counter-insurgency efforts between the Vendée and Spain, Alexander notes what the numbers reveal: 'Hoche had 100,000 men for the pacification of a province, while the Imperial forces in the peninsula barely exceeded 300,000 at the height of the intervention.' In order to secure the gains he made in 1810, Suchet would have needed to station a garrison in every town and decent-sized village, which he could not do. Historian Charles Oman's observations confirmed the existence of this shortage of manpower, and he noted that when towns were abandoned, 'the insurgents would descend and occupy them'. To put the shortage into perspective, of the 26,000 troops under Suchet's command, only 12,000 could be used for the three sieges in western Catalonia. The rest were needed to secure what had already been taken in Zaragoza and the Ebro River valley.[10]

Suchet's last major siege of 1811 was Tarragona. The ancient Roman town had a long history of occupation by Vandals, Visigoths and Muslims before becoming part of the Kingdom of Aragon in 1164. In 1641 the French had assisted the Catalans in taking the city from the Spaniards. The summer campaign of 1811, however, was quite a different matter, and Napoleon believed that taking Tarragona was 'the only means of preventing the insurgents from invading Upper Catalonia'. Suchet was also motivated by a promise from Napoleon that he would 'find his marshal's baton' in Tarragona, and he duly became the first French general in Spain to achieve that honour.[11]

On 29 June, after a siege of two long months, and despite harassment of the French by British naval cannon fire, the city fell. Suchet's forces suffered more than 3,000 losses, and the enraged soldiers took revenge on an equal number of inhabitants when they stormed the city. The scene, worse than Lerida and reminiscent of Zaragoza, was stunning in its savagery. Suchet wrote that the soldiers' 'excitement had reached the highest pitch; [and] it was not possible in so short a time, amid such a scene, to moderate them by words'. Essentially, the general denied culpability for the slaughter. 'They were inebriated, as it were, by the noise, smoke and blood, by the recollection of danger, by the desire of victory, by the thirst of revenge … after so obstinate a resistance, their rage knew no bounds.'[12]

Oman described the sack of Tarragona by telling how the French went from house to house murdering people in 'something that almost amounted to the systematic massacre of non-combatants'. He estimated that half of the 4,000 people lying dead in the streets were civilians. Suchet's words regarding Tarragona, although true in one sense, were misleading in that 'so short a time' referred to the initial storming of the city, not the overnight melee of rape and pillage he allowed his vengeful soldiers to engage in. Oman wrote that '450 women and children were among the slain … the victorious stormers generally gave quarter to any man wearing a uniform, and let off their fury on priests and unarmed citizens'. Oman also disputed Suchet's recollection of the slaughter occurring in 'so short a time': 'Plunder was even more general than murder … drunkenness and rape … riot and slaughter went on all night, and it was not till the next day that order was restored.'[13]

When news of the Tarragona massacre reached Britain, *The Times* called Suchet 'the most inhuman Frenchman who has passed the Pyrenees' and claimed he would be known 'as the soldier of Robespierre, and execrated for the atrocious cruelty with which, under the orders of the monstrous tyrant, he spilt the blood of his countrymen, [and] has poured out the remains of his barbarity upon unfortunate Tarragona.' Exaggerated stories of the sack had been spread, but 'the relations of the excesses committed by the French in Tarragona have rendered them horrible, even among the others which the peninsula has witnessed'. *The Times* did not hold back in its disgust:

> In a few hours, more than 6,000 persons of all classes were equally and cowardly assassinated. Neither the old, the servants of God, women, nor infants lately born, were spared; the soldiers robbed and plundered in the most violent and atrocious manner; they violated maidens, nuns, children, widows, married women, and committed such abominations that the pen refuses to record them.[14]

Outside observers followed the protracted war with interest. The Spanish resistance had become known throughout the western world, and despite their successful sieges, the image of the French took a battering. In his frequent conversations with a confident French ambassador in Moscow, US Minister to Russia John Quincy Adams noted sceptically in his diary that he was happy to hear 'there would be no war between this country [Russia] and France, for I had for a long time been afraid there would'. However, Napoleon was still planning an invasion of Russia and impatiently waiting for Suchet to complete his offensive and free up the necessary troops and supplies. Adams wrote that the ambassador believed the emperor 'intended first to sweep all clear in Spain, to wear out all the guerrillas, and take Valencia and Cartagena, which would not cost so much trouble as Tarragona. Cadiz would … be the last hold.'[15] However, Napoleon was deluded in his belief at this point, since attrition was favouring the insurgency.

Like Suchet, Napoleon viewed the sieges from a propaganda rather than strategic perspective. In a mid-June speech made to the Corps Législatif he bragged that 'most of the fortified towns in Spain have been taken by memorable sieges; the rebels have repeatedly been beaten in battle. England understands that the war is coming into its final phase.' It was a denial of reality and a repudiation of the military doctrine that had made him master of Europe. He did not control the seas, nor did his soldiers control the countryside. Nevertheless, the emperor refused to abandon plans he viewed in epic and historic terms: 'Our struggle against Carthage … will now be settled on the plains of Spain. A clap of thunder will put an end to the Spanish business … It will avenge Europe and Asia by ending this second Punic War.'[16]

On the other side of the Atlantic the Spanish rulers of Mexico, who were winning their own war against an insurrectionary movement inspired by the new tactics, remained cautiously optimistic about events back home. Reports trickled in, sent through the Junta Superior of Aragon, of Espoz y Mina's 'brave defenders of the homeland'. The reports were detailed and confident, and bolstered the spirits of those lamenting the unravelling of their empire:

> In all the other points the Spanish enthusiasm and the allied armies are observed unchanged, because despite having been seized by the French, at the cost of much blood, the Plaza of Tarragona … emulates that of Zaragoza and Gerona, and the courage of our generous warriors has been increased with this. Espoz y Mina cheats them without intermission, and divine providence has visibly protected him in various actions undertaken against the desperate *gabachos* [foreigners] that persecute him as desperate. The other guerrilla *partidas* circulate with the same vigour.[17]

Suchet's victory at Tarragona and his promotion to the rank of marshal illustrate an important dichotomy. As the French relished victories pleasing to Napoleon, the guerrilla war took on an intensity which made their victories ever hollower and their hold on the country more precarious. In essence, two separate wars were fought, one conventional and one unconventional. Ultimately, the French were in denial of the effectiveness and motivations of the insurgents – believing each new city they took was one step further towards the ultimate collapse of the resistance. For the Spanish, on the other hand, the war was an existential crisis, and no amount of terror could reduce their determination to resist. Unfortunately for both sides, Napoleon only realized this at a late date. Despite Suchet's victories in 1810 and 1811 at Lerida, Mequinenza, Tortosa and Tarragona, the insurgency he left behind in the north-east only intensified. These victories were hardly significant strategically, since the guerrillas were becoming stronger in the precisely same locations where Suchet had spent the entire year of 1809 working diligently to suppress them. In retrospect, his pyrrhic victories did not strengthen the French hold on Spain, but only resulted in the army becoming terminally overstretched.

One month after taking Tarragona, Marshal Suchet led two divisions into the hills west of Barcelona to storm the sacred Catalonian site of Montserrat. According to him, it was 'a position of great importance from a military point of view' because of its location on the heights along the main road linking Barcelona and Lerida in the centre of the province. Writing in his *Memoirs*, Suchet considered the Montserrat and Tarragona victories to have had a 'strong moral effect' upon the 'warlike' Catalonian population. Time was limited, however, as Napoleon 'was all impatience at Paris' due to his plans to invade Russia. Because of a growing shortage of troops, Napoleon needed to strip forces from Iberia to bolster the numbers intended to invade Russia. In late August, the same day that Napoleon officially annexed Catalonia to France, Suchet received a communication from the emperor specifically instructing him to be at 'the gates of that city' by mid-September. Suchet's 20,000-strong army began the siege of Valencia in early November and seized the city after two months. The decision by General Blake to surrender was controversial, but given Valencia's dwindling supplies and scant defences, French desire to avenge the *dos de mayo* mob killings, and Suchet's record of brutality, the decision probably reduced civilian deaths.[18]

Despite Napoleon's grand plans and Suchet's successful sieges, the war's most important siege, of Cadiz, ended in failure. Michael Glover, an historian of the Peninsular War, describes the effort to take that city as an 'illusory' impossibility. From February 1810 to August 1812, the French laid siege to the capital-in-exile with more than 60,000 soldiers, in the hope that reducing

Napoleonic Spain
February 1809–March 1812

it would stamp out resistance. During these two years the French supply lines stretched north-to-south throughout the entire country – affording numerous opportunities for insurgents to attack convoys, couriers and small detachments. Lord Castlereagh, the Leader of the House of Commons and Foreign Secretary, outlined the reasons why Napoleon continued the siege despite its futility. His assessment underlines Glover's assertion that there was 'no real hope that they would ever take the place'. Instead, as *The Times* noted in late 1812, the massive effort was carried on for 'the moral effect … because it was seen, that while Cadiz was in possession of the French, the world would suppose that Spain was completely in their power'.[19]

Lessons from the Sieges

Dozens of Spanish cities were devastated by sieges, assaults and occupations. Zaragoza was almost completely levelled, Tarragona and Lerida were brutally attacked, and Astorga, Cadiz, Gerona, Figueres, Pamplona, Tortosa and Valencia all suffered in such operations. Badajoz lost 4,000 civilians after Wellington's army – Spain's allies – brutally pillaged that city after bombarding it. The effects on these cities were lasting. David Gates explains that before the outbreak of the war in Spain 'full-blown sieges were unheard of in the Napoleonic Wars. The emperor's whole strategic doctrine was founded on brisk manoeuvre aimed at the destruction of an adversary's army.' For many reasons, Napoleon abandoned all his previously sound strategy in Spain, including the successful counter-insurgency tactics used in the Vendée. Gates also claims that 'Napoleon's military and diplomatic policies were out of step' with a politically unpopular puppet king. The second reason he gives for the French defeat is 'a failure of strategic doctrine, as, if only from a geographical perspective, the Peninsula was an environment quite unsuited to the French way of war'.[20]

Gates is correct, but he omits Napoleon's sieges of Gaeta, Magdeburg, Hamlin, Stralsund and Danzig in 1806 and 1807, Riga in 1812, and Breda in 1813. Many of these sites, along with cities such as Hamburg and Antwerp, were later defended towards the end of the war. Nevertheless, Gates accurately points out what Halleck himself meticulously concluded before US forces invaded central Mexico – that Spain was exceptional because of the sheer time, resources and manpower expended in taking dozens of cities. Moreover, the sieges not only sapped the resources of the French, they also contributed to the anger felt by the Spanish.

The Americans, before embarking on their campaign to attack the Mexican capital in 1847, would remember the mistakes made by the French. Henry

Halleck was not arguing against seizing important strategic points, only that the French spent too much time, money and resources taking *every* point. With the invasion of central Mexico in mind, Halleck believed it was important to remember that even though Napoleon was able to occupy Spain for years, 'it required ... the expenditure of millions in blood and treasure' to keep it under control. In effect, the defenders wore down the French by forcing them to engage in long drawn-out operations that did nothing to strengthen their strategic hold on the country:

> Those works which had been given up to Napoleon previous to the opening of hostilities contributed very much to the success of his arms; while those which had been retained by Spain and her allies contributed in an equal degree to fetter and embarrass his operations. Some of these, like Saragossa, Tarragona, Gerona, Tortosa ... with their broken walls and defective armaments, kept the enemy in check for months; and, by compelling the French to resort to the tedious operations of sieges, did much to weaken the French power on the peninsula.[21]

The Americans learned a critical lesson in not attempting to capture every Mexican city. In contrast with Spain, Monterrey and Veracruz were the only two major population centres besieged and attacked. Other cities, such as Puebla, gave way to the invaders. Had the large capital city of Mexico resisted, many more American soldiers would have been killed. As Vattel admitted, sieges were a necessary evil in war. They were used to gain footholds by seizing strategic ports or taking capitals, often resulting in the enemy leadership accepting defeat. They were not, however, important to a general whose objective was not the permanent conquest of a country, but the political resolution of a conflict.

Prolonged warfare during an occupation is problematic for an invader. The population begins to believe the occupiers have no intention of leaving, which makes it much more difficult to win the compliance of those who might otherwise have remained neutral. If the occupiers cannot provide some sense of normality, they risk alienating potential allies. When the people perceive the occupiers are on the defensive, it becomes nearly impossible for the occupiers to recruit personnel essential for administrative functions. In only rare cases will a population consider the ruling invaders more likely to promote their general wellbeing.

During a prolonged insurgency everything becomes more burdensome: communications between headquarters and smaller units is negatively affected, supplying and replacing soldiers in the field becomes more dangerous, and the maintenance of basic economic activity and services deteriorates as the guerrillas disrupt the invaders' efforts to pacify the country. In short, the system breaks down. Piecemeal destruction is exactly what the French experienced as collaborating local governments outside of the capital lost control. One by one, smaller garrisons were forced to abandon their posts for the safety of larger command centres. Although Madrid was retaken briefly after it was abandoned by the regime in 1812, the cities of Calatayud, Huesca, Cuenca and Guadalajara were retaken by the insurgents. Navarre and the corridor to Madrid were under constant attack by Espoz y Mina. The northern coast, separated from the interior by rugged mountains, was lost to government forces. With these and other districts falling under the control of the resistance, the authority of the central government collapsed.

Breakdown and Blockade

The provincial nature of the war made matters worse for the occupiers. Although the French courier service had developed an efficient system adjusted to the realities of conventional warfare in theatres outside Spain, it was ill-suited to an uncontrollable countryside. Unaccompanied couriers carrying essential strategic information were targeted. The result of poor inter-provincial communication was a series of provincial wars within a national arena – often with little cross-border coordination. Suchet wrote that 'the *partidas* could usually escape a sweep in one province simply by retreating to another area where the pursuing French could expect no assistance.' This was especially true in Navarre, Aragon, and Catalonia. 'In every direction, the communications are extremely difficult … provinces are isolated from each other, the towns and villages separated by immense distances.'[22]

By 1811 all the advantages previously held by the more experienced French Army had been wiped out. Guerrilla forces in Aragon and Navarre, led by Espoz y Mina, had coalesced into a formidable force that included two cavalry units, nine infantry battalions, and even engineer and artillery units. The most important asset of the guerrillas in that transition was their home support, and Mina's self-sufficient logistics organization was nothing like the ad hoc groups in the early years of the war. Other advantages the *partidas* exploited included their ability to disperse rapidly and re-form when needed, intimate knowledge of the land, faster movement due to their light equipment, and the ability to launch attacks at the time and place of their choosing (which mitigated the effect of French cavalry). Espoz y Mina was careful not to engage the enemy when outnumbered or outgunned – a critical maxim of guerrilla warfare. 'When our forces could not compete' with numerically larger forces, he wrote, 'we shielded ourselves within the mountains and crags, which were very strong natural parapets when the forces were balanced.'[23]

Alexander notes that handicaps on the French side included: 'heavy desertion' and the heavier equipment of their soldiers, burdensome artillery (and wagons) impeded by inclement weather, and a lack of knowledge of the land – including poor maps. Another problem occurred when pursuing guerrillas. Following an engagement, some troops needed to stay behind to protect the wounded, otherwise guerrillas would simply double back and take them out. To prevent this, commanders often kept field detachments closer to garrisons to maintain support nearby, as well as to offer reinforcement to vulnerable posts. When pursuing guerrillas into the mountains, any wounded soldier left behind without protection became an easy target. In this regard, Suchet was honest about the efficacy of the guerrillas:

> These numerous bands, spread over so vast a circumference, began to operate in a simultaneous and uniform manner. They destroyed our stragglers, and frequently even our detachments when they were small in number and off their guard; they spread terror throughout the country, harassed our partisans, compelled all young men to re-enlist in the Spanish armies, intercepted the couriers, arrested the convoys and obstructed the return of the contributions or provisions we had raised.[24]

The growing success of the insurgency coincided with a breakdown in provincial administration, and the conflict became untenable for the invaders after 1811, when guerrillas reached parity with them. Alexander's research into French military correspondence led him to conclude that 'Napoleon's creation of independent military governments did not encourage coordinated activities'. Compounding this administrative provincialism were deteriorating troop replacement methods. In Spain, replacing men became a major burden in an unexpectedly long-term campaign. Essentially, 'Napoleon mortgaged the future to replace the catastrophic losses suffered in 1808'. Unable to replace large numbers of troops in order to occupy and hold vast areas of Spain in the face of a growing insurgency, the French became 'locked in a vicious battle of attrition'.[25]

Even though the French *levée* system trained and assimilated new conscripts into the army, it could not cope with the unanticipated duration of the conflict. French officials were not ready to face a protracted war in Spain – a war requiring hundreds of thousands of troops to confront an insurgency *and* occupy vast territories. This was especially true in the vital logistic corridors connecting the army to France. In Alexander's words, Napoleon's army had 'expanded beyond the limits of his managerial bounds, and his troops suffered the consequences'. Compounding the shock to a system predicated on conventional tactics was a shortage of officers, which had been apparent as early as 1807. In large battles in northern Europe, a small number of talented officers might have been enough to turn the tide on a battlefield where troop numbers were comparable to the population of a small city. In Spain, however, the lack of lower-level talent on small posts in isolated locations meant that engaging in counter-insurgency sweeps of the countryside became an impossibility or, at the very least, more dangerous than simply defending a fortified position. As early as 1809, the shortage of officers with experience in Hoche's counter-insurgency methods, along with shortages of men (veterans or conscripts), meant that it was only a matter of time before the French were bled dry. Other serious logistics problems existed. Disorganization in the rear stymied progress, and as early as 1809, the main depot supplying the war at Bayonne was reported to be in 'great disorder'.[26]

The lack of horsepower also became a problem. A shortage of horses in Iberia affected both cavalry units and the army's ability to transport artillery and heavy guns the distances required to launch offensive operations. The inability to replace dead or injured horses meant fewer wagons and fewer supplies reaching the soldiers. Due to its employment in dozens of sieges, the replacement of artillery was similarly affected. Logistically then, by the time Napoleon began planning his ill-advised invasion of Russia in 1811, the French army in Spain was exhausted from a lack of men, supplies, horses, cannons, experience and everything else needed for a successful long-term occupation. Materiel not sent to Spain was being diverted to the transport companies being assembled to march across Russia.[27]

The French were not the only ones engaged in sieges during the war. On 14 December 1811, Espoz y Mina issued a decree implementing an economic blockade of Pamplona. 'Navarre is filled with wretchedness,' the decree began. 'Fathers have seen their children hanged for their heroic conduct … sons have seen their fathers consumed in prison, for no other crime than that of being the parents of such valiant defenders.'[28] The decree legitimized a siege of terror designed to starve the garrison into submission. The decree forbade all goods from entering Pamplona 'under pain of death; and that all persons attempting to enter it shall without ceremony be fired upon, and if wounded and taken, immediately hanged.' Mina allowed people to leave Pamplona, but no one could enter the city. The five-article decree forced the remaining citizens to choose sides. Article Three warned, 'Any officer, soldier, or person of whatever description, who assists or suffers a Frenchman to escape, shall infallibly be shot.' Dissent was not an option either, as the chieftain repeated that anyone voicing opposition to his dictates 'shall be shot, and their property distributed among the division'. Lastly, to drive the point home about the prohibition on aiding the French, Mina added a fifth article: 'The house in any town in which any Frenchman is concealed shall be burnt, and its inhabitants shot.'[29]

The only ways out of the city for a Frenchman were to fight or surrender – since deserters could not rely on locals to aid their escape. Two months into the blockade, scarcity of supplies forced the French to make dangerous foraging expeditions in the environs of Pamplona. Despite the suffering the siege inflicted on its citizens, Espoz y Mina believed it was 'a well designated moral blockade' justified by the right to defend Spain in a conflict in which the traditional rules of war were jettisoned. General Reille tried in vain to countermand the decree's effectiveness with his own, equally stern proclamation, calling Espoz y Mina a 'gang leader' who despised the citizens of Pamplona.[30]

What Espoz y Mina instituted was more than just a blockade. In response to the executions of Spanish military and civilian prisoners, the decree also announced (Article One) that war 'without quarter, is declared against all French soldiers and officers, including the Emperor himself'. Article Two was equally explicit about the ugly direction the war took in 1811: 'The French officers or soldiers, taken with or without arms in any action, shall be hanged, and their uniforms placed in the high roads.'[31]

A 'Detestable System'

In the spring of 1811 the ambush of a large French convoy by Espoz y Mina's forces at the Basque mountain pass of Arlabán represented another turning point in the war. The attack was disconcerting to French officials because the Vitoria to Irun supply corridor was vital to efforts elsewhere in the peninsula. When news of the attack reached Paris, the emperor expressed his dismay but also gave a stubbornly conventional response, writing to Berthier that the 'passage of the Ebro must be secured'. In addition to fortifying Miranda with guardhouse towers, ten large towers were ordered to be built between Vitoria and Irun as 'outposts to reconnoitre the heights, and to keep us always the masters of them'. Napoleon informed Berthier that General Reille 'should pursue Mina, and do all he can to destroy the *banditti* and pacify Navarre … [he] must make an end of the *banditti*, terrify them, shoot them by the hundreds, disarm the country.' After Arlabán, French counter-insurgency efforts were stepped up in a desperate attempt to subdue Navarre; 20,000 troops were borrowed from the district of Biscay to put down the Navarrese insurgents, thus doubling the number of soldiers deployed to capture or kill El Empecinado a month earlier. Taken together, the two actions demonstrate the seriousness with which the French viewed the guerrilla threat, and Napoleon grew so impatient that he wrote to Berthier in November to 'order General Caffarelli to proceed with his division against Mina; to pursue him in every direction till he is utterly routed'.[32]

The fact that the population mostly supported the rebels bolstered their intelligence-gathering capabilities. Conversely, the occupying army's military intelligence system was regularly undermined. Couriers unaccompanied by large escorts disappeared, and critical information arrived too late to be strategically useful. Insurgents intercepting imperial communications became privy to the thinking of and decisions made by the upper echelons, which only worsened the situation of the occupiers. It was death by a thousand cuts. One historian claims that one out of every two French soldiers 'in Spain were thus usually tied up in protection of their communications'. Even if it was only half that number, it would still represent an astonishing percentage of imperial manpower devoted to maintaining communications.[33]

Having denied the military reality since the beginning of the war, in November of 1811 Napoleon finally recognized the situation as it truly was. In a letter to Berthier (who was on the verge of a nervous breakdown) Napoleon addressed the ineffective 'detestable system' he had micromanaged for three years by invoking the counter-insurgency tactics used in the Vendée. He lamented the fact that 'immense forces are stationed in the villages to resist troops of banditti' and ordered that 'only the principal posts should be occupied, and moveable columns sent from them'. Switching strategies was too late to be effective, however, and rather than regroup, Napoleon redirected his focus onto the coming campaign in the north. As soon as Suchet took Valencia, Napoleon ordered a crippling withdrawal of his best units to amass the army of 500,000 men which he believed would conquer Russia. The Spanish knew about the troop draw-down and the impending Russian campaign, because the citizens of Irun and other border towns had been counting the number of French soldiers coming into and leaving Spain since the beginning of the war. The momentum was turning toward the insurgents.[34]

Gains made by the insurgents wore down the occupiers, and desperate measures ensued. In May the authorities implemented a policy of executing captured prisoners. This marked a major escalation in hostilities and a departure from the conventional rules of war. Since the guerrillas held untold numbers of French prisoners, it was a disastrous move, and both El Empecinado and Mina informed Joseph that French prisoners would receive the same fate.[35] Summary executions of Spanish traitors (*chacones*) working for the French had been carried out by the insurgents since the beginning of the war, but reprisal executions of French prisoners increased dramatically in 1812 in response to Reille's rule in Navarre. Later, after Napoleon replaced Reille, an accommodation was reached between Mina and the new governor-general, and reprisal executions ceased at the end of 1812. Extreme violence was thus reduced towards the end of the war, but there is no telling how many had been killed by then.[36]

In 1812 Mina made major inroads against the French. The Navarrese farmer had become so formidable that Suchet ordered a division from Valencia to assist Reille, but it was a futile gesture. Reille's Army of the Ebro was useless against an enemy that refused pitched battles, struck wherever and whenever it could, and dispersed and regrouped at will, supported by the population. The French garrison at Pamplona was essentially 'under siege' on an island surrounded by insurgents. Nor was Mina interested in trying to win the war outright, but instead focused on slowly bleeding the French. Alexander writes that through 'a combination of partisan persistence and attrition, the combat superiority that the French initially had enjoyed gradually disappeared; by 1812 the partisans were nearly on an equal footing with the best French regulars.' The Zaragoza-Madrid route became untenable, and the provincial nature of the conflict became more extreme that summer, when Suchet forbade Reille in Navarre from using his troops in Aragon. Thus, the inability and unwillingness of French commanders to coordinate their efforts to fight the guerrillas was a major Achilles heel. These factors, coupled with Wellington's desire to begin fighting again after a long hiatus, turned the tide of the war.[37]

Joseph was in no less precarious a position in Madrid. When Wellington returned, the combined action of conventional forces and seasoned insurgent groups ripped apart the logistics and communications sinews of the occupying army. In his 1986 work, *The Spanish Ulcer*, David Gates notes that guerrillas were 'a priceless source of information' for the British from 1809, and quotes Wellington: 'The French armies have no communications … whereas I have knowledge of all that passes on all sides.' By the beginning of 1812, 'hardly any correspondence between King Joseph and Marshal Mormont reached its destination'. Wellington's victory at Salamanca in July thus represented the fruits of that vital relationship.[38]

By 1812 the combination of the two forces, after years of grinding on the French, had worn the occupiers down. Oman commented that the blame rested with Napoleon, who despite the obvious situation of Spain, had 'continued, with all serenity to ignore tiresome hindrances, and to issue orders grounded on data many weeks old, often on data which had never been true at any moment, but which suited him to believe'. Stubborn refusal to accurately assess the military situation in Spain, along with embarking on the Russian campaign, hastened the French 'catastrophe of 1812'.[39]

The year 1812 was also when the British government, which theretofore had been reluctant to officially sanction the guerrilla war in Spain, changed course. While newspaper reports of the guerrillas' activities reached the British public, the government had remained quietly sceptical about the unconventional efforts of the partisans. All that changed on 7 January 1812, when British support for the insurgent 'system' was announced at the opening of the parliamentary session; the Lords Commissioners and Prince Regent (the future George IV) gave speeches to both houses proclaiming that 'his Royal Highness is persuaded that you will admire the perseverance and gallantry manifested by the Spanish' and that a 'new energy has arisen among the people.' Britain's leaders were ecstatic, because after years of doggedly fighting the French, progress was finally being made:

> In Spain the spirit of the people remains unsubdued; and the system of warfare so peculiarly adapted to the actual condition of the Spanish nation has been recently extended and improved, under the advantages which result from the operations of the Allied Armies on the frontier, and from the countenance and assistance of his Majesty's navy on the coast.[40]

On 12 August the allied army headed by Wellington liberated Madrid. Two weeks later, the siege of Cadiz was lifted. The following month, Joseph managed to muster a combined force in Valencia to briefly retake Madrid, but the war's outcome was now inevitable. While Joseph re-established himself in Madrid, Napoleon's army was in full winter retreat across western Russia. Speaking to his close personal aide General Armand de Caulaincourt on the way back to Paris, the emperor displayed unusual candour in admitting, 'It would have been better to have wound up the war in Spain before embarking on this Russian expedition.' He also confessed, uncharacteristically, that 'the war in Spain itself, it is now a matter only of guerrilla contests'.[41] Shortly afterwards, news of Napoleon's massive defeat in Russia reached the peninsula. 'Simple calculations were presented to me at the same moment that I came to know the fatal outcome for Bonaparte of the Russian campaign,' Espoz y Mina wrote in his *Memoirs*. With the British engaged again, these calculations presaged the destruction of the French Army: 'After the successful defeat of the Muscovite czar's enemy ... their strength could be counted at the beginning of this year from eighty to one hundred thousand men in all, spread out in a vast space.'[42] Joseph abandoned Madrid on 17 March 1813, and left Spain for the last time on 28 June. The long retreat followed the same route he had used to enter the kingdom in 1808. After five years of war, the French were pushed back over the Pyrenees.

Defeat and Retrospection

French defeat was apparent in 1812. Shortly after Suchet's triumph in Valencia, an optimistic Napoleon saw his plans crumbling and commented that the 'most distinguished officers looked upon it is a disgrace to be sent to the Peninsula'. The emperor himself admitted, 'It was easy to foresee that the period was not far distant when the French would be obliged to recross the Pyrenees.' Despite throwing 300,000 soldiers into Spain, the country had not been subdued. With the advantage of hindsight from his exile on a far-flung island in the South Atlantic, Napoleon confessed that he had underestimated the Spanish. He summed up the entire campaign by highlighting the early victories of Suchet and other generals, but then coming to a brutal conclusion:

> At first we were uniformly successful, but our advantages were so dearly purchased that the ultimate issue of this struggle might have easily been foreseen, because when a people fight for their homes and their liberties the invading army must gradually diminish, while at the same time the armed population, emboldened by success, increases in a still more marked progression. Insurrection was now regarded by the Spaniards as a holy and sacred duty.[43]

Antoine-Henry Jomini, a highly respected author and a colonel who served under Marshal Michel Ney during the early period of the Peninsular War, was admired by both Napoleon and Scott for his 1805 work, *Treatise on Grand Military Operations*, a text which informed the early West Point curriculum, leaning heavily, as it did, towards the French military school. In 1838 Jomini published his most acclaimed work, *The Art of War*, which echoed the emperor's explanation of what went wrong. Like Napoleon, Jomini witnessed Spanish resistance at first hand and believed the defeat of the greatest army in the world boiled down to the inability to suppress a population supporting partisan forces defending their homeland:

> No army, however disciplined, can contend successfully against such a system applied to a great nation, unless it be strong enough to hold all the essential points of the country, cover its communications, and at the same time furnish an active force sufficient to beat the enemy wherever he may present himself. If this enemy has a regular army of respectable size to be a nucleus around which to rally the people, what force will be sufficient to be superior everywhere, and to assure the safety of the long lines of communication against numerous bodies? The Peninsular War should be

carefully studied, to learn all the obstacles which a general and his brave troops may encounter in the occupation or conquest of a country whose people are all in arms.[44]

Other scholars have examined the conflict. Carl von Clausewitz, a veteran of the Napoleonic Wars who spent much of his career educating a new generation of cadets at the Prussian War College (*Kriegsakademie*) in Berlin, was one of the earliest students of guerrilla warfare. His lectures between 1816 and 1830 were later compiled and published in 1832 after his death as the seminal work *On War* (*Vom Kriege*). Clausewitz stressed the psychological factors which Napoleonic tacticians such as Jomini often overlooked. One of his most famous precepts, 'War is only the continuation of political methods', relates to the desirability of winning 'hearts and minds'. This developing approach to combating insurgency links to the maxim first attributed to Cato the Elder:

But now, if a war is not so decisive in its results, if its operations are not so comprehensive as is consistent with its real nature, then the requisition system will begin to exhaust the country in which it is carried on to that degree that either peace must be made, or means must be found to lighten the burden on the country, and to become independent of it for the supplies of the army. The latter was the case of the French army under Buonaparte in Spain, but the first happens much more frequently.[45]

Clausewitz's sentiments were reflected in the opinions of contemporary observers, such as those in March of 1813 of the former British Secretary of State, Marquess Richard Wellesley. Although the Duke of Wellington's older brother understood the military tide had turned, he was critical of the way the British conducted the war – with alternating advances from and retreats to Portugal: 'What is this system of protracted warfare, which … never begins, but which is never to end; which is to linger on at its ease from year to year … and all the miseries without its successes?' Wellesley described a new type of war of attrition against an occupying force and recognized the fatal fallacy of Napoleon's self-sufficient provincial military system: 'Instead of superintending the army in person, its general was compelled to abandon it; to leave it to conflicting powers – to authorities ridiculous and contemptible.' Essentially, the governors-general could not work together, and only did so after it was too late. 'Their commander in the south [was] not able to assist, or draw assistance from, the commander in the north; and the general in the north [lacked] the assistance and co-operation of the commander in the south.' He lauded his brother's victories but recognized that the Spanish had forced the French to 'spread out over a large surface' and occupy the entire country, which reduced the threat they posed to the British army:

> They could not present themselves in any united body to the whole of your [British] army; that they could not oppose to you the whole body of their force. Your system, therefore, shall have been, to have had a force able to maintain active operations in the field, and another force competent to keep in check the main body of the French army.[46]

Zaragoza was liberated in 1813. Shortly after the main French force left the city in early July of that year, Espoz y Mina entered it in triumph. But the war had a devastating effect. After enduring eight months of siege, destruction, pillage and occupation, Zaragoza needed to rebuild what it had lost. Many of the ruins from the war, with their bullet holes and shell damage, are still there to see. Zaragoza thus became a symbol of the defiance, independence and heroism of a people who refused to be conquered. It represented not just the geographic and strategic failure of the French in subduing Spain, but the spiritual persistence and determination of the Spanish people.

The destruction of the French Army by the Spanish guerrillas during the Peninsular War changed the trajectory of modern warfare. Until that time the French had been undefeated in battle. The invasion of Spain and imposition of Napoleon's brother on the throne were the catalysts that upended that record. Rather than accede to the more powerful occupier, the Spanish rose to challenge the invaders by waging a national war. The 2 May uprising in Madrid and the resistance forged during the sieges of Zaragoza became symbols of popular defiance in the face of a militarily superior foe. When conventional military means failed, the Spanish changed tactics and launched an unprecedented guerrilla campaign that overturned the rules and laws of regular warfare. The insurgent war was initially fostered by the ad hoc central juntas of Spain through regulations and later the *Corso Terrestre* ('land privateering') – a proclamation that legitimized and incentivized the interception of enemy supplies and communications by small *partidas* throughout the occupied provinces.

The tactics employed by the small units organized under the auspices of the *Corso Terrestre* were antithetical to those of Napoleon's larger armies and to the military doctrines of the era. Various stratagems such as avoiding direct confrontation with larger forces, striking unsuspecting units in surprise attacks, and dispersing and re-forming, became the norm for insurgent forces in Spain. This 'swarming' strategy, later employed in other conflicts such as the Mexican War of Independence, forced the occupiers to be on their guard at all times. In eschewing conventional military engagements, the guerrillas undermined the enemy by compelling him to protect convoys and couriers with heavily armed escorts. Because of this, soldiers that might have otherwise been used in counter-insurgency or offensive operations against the British had to be deployed to keep logistics going, and these obligations became a constant burden undercutting the army's basic capabilities.

The efficacy of guerrilla warfare during the conflict contrasts with the stubborn belief of Napoleon that conventional warfare would eventually bring victory. The strategy of occupying the entire country undermined the French because it forced Napoleon to send troops to nearly every corner of the peninsula. Once the French forces were dispersed, it became easier for guerrillas to attack smaller isolated garrisons in locations strategically unnecessary to the regime's main goals of destroying the government in Cadiz and driving the British from Portugal. Napoleon micromanaged the conflict from a distance, lacked the insight to adapt to new methods, and only realized his army was critically weakened at a late stage in the war. Ultimately, fraying communications and a lack of strategic intelligence undermined the French ability to adapt to the ever-changing military landscape. In the end, Napoleon's top-down method of waging war not only undermined the gains made by his generals in theatre, but was incapable of tackling guerrilla warfare.

The policy of terror implemented by Napoleon from the war's inception only aided the insurgents' cause. Executions, forced exiles, kidnappings, imprisonment and surveillance became the norm. Although justifiably legal, the effect of these policies was exacerbated by the sacking of cities and towns under siege, which only served to further inflame the population. By stubbornly escalating violence against the people, Napoleon fuelled the very insurgency undermining his hold on the country. Popular resistance was further stimulated by the unsavoury treatment of the Catholic Church and clerics – many of whom were already opponents of French secularism. The inability to gain the support of such an influential institution posed a major problem, and because of previous conflicts with the French, the occupying force faced an uphill battle in winning over neutrals at the onset of the war. Taken in total, harsh French treatment of Spanish combatants, ecclesiastics and civilians undermined efforts to win over the domestic allies and collaborators essential for a successful long-term occupation.

Severely punishing those deemed critical of the French regime, of sympathizing with insurgents, or of aiding them, was the biggest mistake made by the French. This policy, which percolated from the top throughout the military command structure, alienated the regime and occupying army from a population already dubious about French intentions. Execution, imprisonment and exile of those associated with the insurgency turned the war into an existential threat and made enemies of people who might otherwise have remained uninvolved. Confiscation of wealth, whether from churches, convents, parishes or private individuals, convinced a critical majority of Spaniards (lay and clerical) that French intentions were hostile to their interests – despite all the rhetoric to the contrary by the regime. Napoleon's personal animus towards the Spanish was therefore redirected against the people of Spain by his generals, their colonels, their captains, and all the way down the command structure, for the duration of the occupation.

In examining other wars, turning points can be seen at which insurgent forces begin to reach military parity against an invader. From examples as diverse as the British during the American Revolutionary War or the Russians fighting the Afghans during the Cold War, the insurgency grinds down the logistics network and morale of the invading army, while the invader is forced to enact counterproductive counter-insurgency policies to root out rebels or sympathizers among the general population. In such situations time is the enemy of the invaders. Once this turning point is reached, there is little an army can do (apart from massacring the entire population) to win the compliance of a people whose sons, fathers and mothers are engaging the enemy. Politically, that point arrived early in the Peninsular War. Militarily, it came in 1811, when the guerrillas reached parity with the French. By the time the British reasserted themselves in 1812 with their rested army, the combined action of insurgents and conventional forces hastened the destruction of the French Army.

In 1840, many years after the Napoleonic Wars and six years before the US Army invaded Mexico, an article appeared in *The Times*:

> If France is henceforth to carry on an aggressive war, she must do so out of her own proper cost. The age for making 'war support war' according to the cool phrase of Bonaparte and for grinding an oppressed people to death, or goading them to madness, by a system of savage robbery, under the name of 'contributions' for the maintenance of an invading horde – that day will not speedily return. The bones of Napoleon will not have brought back with them the matchless skill which he commanded for wholesale desolation throughout the earth.[47]

When Napoleon told his brother Joseph, 'At Madrid you are in France', he displayed tragic hubris. The Spanish may not have been able to agree among themselves about liberalism, enlightenment or absolutism, but they were united against an invader who did not respect their religious institutions or their true king. Exacerbating that hubris on the part of Napoleon was his belief that he could relive Cato the Elder's glory by adopting his ancient maxim, *bellum se ipsum alet* – 'the war will feed itself'. This was one of many lessons the Americans learned before penetrating the heart of Mexico.

Part II

The Mexican-American War

In great wars of invasion it is sometimes impracticable ... to provide for the immense forces ... by any regular system of magazines or of ordinary requisitions: in such cases their subsistence is entirely intrusted [sic] to the troops themselves, who levy contributions wherever they pass. The inevitable consequences of this system are universal pillage and a total relaxation of discipline; the loss of private property and the violation of individual rights, are followed by the massacre of all straggling parties, and the ordinary peaceful and non-combatant inhabitants are converted into bitter and implacable enemies. In this connection the war in the Spanish peninsula is well worthy of study. At the beginning of this war Napoleon had to choose between methodical operations, with provisions carried in the train of his army, or purchased of the inhabitants and regularly paid for; and irregular warfare, with forced requisitions – war being made to support war.

Henry Halleck, *Military Art and Science*, 1846

Chapter 3

The 'Second Saragossa'

I n early 1845 the incoming American administration led by President
James K. Polk worked to finalize the annexation of the Republic of Texas
– a breakaway state formerly part of Mexico. That July, Polk sent soldiers
under the command of General Zachary Taylor into the disputed region
between the Rio Grande and Nueces Rivers, and later dispatched envoy John
Slidell to Mexico City to negotiate the purchase of that area. On 13 May 1846,
a little more than two weeks after skirmishes broke out on the northern side of
the Rio Grande, the US Congress approved Polk's assertion that a state of war
with Mexico now existed. Despite the controversial origins of the war, the US
Army launched an invasion of northern Mexico.

The invasion led by Zachary Taylor was one of the two major theatres of
the conflict. The other – excluding the naval forces and soldiers sent by Polk to
California and New Mexico – was the attack directed at the heart of Mexico
to force the Mexicans to sue for peace. The campaign to seize the capital, led
by General Winfield Scott, commenced in April 1847 with an amphibious
assault on the coastal city of Veracruz. Leading the defence of Mexico was
former president General Antonio López de Santa Anna – who returned from
exile in Cuba to unite his fractured country. As Mexican unity fragmented
in the spring of 1847, domestic and foreign guerrillas began attacking US
forces along the line between Puebla and Veracruz. In the United States the
war remained controversial, but when fighting commenced, much of the
American press promoted the conflict by framing it as a romantic endeavour
pitting enlightened republican warriors against the corrupt and despotic rulers
of Mexico. Underlying that general theme was a growing interest among
Americans in Spanish history and more specifically the Napoleonic War
in Spain.

Veracruz

On 9 April 1847, the *New York Herald* printed a short article about a ship
named *Oregon* that had set sail from Veracruz the month before. The piece
stated that after heading 'three or four hours' in open water towards New

Orleans, 'heavy firing was heard in Veracruz, and from the sound, it came from the Americans'. Indeed, it could not have had any other source. The bombardment of Veracruz in March ushered in the second phase of a war which had started almost exactly a year earlier. The *Herald* promised its readers more updates, adding keenly that 'Veracruz is to be the second Saragossa!'[1]

The assault on Mexico's main port city was received with both eager praise and great consternation by a politically divided America, and both pro- and anti-war advocates in the United States found ways to compare the event to the actual siege of Zaragoza a generation earlier. Northern anti-war newspapers focused on 'the immense horror of the scene, [where] 500 women and children perished with their ruined homes and slaughtered husbands and fathers'. While acknowledging that General Winfield Scott 'invited' civilians to leave before the bombardment, the anti-war press often praised the Mexicans defending their homes with a reference to the defiant city's most famous heroine – Agustina. 'We know something of the brave stock from which they sprung ... that nerved women's hands to join the awful strife at Saragossa? Better ... to die with their defenders, than to live widowed and fatherless.'[2]

The use of feminine imagery was common. One North Carolina newspaper published an article entitled 'Female Patriotism' while noting that the idea of Agustina had inspired a woman from Alabama to inquire about how 'to join our forces in Mexico'. The article claimed she was motivated by patriotism and 'determined, if possible, to do her part towards sustaining the honor of her country' by enlisting in an infantry, artillery or dragoon company. The writer asked, 'After this, who shall say that the spirit of Joan d'Arc has fled, or that the patriotism of the Maid of Saragossa does not still burn in the bosoms of some of her sex?'[3]

Newspaper editors and columnists asked themselves and their readers whether a defiant Spanish spirit existed among the Mexicans. The *Liberator* of Boston, opposed to the war along with much of New England, confirmed the presence among the Mexicans of a Spanish-inspired hostility to invaders harking back to the days of Hannibal and the Punic Wars: 'The Spanish blood is as remarkable, in its way, as the Anglo-Saxon. It has been very hard to conquer, from the siege of Saguntum down to that of Saragossa.'[4] Comparisons with the Carthaginian siege of the ancient Spanish city of Saguntum lent the modern siege epic and Iberian credentials. During the war, ancient military campaigns were commonly cited by a press eager to sell the conflict to the public. The *Buffalo Commercial* made a case for expecting further opposition by claiming that 'everybody knows that the very women of invaded countries, and especially when those women are of the Spanish race, fight for their firesides like so many born devils.' The upstate New York newspaper claimed that 'ladies are instinctive soldiers', while again referencing 'Joan of Arc or the Maid of Saragossa' as examples:

> Witness how she of Saragossa, Agustina, one of the beauties of her city, shone in its two sieges … among the most desperate of its unconquerable defenders, and verified how, when people strike for their hearths and altars, you have 'The man nerved to the spirit, and the maid waving her Amazonian blade'. We may meet, in overrunning Mexico, a fierce … feminine resistance of this old Numantian sort.[5]

Comparisons between the two sieges continued to be made in reports long after the walls of Veracruz were breached by cannon fire. When news reached New Orleans – the closest major American city to the war – the information was relayed rapidly to the eastern United States via couriers and the newly-invented (and developing) telegraph system. Many newspapers shared reports and stories. One of Natchez's main papers, the *Mississippi Free Trader*, noted how Veracruz's 'main streets had been barricaded, the pavements broken up, and cannon placed in position to enfilade them … every house was a fortress, and the city was capable of presenting a resistance equal to that of Saragossa.'[6] The *New York Herald* reported that, as in the French siege of Zaragoza, 'every house here was a fortress, loopholed, in readiness to envelop our columns in murderous fire, the moment they should attempt to penetrate its interior'.[7] Many of the reports of the siege of Veracruz employed similar phraseology to describe the scene.

So where did the Americans acquire these romantic and fanciful historical notions? In his 1985 work, *To the Halls of the Montezumas*, historian Robert Johannsen demonstrated that many historical works during the war 'suggested parallels between the Mexican War and the Napoleonic wars that broadened support for the conflict'. These works included Joel Taylor Headley's *History of Napoleon and his Marshals* (1846), William Hazlitt's *Life of Napoleon Buonaparte* (1847) and Adolphe Thier's *History of the Consulate and the Empire of France under Napoleon* (1845). Johannsen elaborated on how entrepreneurial publishers reprinted new editions of various English historical works on the Peninsular War by authors such as Archibald Alison, Charles Vane and William Napier, and that excerpts from these were published in US papers. Headley's *Napoleon and his Marshals* was even 'dedicated to [Winfield] Scott, whom Headley admired and thought would soon become the Napoleon of the Mexican War'. These books, among a myriad of other works including dime novels and magazine stories, 'aroused the mid-century's romantic imagination'.[8]

Newspapers ran stories throughout 1847 comparing the siege of Veracruz to contemporary accounts of the siege of Zaragoza – often with racial overtones: 'To give our readers some idea of the indomitable pertinacity of the Spanish race when their homes and their altars are assailed,' the *Buffalo Commercial* read, 'and to show what the thirty Mexican departments would probably do on their own account' if the Americans widened the war. The newspaper ran an excerpt from Headley's book on Napoleon, noting that it had been taken from Marshal Lannes' account (italics added):

> Unyielding to the last, the brave Saragossans fought on... rushed up to the very mouth of the cannon, and perished by hundreds of thousands in the streets of the city. *Every house was a fortress*, and around its walls were separate battlefields, where deeds of frantic valor were done. Day after day did these single-handed fights continue, while famine and pestilence walked the city at noonday, and slew faster than the swords of the enemy. The dead lay piled up in every street, and on the thick heaps of the slain the living mounted and fought with the energy of despair for their homes and their liberty.[9]

Zaragoza was also portrayed as a general symbol of defiance against an aggressor *before* the siege of Veracruz. The northern Mexican city of Monterrey, captured by General Zachary Taylor in September of 1846, was also used to invoke the spirit of Zaragozan resistance. Many papers ran stories claiming the capture of Monterrey 'brings to mind parallel instances' among historical events, including 'the last great struggle between Rome and Carthage' and 'the Peninsular War of the present century'. William Napier's history of the war in Spain was quoted. Using feminine imagery again, the article described how the 'walls of Saragossa thus went to the ground; but Saragossa herself remained erect, and as the broken girdle fell from the heroic city the besiegers [were] startled at the view of her naked strength.' Thus, the Americans took on the role of the French aggressors, albeit with updated weaponry:

> Mines were prepared in the more open spaces and the internal communications from house to house were multiplied until they formed a vast labyrinth, the intricate windings of which were only to be traced by the weapons and the dead bodies of the defenders ... advantages secured by thus advancing under cover, the American rifle, in the hands of such men as the Texas Rangers and the Western volunteers, was a more efficient weapon in such a contest as this than any which the assailants of Saragossa possessed.[10]

The *Natchez Weekly Courier* reported similar events during the storming of Monterrey: 'Americans had found the streets of the city barricaded with stone walls, but no obstacles, no difficulties were found insurmountable to American valor.' Such descriptions of American courage were typical of pro-war dispatches, despite the fact that 'the enemy thought to have Monterrey recorded in history as the Saragossa of Mexico, and to win unfading laurels in the repulse which they were to inflict upon the American forces.' Indeed, that city, stormed by US soldiers in the fall of 1846, had been labelled by dozens of newspapers the 'Saragossa of Mexico', before being replaced by the more fitting Veracruz the following year. Nevertheless, the fact that Americans had been fighting within the walls of a foreign city was close enough to render a comparison feasible. 'The fiercest of the fight was in the very streets of the city, and there the deadliness of Texan retribution found no obstruction to its revenge in the walls of stone which had been reared to oppose its advance.'[11]

Seeking international recognition, the American press constantly compared the US Army's achievements to those of European powers: Americans 'cannot look back on the career of our army in Mexico without a thrill of honest pride! Such prodigies of valor, such heroic perseverance has never been passed in history, and has only been equaled by the fabled deeds of the Paladins of old.' Newspapers worked diligently to ensure that 'future analysts will tell the story of the war' and portray the 'miraculous' American efforts against insurmountable odds in the best possible light. The US Army's achievements in Mexico, according to the pro-war press, even surpassed the 'prodigies performed by the old guard' of Europe. The former French emperor was often the object of these epic comparisons: 'Napoleon often won battles against armies thrice his own number; Taylor and Scott have conquered against fourfold odds. The victories of Napoleon were achieved by veteran troops; our successes have been gained chiefly by volunteers.' The *Daily Picayune* of New Orleans, an important source of war news in the eastern USA, claimed that General Zachary Taylor's victories had proved 'to the world that he is the 'second Napoleon'. Others wrote that Scott was 'always admired' as a general, but that 'Old "Rough and Ready" however will still remain with us, to all who know him [as the] "Napoleon" of the army.' Taylor would become the next president as a result of his military fame.[12]

If the American pro-war press was not comparing Taylor or Scott to Napoleon, it was criticizing the Mexicans for failing to put up a resistance akin to that of their Spanish cousins: 'New Spain is as like Old Spain as ever a child was like a parent. If the Mexicans had been blessed with a little Bailén, the whole scene would be a wonderful representation of the peninsula in 1809.' Some even compared Santa Anna's flight after the Battle of Cerro Gordo to the end of the Peninsular War: 'Santa Anna is said to have decamped in good time, leaving his carriage, like Joseph's at Vittoria, to the spoils of his pursuers.' To many editors it did not matter if the Americans took on the role of the Spanish in the analogy.[13]

Other romantic comparisons were widely disseminated. Since it was known that Scott's army was heading to Mexico City, newspapers in the early phases of the war likened the US Army to Cortez's band of conquistadors:

> The Anglo-Saxons were cut off from all succor and support from home … The Yankee invaders found the valley bristling with bayonets … They had before them a city of 200,000 inhabitants – a city in which every house was a fortress – they had a population incited against them by a thousand and one idle tales and calumnities – by stories of brutalities and excesses they were said to have committed, and which they were advancing to repeat; a population which had learned the sieges of Saguntum and Saragossa by heart, and in their exceeding pride of valor doubtless thought they were to rival if not excel the deeds enacted by the defenders of those valiant cities.[14]

Even General Scott, not known to be overly romantic by nature, employed some historical parallels in a report to Secretary of War William L. Marcy outlining his lack of logistical support from Washington DC during the invasion: 'Thus, like Cortez finding myself isolated and abandoned again like him, always afraid that the next ship or messenger might recall or further cripple me, I resolved no longer to depend on Veracruz or home, but to render my little army "a self-sustaining" machine … and advance to Puebla.'[15]

Reprinted accounts of the Spanish Conquest of Mexico appeared almost as often as excerpts from popular works on the Peninsular War or vivid tales of Napoleon. One of the most acclaimed books during the war was William H. Prescott's *History of the Conquest of* Mexico (1843). This 'immensely popular' work was even read by American soldiers fighting in Mexico. The book, Johannsen writes, 'published just two and a half years before the war, had turned public attention towards Mexico, stimulated interest in that country, and familiarized countless Americans with the titanic struggle between Cortez and Montezuma'. Although Prescott opposed the war, his widely read book 'had much to do with stimulating' it. Indeed, many American readers of Prescott drew historic parallels between the civilizing sense of mission among the conquistadors of Spain and the US Army's efforts in Mexico – particularly after comparisons between the two became more acute following the siege of Veracruz. Prescott wrote, 'The Spanish cavalier felt he had [a] high mission to accomplish as a soldier of the cross. However unauthorized or unrighteous the war he had entered may seem to us, to him it was a holy war. He was in arms against the infidel.'[16] This kind of romantic imagery was in high demand among American readers in the mid-1840s.

The *Weekly National Intelligencer* among others printed a story on 31 July entitled 'Romance of Louisiana History' over columns on the war. This feature was a long excerpt from *De Bow's Commercial Review of the South and West*, a widely circulated magazine that sprang up in New Orleans during the war in response to demand for Spanish- and Mexican-related literature. The focus of *De Bow's* was the frontier beyond New Orleans. 'Poetry is the daughter of the imagination, and imagination is perhaps the highest gift of Heaven,' the excerpt began. To 'conceive an Alexander, a Caesar, a Napoleon ... or any of those wonderful men who have carried as far as they could go the powers of the human mind ... which enter into the composition of poetical organization.' The article went on to posit the existence of 'Grecian figures and letters' in native American pottery, Phoenician visitors to the New World, and Tacitus' descriptions of 'ancient barbarian tribes of Germany', before jumping to the sixteenth-century exploits of the conquistador Hernando de Soto in the Gulf of Mexico:

Here is chivalry, with all its glittering, its soul-stirring aspirations, in full march, with its iron heels and gilded spurs, towards the unknown and hitherto unexplored soil of Louisiana. In sooth, it must have been a splendid sight! Let us look at ... those bronzed sons of Spain, clad in refulgent armor! How brave that music sounds! How fleet they move, those Andalusian chargers, with arched necks and dilated nostrils ... Blest be the soul of the noble knight and of the true Christian![17]

Anti-war advocates decried such depictions of Americans as new conquistadors gloriously fighting for civilization. They sternly warned that America was bound to become embroiled in a conflict it would be unable to extract itself from – especially since Scott's army was heading towards the capital of a foreign country about which Americans knew little. To naysayers, this was the prosaic history of the Peninsular War being re-enacted in North America. Yet even anti-war diatribes were couched in romantic tones. In a speech made on Christmas Eve 1846, Ohio Congressman Joseph M. Root warned of becoming mired in Mexico: 'Suppose we presented ourselves before their last refuge – what then? We should there find that old genuine Castilian spirit that shone so brightly in their fathers in Old Spain. The cry would be no surrender! No Capitulation! But war to the knife!' Like other anti-war advocates, Root argued that the conflict might easily spiral out of control and turn into something akin to the war in Spain. 'They might there behold, as was seen at Saragossa, the priest laying aside his sacerdotal garments and hallowing the war by participating in it.'[18] Similar concerns were voiced elsewhere. 'Is there an instance in all history of a nation, and a nation thoroughly united as is Mexico, with a population of eight millions, and abundantly supplied with all the munitions of war, having been conquered?' Napier's history of the war in Spain was cited as an ominous warning:

> It is remarked by Napier ... that 'no country in Europe is so easy to overrun as Spain – none so difficult to retain'. The ultimate fate of the legions of Bonaparte confirms this truth. Where else, in history, do we find a war to have continued for eight hundred years, as did that between the Goths and the Moors?[19]

Strategic questions were asked about the feasibility of seizing the Mexican capital: 'Are we to march to the city of Mexico and then march back? How long must we remain there?' More importantly, people were inquiring about the amount of time it would take to provision the army on foreign territory: 'Garrisons must be left at Tampico, at Veracruz, Jalapa, and Perote, of two thousand men at each place.' Indeed, these were the same questions Scott and the war planners asked themselves before seizing Veracruz. 'How many [soldiers] at Puebla – a city of ninety thousand inhabitants and in the center of the most dense and warlike population of Mexico – in the neighborhood of the renowned and warlike Tlascalans.' Since Puebla was the largest city between the capital and the coast, some surmised the garrison there would require at least 'six or eight thousand men'. To the observer steeped in romantic history, these considerations called to mind the Napoleonic conflict in Spain – the last major war of a similar nature in contemporary memory. The best laid plans would be undone if 'resistance is offered ... the thousand natural defiles which the route presents, with more than one walled town to be stormed ... To collect these troops, concentrate at Veracruz, march to the city of Mexico, and remain there ... will require at least a year.' Many Americans were led to expect the worst-case scenario, because Mexicans were 'the descendants of the heroes of Saguntum, Numantis, and Saragossa'.[20]

The *Louisville Morning Courier* of Kentucky, one of the most informative newspapers about the war, echoed similar concerns about the plan's feasibility by arguing that difficulties taking Veracruz could critically hamstring the entire endeavour at its inception: 'It may not be too late to withdraw our armies from the present plan of operations, and land to the left or right of

Veracruz, without any probability of the garrison interrupting their march to the Capital.' The US Army had two main routes to Mexico City, 'either by Perote, the route selected by Cortez, or by Puebla, the present stage route'. The editorial stressed that a 'speedy peace' was important to overall success, and used the example that 'in Europe, especially in the day of Napoleon, the capture of the capital led to a general submission by the country'. However, capturing the capital did not always guarantee peace, as anti-war opponents and war sceptics began reading non-British accounts of the war in Spain:

> But there is reason to apprehend that the enemy may adopt the Fabian policy, of avoiding a general battle, and resort to the guerrilla system, so fatal in its effects to the army of Napoleon in Spain. The Mexican inherits the pride and obstinate valor of the Castilian, and is superior in the use of the lance … Wellington, in the war of the Peninsula, was not more indebted, for his victories, to his own genius and the valor of his troops, than to the partisan efforts of the Spanish peasantry, who intercepted communications … and thus saved Wellington from destruction. To meet this kind of warfare, we should increase the regiments of riflemen – mounted if possible, and corps of light artillery.[21]

The *Free Soil Courier and Liberty Gazette* of Burlington offered scathing criticism of the war, along with a corresponding political message. In an editorial entitled 'Historical Parallels,' the Vermont newspaper began with a subdued attack on President Polk by noting that the 'crowned bandit Napoleon was the embodiment of the aggressive Democracy of France. In violation of international law, of solemn treaties, and all principles of equity, he sought to extend the limits of his empire.' The *Gazette* continued by asking its readers, 'Does history afford no example of our present condition, no warning of our future?' Historical parallels served as important 'illustrations of principles' not to be dismissed: 'Napoleon invaded Spain, a nation distracted and seemingly incapable of resistance, and overcame its territories with facility.' But these initial victories came at a price:

> He did not conquer, though he overran the country … six hundred thousand Frenchmen entered Spain at different times. Of these, about two hundred and fifty thousand returned to their country … Our victories will be our losses. We may take Veracruz and the city of Mexico, fortify or destroy them. We shall obtain no foothold in the country. Our armies will daily diminish from the pestilence, if encamped in large bodies; and,

if scattered over the country, will be destroyed in detail by the various guerrilla bands, or rancheros, who will hover like a dark cloud over them.[22]

Other New England newspapers offered similar sentiments. Although many admitted the siege of Veracruz was a military success, they were still not convinced the war could be won. 'Is peace conquered?' they asked. 'True, another stronghold has gone down before the ruthless invader, but there are distance and time, thirst and the plague, in the field yet.' In addition to the environmental obstacles opposing Scott's army, there were 'scattered Mexicans crowding their mountain passes, in guerrilla bands, that hang around an army like vultures, aloof and unseen till the hour to swoop, and away again to their eyrie'.[23]

The *Louisville Morning Courier* used similar language in offering an historical parallel. In an article entitled 'The Guerrilla Chief', G.H.B. described how the 'wars of France and Spain have been proverbial in modern warfare for their sanguinary acts of destruction. The invasion of Napoleon has instances marked by desperate resistance and uncompromising severity.' The writer described how the people of the Sierra Morena in Spain 'had become noted for their unsubdued spirit' of resistance against the invaders. 'Driven one day from the bosom of their pleasant homes into the recesses of wild crags – on the next they would swoop down suddenly like an Alpine storm up on their invaders, men, women and children vying in mutual fortitude and courage.' The article gave an account of a popular guerrilla leader named Juan d'Estano who was caught and executed – further enraging his countrymen. 'The blood of Juan d'Estano seemed to have found a thousand arms of revenge. Not a hill or mountain but was a tower of insurrection.' The fabled guerrilla was then replaced by his 'superhuman' brother, himself bent on revenge, and 'woe indeed to the captives who fell into the hands of his ruthless band'. The 'old and experienced veteran' opposing insurgents soon found himself 'not sufficiently accustomed to the wonderful acuteness and endurance of the guerrillas', and was eventually defeated.[24] Stories of this kind ran side by side with news reports during the Mexican war – as Prescott's American paradigm took root from the European Black Legend in North American soil.

Most major publications sceptical of the war employed more rational arguments, while utilizing historical comparisons to drive home their points. The *New York Herald* soberly explained that nearly 'all the newspapers in the country, for years past, have told us the Mexicans would not fight at all, and that a few thousand US troops could proceed quietly to, and capture the city of Mexico itself and "revel in the halls of the Montezumas".' However, the *Herald*'s writers noted that a 'discovery seems to have been made, during the short period of operations by our army of occupation, that the city of Mexico cannot be taken without the shot of a gun, and we begin to doubt our own invincibility'. The *Herald* warned against the base instincts many foreign soldiers (French and English) succumbed to while fighting in Spain – the desire to plunder. Many of the volunteers 'are influenced by a hope of extensive plunder, and the indulgence of other gratifications' which marked the Peninsular War. 'This plundering disposition, if indulged in', would create 'an inevitable tendency to unite the Mexicans … whilst their enemies, from this very cause, will become, to a certainty disunited.' This was a strong argument for maintaining discipline. Without it, the New York paper argued, US forces might become embroiled in something beyond their control:

> The example of Napoleon in Spain, with one of the most numerous and courageous armies, and the best marshals and generals the world ever saw, will then be realized on this continent, with precisely alike results. An interminable guerrilla warfare will be carried on with disastrous and fatal effects.[25]

Pro-war advocates were not convinced Americans would have to contend with a defiant, Spanish-style opposition, and they sought to distinguish Mexicans from their former Iberian rulers while criticizing anti-war proponents. Arguments were frequently couched in racist language, claiming Mexicans were not nearly as formidable as Spaniards. The *Evening Post* of New York, a rival of the *Herald*, wrote:

> The advocates of peace, as they style themselves, among us, are perpetually harping upon the Mexicans as if they were Spaniards, or Europeans, or of European descent; and talk of Zaragoza and Badajoz, and guerillas, as if the history of Old Spain were to be re-enacted on our continent. One would really suppose that by this time the delusion would have dissipated. One Maid of Zaragoza was worth all the Mexicans that were ever cradled.[26]

The *State Indiana Sentinel* ran a speech by Senator Edward A. Hannegan towards the end of the Veracruz siege comparing Napoleonic Spain and the holy wars in Iberia. This pro-war ally of Polk who would later push to annex all of Mexico argued that the US 'must seek peace with our armies in their seats of power and wealth, the homes and palaces of their rulers' to successfully prosecute the war. The Indiana senator supported plans to seize the Mexican capital while forecasting a speedy conclusion to the war: 'The road to the city of Mexico is the road to peace. Their capital and other principal cities in the hands of a well-appointed army ... will insure us peace before the autumn leaf has fallen.' Like other hawks, he dismissed the myth of a fiery, Spanish-style militancy among Mexicans based on the 'indomitable resistance to the Moors several centuries back'. Hannegan said the comparison with the Spanish was 'worth nothing' because only one-fifth of the population consisted of Spaniards with an 'inherent obstinacy in conflict'.[27]

US newspapers often responded to criticism from foreign publications, especially British ones. The New Orleans *Delta* reprinted several excerpts from British papers downplaying American military achievements in Mexico, one of which stated, 'The genius of a Carnot and a Napoleon could not get [American] armies out of their difficulties, and ... Mr Polk is not a Carnot, nor Gen. Taylor a Napoleon.' The editors of the *Delta* replied to the British that they had 'long since grown indifferent to their slander'.[28]

The *Richmond Enquirer* responded to British criticism of the siege at Veracruz. 'The slaughter of women and children, and of neutral persons at Veracruz is especially dwelt upon in the English press,' the article ran, 'but this was a necessary incident to the siege, and was no novelty in warfare. Besides, with unusual clemency ample time was given for the removal of such persons.' The article pointed out the hypocrisy of mentioning civilian deaths by referring to the British bombardment of the city of Copenhagen in 1807 – before returning to the subject of Spain. 'In the celebrated siege of Saragossa, that city contained not only its own inhabitants, but an immense multitude of the neighboring peasantry; yet the French were never blamed for assaulting it.' The *Enquirer* argued that the carnage at Zaragoza held little similarity to Veracruz: 'Regardless of the havoc which necessarily ensued, they threw into the crowded town thirty-thousand cannon shot, and sixteen thousand bombs.' The article quoted historian Archibald Alison's account:

When the French troops entered, says Alison, 'six thousand dead bodies still lay unburied in the streets among the fragments of buildings, or around the churches; half the houses were in ruins ... Fifty-four thousand human being[s] had perished during the siege; of whom only six thousand were killed by the sword or fire of the enemy, the awful plague had carried the rest.' Such were the results of the siege of Saragossa ... acknowledged to be one of the most glorious events in the history of the war.[29]

With an accurate and objective comparison in mind, the editorial dismissed the accusations of wanton brutality by the Americans and Scott, and claimed they had effected their strategic objectives with the least possible number of civilian deaths. In other words, the comparison with Zaragoza fell flat. 'Criticisms upon the siege of Veracruz become ridiculous, when its attendant circumstances are compared with such wholesale slaughter as Napoleon and Wellington never hesitated to undertake, if it was necessary to accomplish a military end.'[30]

The *New York Herald* concurred: 'The defense of the breach should have been desperate, for the Mexicans had their interior fortress to retreat to.' However, the carnage of Zaragoza was not repeated, despite attempts to portray it as such. 'Infinite was their disgust that we did not storm the city, as the English did at Badajoz … and like the French at Saragossa, fight from street to street, from house to house.' The *Herald* noted the unromantic nature and exemplary result of the siege, while stating, 'If the science of war consists in the proper adaptation of the means to the end, the projection and execution of the siege was eminently scientific.' According to the paper, the loss of life involved in capturing the port city was nothing to be ashamed of. 'With these convictions, let us exult our brilliant victory, and cheerfully commit it to the military criticism of this country and of Europe.' The article finished with its own rebuke of those who 'looked to bloody results and superhuman exertions, as evidence of a well conducted enterprise … forgetting that this ease and no loss were the results of a rightly planned attack.'[31]

Others took the same position, while acknowledging Scott's meticulous preparation for the landing and assault: 'But Gen. Scott seemed to think that, if by display of military skill he could effect the same result – the reduction of the city and castle with but little loss of life – the reflecting and humane would appreciate his motives and his conduct.' The trade-off was worth it. 'In a word, he generally surrendered the brilliant for the solid – the evanescent praise of popular excitement to the more discriminating judgement of posterity.' That is not to deny that the Americans were making plans to storm the city. After breaching the walls in two spots, a massive storming party was planned if the Mexicans did not surrender, in which case 'the disgraceful and sanguinary scenes of Badajoz and Ciudad Rodrigo would most assuredly have been reenacted; and humanity revolts at the idea'. With the city taken at minimal loss of life, the next phase of the operation commenced. After all, that was the objective of landing at Veracruz, despite attempts to romanticize the siege by turning it into a violent reenactment of the Peninsular War: 'What we wanted was the place, as a mere means to secure a great ulterior object … is it not then a matter of congratulation rather than censure, that this has been attained with so little delay, and with so small a sacrifice of life?'[32]

In fact, avoiding mass slaughter was Scott's original intention. While consulting with his war cabinet following the bloodless landing of 12,000 soldiers from more than eighty vessels, Scott offered two options for conducting the second phase of the operation: the first was a slower, 'scientific' siege; the second, storming the city at night, would 'result in an immense slaughter, with the usual terrible accompaniments'. Scott wrote in his *Memoirs* that he found the second option 'most revolting', and he told his cabinet that he was 'strongly inclined – policy concurring with humanity – to forgo their loud applause and *aves* vehement, and take the city with the least possible loss of life.' Indeed, the loss of life was nothing as compared to Zaragoza.[33]

Following the city's capitulation, the next phase was to march the army into the interior, where it was intended to work with General Taylor's northern forces. The route inland had been carefully selected in Washington during the planning phase and followed that taken by Cortez in the early sixteenth century. First, the Americans would move north-west past the National Bridge (*Puente Nacional*), a location given that name because across it ran the fortified 'royal road' – often called the National Road – which connected Veracruz to the capital. The royal road was key to maintaining communications between Mexico City and the outside world, and it was critical for Scott as well. From there the army would march uphill through Cerro Gordo, a formidable mountain pass, before arriving in Jalapa – 1,400m above sea level. After Jalapa, the army expected to march uphill another 1,000-plus metres into the Sierra Madre before reaching the town of Perote. From here they would descend south-west almost 200km to Puebla – the largest city between Veracruz and

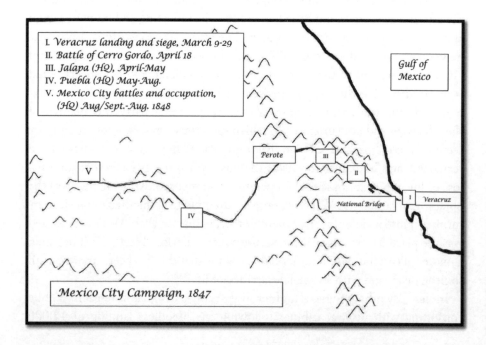

I. *Veracruz landing and siege, March 9-29*
II. *Battle of Cerro Gordo, April 18*
III. *Jalapa (HQ), April-May*
IV. *Puebla (HQ) May-Aug.*
V. *Mexico City battles and occupation,*
    (HQ) Aug/Sept.-Aug. 1848

Gulf of Mexico

Perote   III
         II

National Bridge   I   Veracruz

V

IV

Mexico City Campaign, 1847

the capital. At Puebla, the US Army would be roughly two-thirds of the way to its destination.

The military operation therefore depended on logistics. Scott estimated the army needed 1,000 wagons and a herd of 8,000 mules. In the words of a young Ulysses S. Grant, it was 'absolutely necessary to have enough to supply our army to Jalapa'. While waiting in Veracruz, hundreds of wagons and draught animals 'were expected from the North', but were 'arriving slowly'. The animals, according to Scott, were 'never in sufficient numbers'. In addition, every division was required to carry by wagon 'subsistence for men equal to six days, and oats for horses equal to three'. Once they were beyond the dreaded yellow fever zone at Jalapa, Scott believed supplies could be obtained for the next stage into the Sierra Madre. Scott wrote that Jalapa was a 'productive region abounding in many articles of food as well as in mules'; the latter were needed to bring up the remaining transports left in Veracruz and continue the march towards the capital. Once the bulk of the army had moved on, a garrison was left behind in Veracruz to ensure the port and logistics lifeline stayed in American hands.[34]

Despite the success of the risky (yet unopposed) amphibious landing and the relatively bloodless seizure of Mexico's main port, some were far from convinced of the plan's feasibility – especially war sceptics in New England. Boston's *Liberator*, a staunch anti-war and anti-Polk publication, ran an editorial comparing Scott to both Cortez *and* Napoleon: 'The force of desperation is, undoubtedly, one of the strongest that can bind men together, and impel them upon a more numerous enemy.' According to them, this 'was the secret of Cortez's success, and this is no small part of that of this new Brummagen Cortez of ours.' While the editorial admitted that Scott might have achieved a foothold in the country, it still maintained, 'Mexico is not fallen; she may still recover her losses and roll back the barbarian hordes of this invasion.' To make the point, the paper switched analogies: 'Napoleon is said to have taught Europe how to conquer himself. General Scott, though no Napoleon, may teach the Mexicans in a like manner, the necessary lesson of union and subordination.' In other words, the *Liberator* was claiming that the Mexicans would adjust their tactics and learn how to defeat the US Army. By adapting to the American mode of war, 'It is impossible that they should not be able to crush any force we can send against them.' These anti-war diatribes were excoriated by pro-war Americans, who viewed them as treasonous. Critics often cited them as providing the enemy with moral support and prolonging the war, since Mexicans were reading US publications and were keen to exploit the political divisions in the USA. To pro-war advocates, anti-war newspapers like the *Liberator* were aiding the enemy when they printed the opinion, following what Palafox said at Saragossa, that the Mexicans 'have the cause, which all but the most ultra of peace men consider as the holiest, and a justification of war, even "to the knife".'[35]

Historical parallels between the wars in Mexico and Spain were not just a romantic fabrication of the American mind. If Mexicans were reading about American divisions at home, Americans were also reading about what Mexicans themselves were saying about the war. Excerpts from Mexican papers and speeches were reprinted in American newspapers, as Americans on both sides of the pro- and anti-war political divide were eager to hear what the enemy was saying to itself and to the outside world. Many of these reports first came via New Orleans newspapers such as the *Picayune* and *Delta*.

The *Weekly National Intelligencer* reprinted a 2 May article from the *Picayune* quoting excerpts from Mexican newspapers such as *El Republicano* and the country's main governmental organ, the *Diario del Gobierno de la Republica Mexicana*. Mexico was fraught with deep political divisions between federalists, centralists and monarchists, and these divisions were reflected in the papers' editorial stances. However, they could all agree on opposition to the Americans, the war, and particularly the attempt to take Mexico City.[36]

The *Intelligencer* noted the election of Pedro María de Anaya as the new president and *El Republicano*'s belief that he was capable of 'unit[ing] all parties' in Mexico. With the 'enemy conquering and menacing, we conjure all Mexicans who love the honor and existence of their country that henceforth they have but one part – that of independence … Vengeance and War.' The *Intelligencer* noted the *Diario*'s recent opinion that 'one source of the weakness' of Mexico was that 'different states seem to be providing means to each to defend its own territory' rather than fighting in unity. Akin to Spain in this regard, nineteenth-century Mexico had its own provincial differences to overcome in order to repel the invaders. The article reprinted an extensive excerpt from *El Monitor*, another popular Mexican newspaper, noting that 'Mexicans are counselled to change their mode of conducting the war, and instead of confining themselves to defenseless cities … advised to guard the many natural passes and strong defenses … and to carry on fierce partisan warfare.' Although the Mexican Army under Santa Anna had not yet been routed by Scott's force, conversations among Mexicans about changing the war's strategy were beginning to become common. *El Monitor* elaborated:

> Shall we expose delicate women and innocent children to cruel deaths, and still more cruel outrage, by keeping up this disastrous system of warfare? … will this be a motive why we should leave open and unprotected the gates of our capital, and allow the enemy to penetrate into the very heart

of our Republic, to carry on their customary depredations? ... I will not propose what I wish to see – that is, that the Mexicans should imitate the Numidians and Carthaginians, when attacked by the Romans in ancient times; or should follow the example of the memorable Saragossa, which ... was reduced to a pile of ruins, burying 100,000 combatants beneath them.[37]

Other drastic measures to prevent the Americans from achieving victory were considered. Using the example of the Russians during the Napoleonic Wars, the *Diario* cited their 'heroic example' when they 'set Moscow to fire to remove that sanctuary from the conqueror Napoleon', and declared that this sacrificial act 'speaks very loudly in favor of the patriotic fire that encourages the people when they see their religion, their freedom, and their imprescriptible rights are threatened.'[38] Some Americans concurred with the possibility that the Mexicans could 'resort to the devastation of their own country, wherever it can be made to fall on the heads of our forces'. They also agreed that the Mexicans might contemplate the sacrifice of their capital in a 'patriotic fire', like the Russians in 1812, noting that the Spanish-Mexican publicist and diplomat, Juan de la Granja, had recommended to his friend Santa Anna that he burn Mexico City. Another publication made a similar (albeit sceptical) argument after Veracruz that Scott's march to the capital 'is about as visionary as that of Napoleon upon Moscow'.[39] Santa Anna joined in such comparisons by invoking commonly used Spanish and Mexican rhetoric prior to the Mexico City battle:

Mexicans! The conquest made you kindred to that noble race, illustrious by the memory of Numantia and Saguntum, and which in more modern times has presented examples for your imitation in the defense of Zaragoza and Gerona. The epoch has arrived for you to prove that the descendants of heroes are also heroes under the beautiful sky of the New World.[40]

Political leaders in the United States rarely missed the opportunity to express their own romantic views of the war. Ohio Senator Thomas Corwin's staunchly anti-war speech was published after the landing at Veracruz. First citing Tamerlane, Alexander the Great's 'drunken' death in Babylon, and the 'lovely Mexican girl' Dos Amades, who died heroically at Monterrey 'carrying water to slake the thirst' of a wounded US soldier, the senator then launched into a Napoleonic analogy: 'Suddenly we see, sir, six hundred thousand armed men marching to Moscow. Does his Veracruz protect him now? Far from it ... and finally the conflagration of the old commercial metropolis of Russia.' That

Scott's army was considerably smaller than Napoleon's was not important. Carrying the analogy further, in a criticism of Polk's apparent lust for power, Corwin cited Napoleon's final status as 'a prisoner on the rock of St. Helena', before comparing his empire's demise to America's unavoidable fate:

> Her 'eagles' now no longer scream along the banks of the Danube, the Po, and the Borysthenes. They have returned home, to their old eyrie, between the Alps, the Rhine, the Pyrenees; so shall it be with yours. You may carry them to the loftiest peaks of the Cordilleras, they may wave with insolent triumph in the Halls of the Montezumas ... but the weakest hand in Mexico, uplifted in prayer to the god of justice, may call down against you a power.[41]

Ultimately, the Mexicans spared their capital from self-immolation. Still fielding conventional forces, they believed they could keep Scott from crossing the Sierra Madre Oriental to seize Puebla. When that effort failed, and Santa Anna's army was routed at Cerro Gordo, the Mexicans looked for other ways to defeat a relatively small but seemingly unstoppable army. As when the Spanish conventional forces had collapsed against a superior French Army, Mexicans began to consider launching a nationwide guerrilla war. The possibility existed of such a war – as the history of Mexico's independence movement demonstrated – *if* the movement could garner popular support.

The reality that Veracruz, or Monterrey for that matter, had not witnessed the carnage exhibited in the real siege of Zaragoza a generation earlier in Spain did not keep the press from conjuring new, future Zaragozas. The *Freeman's Journal* of Dublin, a pro-Catholic publication, eagerly claimed, 'The Mexicans appear determined that General Scott shall fight every inch of his way to the "Halls of the Montezumas".' Indeed, the only reason for taking Veracruz, as the *Mississippi Free Trader* reminded its readers, was to capture Mexico City. As Scott's army marched inland, Mexican 'troops are being mustered from all quarters for the defense of the city – fortifications are going up ... the church bells are being cast into cannon, and every other preparation is toward, to make Mexico a second Saragossa for the invader.'[42] In other words, every Mexican city the US Army approached became a 'second Zaragoza.' As the American invasion of Mexico continued, so comparisons would continue to be drawn with the war in Spain.

Chapter 4

Napoleon's Student: Winfield Scott

The Mexicans had never any apprehension of an effective invasion from [Veracruz] or from Tampico. In respect to either of these routes, they might have expressed what the Russians felt when Napoleon marched upon Moscow: 'Come unto us with a few and we will overwhelm you; come unto us with many, and you shall overwhelm yourselves.'[1]

Lieutenant General Winfield Scott, *Memoirs* (1864)

The years between the Peninsular War and the Mexican War represent a period of profound change in the American military. Professionalization of a nascent national army took place, as updated tactics and strategies were introduced to accommodate innovations and ever-changing rules and strategies in warfare. As military scholars absorbed lessons from the war in Spain, American settlement of frontier regions brought guerrilla warfare out of the shadows, and it received reluctant recognition as an 'illegal' mode of warfare capable of challenging the supremacy of Napoleonic military tactics and the established rules of war. While guerrilla warfare helped create new states in the Americas, it was also used by native tribes in North America to thwart the expansion of the US. On the eve of a predictable war with Mexico, how to reduce popular support for insurgency became a new and important consideration. The rules for achieving military success were changing, and laws were changed to accommodate these new rules. Indeed, the antebellum period marked a major turning point in the history of American warfare, and it is Winfield Scott, the commander of the Mexico City campaign, who best embodies the profound change that took place within the US military between 1808 and 1846. Although a student of Napoleonic strategy and tactics, Scott deviated from traditional military thinking to limit the war in Mexico. In surpassing his predecessor, he essentially ushered in an era in which conciliatory methods became the cornerstone of a new benign counter-insurgency doctrine.[2]

Winfield Scott was a rules man. In 1807 at the age of twenty he learned the importance of adhering to the rule of law when he attended the Aaron

Burr trial in his home state of Virginia. 'I had just ridden my first circuit as an incipient man of law,' he wrote in his *Memoirs*, 'when, like a vast multitude of others … I hastened up to Richmond to witness a scene of the highest interest.' At the time, Scott was as an aspiring lawyer and had not yet joined the army. The treason trial of the former Vice President taught him that law and order in the young republic needed to be enforced if the country was to have any chance of longevity. Since Scott's first profession was the law, this short prelude to his main career affected his long-term thinking as a military officer. Scott also saw something imposing and indomitable in Burr that must have prompted him to change the trajectory of his life, and he described Burr in the courtroom standing defiant and 'immovable, as one of Canova's living marbles'.[3]

During the War of 1812 Scott demonstrated a remarkable sense of right and wrong in military conduct when he was briefly taken prisoner by the British in the Niagara region of Canada. The following year, one of the prisoners taken at the Battle of Fort George in 1813 was an officer who had insulted him during his period as a prisoner at the same fort. Scott saw to it the prisoner was treated for his wounds, and even 'had the pleasure' of returning his enemy's horse after he took it to continue an assault on the fort. Timothy Johnson, one of Scott's principal biographers, wrote that Scott 'no doubt wanted to show his foe how gentlemen behave in victory'. The encounter also served to solidify Scott's sense of proper military conduct in a period when America's military was formally adopting a European pattern. Another notable practice from the war was his employment of agents to create a 'spy network to provide information' on British activities.[4] Scott would later do the same on a larger scale in Mexico – where the term *contra-guerrillas* originated. Ultimately, Scott's experiences in the War of 1812 proved to be valuable training.

Following the war, a young and promoted General Scott requested leave of absence to embark on a trip to Europe as an 'unofficial observer'. Napoleon's empire had recently collapsed after setting the continent on fire, and Scott was witness to the aftermath when he arrived in France following the Battle of Waterloo. Acting Secretary of War Alexander J. Dallas instructed Scott to 'avoid actual service with European' militaries, but he took the opportunity to absorb as much information as he could about military affairs. Having recently fought the British, Scott confessed to Dallas his 'predilection for France' (Scott spoke French) and informed him that Secretary of State James Monroe and the French Minister to the United States promised to send letters of introduction to 'some of the Marshals of France' and even perhaps to the Duke of Wellington.[5]

Europe was an eye-opening experience for the young officer, since it was the centre of expertise in his adopted profession as well as the nexus of events in the western world. The continent, after being at war for twenty years, was settling into new political realities. Scott's *Memoirs*, written many years after the victorious war in Mexico, were, he admitted, partly inspired by the former French emperor: 'Napoleon, on his abdication, turned to the wrecks of his old

General Winfield Scott (daguerreotype created by Matthew Brady's studio c.1849).

battalions about him, and said: "I will write the history of our campaigns" … and I resolved, in my humble sphere, to write also.'[6]

In late September 1815 the French capital was under foreign occupation. 'Nothing can be more complete than the ruin and degradation of France,' Scott wrote to Monroe. He had no doubt that the blame for France's demise rested squarely on Napoleon, and almost fifty years later, after the Mexican War, he wrote that France, a 'great nation, exhausted by the victories of mad ambition, had, in turn, become conquered and subdued'. It was Scott's first experience of the military occupation of a large capital and the plundering that often accompanied such a seizure. Scott told Monroe that the 'Frenchman is the only European without protection in Paris' and that 'the press here is also under British and Prussian governors'. Scott's time in occupied Paris gave him crucial insights which would inform his later role as conqueror of Mexico City.[7]

In a scene which must have harked back to the Burr trial, Scott commented on the treason trial of Marshal Ney and its sombre outcome: 'All the ministers & generals of the allies attend the trial … to ensure his conviction. To witness the execution, tickets for places are already granted.' In relation to the military occupation, Scott noted a series of unpopular 'laws against seditions … supported as it is, by 150,000 foreign bayonets, [to which] the French are obliged to yield'. Here again, the first-hand experience of military rule in Paris in the aftermath of the Napoleonic Wars influenced Scott's conduct in Mexico – particularly is it related to the management of civilians. In a prophetic confession to Monroe, Scott noted he would be 'very well content to remain at home for the remainder of my life – unless I should be required to march out at the head of an army'.[8]

Before returning to the United States, he passed through England. There he spent time assessing British sentiment towards the revolutionary events unfolding in Latin America and met Lord Holland, whose house was a well-known haven for Spanish and French exiles. It was there that Scott was introduced to Javier Mina, the captured (and released) nephew of Espoz y Mina. According to Scott, Mina and forty other Spanish guerrillas wanted to 'join the patriots' revolting against the Spanish in Mexico. Mina's goal was to discover from Scott 'whether an armed ship … would be permitted to touch at one of our ports, & to depart unmolested'. Like many Americans opposed to monarchy, Scott was sympathetic to the revolutionary movements sweeping the Americas. He wrote to Monroe that the 'best friends of freedom in this country, and on the continent, regard the present moment as particularly favorable to the independence of our hemisphere'. Apparently exceeding any formal authority granted him by the US government, the young general informed Monroe that Mina 'would be able to purchase in our ports, the arms … he requires to complete his equipment'. Scott also facilitated

> the means of shipping some 2,000 stand of arms, & now only waits the collection of his associates, some of whom are on the continent. His ship is in this port, & he is not a little apprehensive of discovery … His associates have been banished by Ferdinand at different times … & [Mina] fled to save his life. These gentlemen will constitute an important acquisition to the patriots, particularly Gen'l M. who was the author of the *guirrella* [*sic*] system in the peninsula war.[9]

Mina was granted permission to dock in Baltimore and was further outfitted in New Orleans. But in 1817 he was captured in Mexico and shot for exporting revolution to a country whose leaders were determined to maintain political ties with Spain.[10]

A couple of points can be gleaned from Scott's letter to Monroe. First, that Scott misspelled the word *guerrilla* is not surprising, given the novelty of the term. Also, that he constantly referred to it as a system shows that, militarily, its tactics were considered worthy of study since it had played a major role in victory in Spain. Put together, these demonstrate that – while Scott was at least aware of the 'system' used by Mina and others to attack and wear down the occupation force – he was not entirely familiar with its conventions at an academic level. Nor could he have been. Being a traditionalist, albeit willing to utilize the newest technology and tactics to win battles, Scott was still not yet totally familiar with guerrilla warfare because most military scholars in the early nineteenth century were not considering it. In other words, by 1816, the war in Spain was still too recent for serious consideration by military strategists, whose primary focus was still the study of Napoleonic tactics.

Settlers encroaching on Indian lands in the Ohio valley and further west were undoubtedly familiar with Native American-style warfare reminiscent of the 'system' used in Spain. However, when it came to detailed studies of methods used in the Peninsular War, which generally focused on attacking communications networks, supply convoys and small posts, we are left with little to glean apart from the works of French authors related to '*La Petite Guerre*' in North America during the Seven Years War, the experiences of New Englanders in the seventeenth century, and use of guerrilla tactics in the American Revolutionary War.[11] Although Americans in the early antebellum period invoked the heroism of the Revolution, it was still considered unethical and ungentlemanly to engage in sneak attacks and ambushes. Guerrilla tactics employed by the colonists were downplayed (or conventionalized) in retrospective narratives which lauded Washington and conventional battles more than the raids of Nathanael Greene, Daniel Morgan or Francis Marion. Yet, even when examining the Forage War in New Jersey during the Revolution, a strong case can be made that Washington's use of skirmishing against hungry British and Prussian troops amounted to an adoption of guerrilla warfare.[12] The position was similar to that of French troops in Spain who needed to venture out into enemy-controlled territory to forage for sustenance. Having said that, guerrilla war was honed in the military laboratory of Spain to such an extent that it acquired its definitive name. In essence, guerrilla war certainly existed, but the study of it was still in its infancy while Scott was in Europe.

Changing Ways of War

The question remains, then, did Winfield Scott study the guerrilla tactics of the Peninsular War? The short answer, requiring a more complex explanation, is *not entirely* – at least not until after his experience in Florida after 1836. This is not to say that he did not study the French side of the war – an important distinction. Scott's career trajectory was a two-tiered track, combining his inclination towards law and order with his desire to advance his military knowledge and status in an up-and-coming republic. Military organization was best served in the United States by emulating the dominant military state of the era – France. After all, his trip to Europe was devoted to observing and studying European militaries.

The question is partially answered by Scott's academic focus before and after his trip. During the post-War of 1812 period, while Americans were still sceptical about a national army, the US Army was in the early stages of organizing a force modelled on European lines. At the time, national military bases were using a variety of different training guides. Therefore, whenever separately trained units were combined into larger forces, they were required to relearn whatever system the highest-ranking commanding officer was most familiar with. The federal government took notice of this inefficiency in 1814 and streamlined the system by 'establishing a board of officers charged with the duty of writing a new system of tactics for the army'. Johnson that writes Scott shrewdly 'positioned himself to be [in] the vanguard' of the process, and thus 'expressed his pleasure in adopting the French system as the model for the U.S. Army'. After being appointed to a board charged with implementing the streamlined rules and regulations based on a translation of the French text and 'incorporating changes in terminology' for Americans, Scott departed on his trip to Europe.[13]

Johnson correctly notes that, although many Americans were sceptical about establishing a large European-size army typical of those in the Napoleonic Wars, the burning of Washington DC by the British in 1814 necessitated the organization of a professional force capable of defending national interests. It was at this period that West Point Military Academy (USMA) in upstate New York took on a more prominent role in training officers for future wars. 'Through professionalization the most obvious route to high rank began at the first rung – West Point', and many officers in the Mexican War and Civil War were trained there. This was one of Scott's legacies. 'Scott thought the militia too unreliable. Military success hinged on discipline, and Scott sought to bring order and control to every aspect of military life.'[14]

In a recent article, military historian Michael Bonura called the American adoption of French military methods during a 'pre-paradigmatic period in American tactics' a leading factor in the United States' 'way of war', and used the term as it 'describes its strategic traditions that determine the ways in which military force is used to accomplish political objectives'. The definition includes 'intellectual military traditions, doctrines, and accepted ideas concerning the fundamental nature of war'. According to Bonura, a nation's way of war encompasses the complicated 'relationship between the citizen and state', and the advent of its development amounts to a historical precedent similar to the scientific revolution.[15]

Beginning during the American Revolution with Friedrich Wilhelm von Steuben's *Blue Book*, a more formalized adoption of French methods progressed after French artillery officer, engineer and Napoleonic War veteran Claudius Crozet introduced Simon Gay de Vernon's *A Treatise on the Science of War* into the West Point curriculum in 1816. The work was thoroughly French, having been approved in 1805 by Napoleon himself for French officers before becoming an essential aspect of the nascent US federal officer-training programme. Although the *Treatise* was heavily influenced by engineering theories and focused primarily on sieges, fortifications and lines of operations, the West Point manual included an appendix compiled by John O'Conner, a US Army captain with a penchant for praising the military skills of Napoleon and Frederick the Great.[16]

O'Conner's 100-page addition, entitled *A Summary of the Principles and Maxims of Grand Tactics and Operations*, was influenced by Henri Jomini and represented the beginning of an era in which maxims became important in military education at West Point. As students of military history searched for scientific truisms with the potential to be implemented successfully on the battlefield, such maxims brought order and system to a developing school of martial education. 'The idea of reducing the system of war to one primitive combination, upon which all others depend; and which should be the basis of a simple and accurate theory, presents innumerable advantages.' Simplification, O'Conner believed, 'would render the study of the science much more easy, the judgement of operations always correct, and faults less frequent'. The American captain was not short of praise for Jomini:

> General Jomini has transcended all writers on war, and has exhibited the most extraordinary powers of analyzing and combining military operations. His work forms an epoch in the history of the science, and should be read by every person ambitious of extending their knowledge, or of understanding military history. The writer has ... reduced the hitherto mysterious science of war to a few self-evident principles and axioms.[17]

Like previous military scholars, O'Conner focused heavily on maintaining lines of operation and lines of manoeuvre, noting that 'Napoleon never operated upon any other than one principal line'. Using the 1800 Alpine campaign as a model, O'Conner stated that Bonaparte's decisive direction at that moment was 'sufficient to convince any mind of the importance of the choice of maneuver in war. We see empires saved, or invaded, by the mere combinations of this choice.' Another maxim espoused by O'Conner was that 'retreating troops must concentrate [their forces] or die' from being attacked separately.[18]

Focusing entirely on conventional applications, *A Summary of the Principles and Maxims of Grand Tactics and Operations* also addressed logistics, stating that it 'is better to supply the wants of a siege, or army, by small and constantly successive convoys, than by periodical and large convoys'. O'Conner's advice in this regard did not take the military realities of guerrilla warfare into account, because he claimed that large convoys risked the loss of too much material. The opposite situation later unfolded in Mexico, as Scott needed large convoys (with large escorts) to prevent their being captured. O'Conner wrote that if 'one or two' small convoys were captured 'their loss will not be felt. But a large periodical convoy offers a temptation to the enterprise of the enemy, and is so great an object and so difficult to escort, that the enemy will much venture to destroy it.'[19]

Using Jomini's maxims of war, O'Conner's *Summary* taught West Point cadets the maxim that Napoleon adopted when short of supplies in occupied territory – *war will support war*: any 'army in march to undertake decisive operations can always find resources while in motion. We may therefore, in proportion to the resources, dispense with the train of provisions and transports.' This was the first of many maxims reminiscent of Napoleon's admonitions to his older brother in 1808. 'Genius has undoubtedly a great share in victory,'

O'Conner wrote. 'It presides over the application of acknowledged rules, and seizes all the modifications of which this application is susceptible. But in no case will a man of genius act in violation of these rules.'[20] Among many maxims to reappear during the Mexican War, Cato the Elder's ancient dictum about soldiers living off the land would later play a major role in the Polk Administration's efforts to change the course of the conflict.

Other maxims included 'a saying of the Emperor Napoleon that the secret of successful war consisted of operating against the enemy's communications', the 'fundamental principle' of attacking an enemy's weakest point with a larger force, taking the initiative with movements, keeping 'forces united' while inducing the enemy to 'commit faults,' and pursuing 'a beaten army'. Each of the maxims listed was examined within an historical military context that helped students understand the situations in which it was most applicable.[21]

And what of the novel Spanish way of war (guerrilla warfare) which violated the sacred rules of war? On the last page of the *Summary* O'Conner acknowledged the problems facing an invading army when occupying an enemy country, but he offered limited suggestions about how to tackle insurgency:

National wars, in which we have to fight and conquer a whole people, are the only exceptions to the great rule of acting constantly in mass … The means of guarding against these evils is to have an army constantly in the field, and independent divisions to keep in subjection the country in the rear. In this case the country should be commanded by enlightened generals who are good governors and men of justice and firmness; because their services may contribute much to the force of arms, to produce the submission of the provinces confided in them.[22]

Despite its focus on military education, the curriculum at West Point during the period did not specifically address guerrilla warfare. Rather than study the novel system, Scott concentrated on creating a more effective and highly trained army based on conventional and updated practices. He even implemented a policing system for the army to enforce discipline – itself an innovation. In 1821 Scott published his *General Regulations* outlining his vision for the army. Johnson writes, 'Scott meticulously described policies regarding army discipline, dress, duties of officers, treatment of staff officers, the chain of command, tactical movements, and camp sanitation.' Complementing his creation of a military police, the *Regulations* provided the army with its first comprehensive, systematic set of military bylaws; and as the author proudly asserted, 'There is a due logical connection and dependence between the parts, not found in other books.' That statement demonstrated Scott's ability to push forward the evolution of the army. *General Regulations* was his most important work (to date), and placed his stamp on the character of the future US Army. The introduction to the second edition, co-authored by artillery expert Pierce Darrow, stated that the 1820 'rules and regulations adopted for the army of the United States should be the governing principle for the militia of the several states, so far as applicable to their particular organization'. Darrow also noted 'the system which is now in use in the army [was] called "Scott's Exercise"'.[23]

As the language indicated, the regulations were formulated during a period in American history when states' rights were strong and it was difficult for the federal government to impose itself. Although the title used Scott's name, Johnson says it 'would be more accurate to describe his works as compilations, adaptations, and translations mostly drawn from British and French texts'. That the material was not original did not bother Scott; what mattered was that 'he provided regimentation and system where little had previously existed, and his manuals and regulations served the army well for years'. Scott wrote that it 'was the first time that the subjects embraced were ever reduced, in any army, to a regular analysis', and drew much of the material from the French *Législation Militaire*. Other areas such as strategy, tactics and engineering were compiled from other sources, and Scott commented that 'the English book of *General Regulations* was also composed of independent articles, without connection or system'. In essence, Scott was not creating the system from scratch, he was rewriting and updating it to advance the interests of the military, and by extension his own career.[24]

An examination of the updated version of the *Regulations* published in 1830 illuminates not only Scott's thinking, but the nature of the evolving US Army. Scott, along with notables such as (Colonel) Zachary Taylor, established a committee in 1826 to compile a new version, approved in 1829. The *Abstract of Infantry Tactics* saw an increased focus on the education of a new class of professional military students at West Point and later Virginia Military Institute (VMI), established in 1839. The updated version also used the term 'school of the soldier' for the first time, which reflected the systematic shift toward education.[25]

Unlike the older version of *Infantry Tactics*, the 1830 updated US Army tactical manual dealt with skirmishing. Skirmishing was generally associated with and often used to describe guerrilla tactics in early press reports of the war in Spain. Skirmishers were also key to French successes during the Napoleonic Wars, and other European armies adopted the practice of using open-formation skirmishers to protect the flanks, vanguard and rearguard of marching units from harassment. Since skirmishers were detached, they operated more independently than larger, more regimented units. The introduction of updated skirmishing tactics in the *Infantry Tactics* manual was important. Acknowledging skirmishing was the first step in the evolution of a combat structure ubiquitous among modern armies. In other words, since skirmishing tactics were often used by smaller guerrilla units to harass larger forces, the 1830 *Infantry Tactics* manual demonstrates that Scott at least acknowledged the efficacy of those tactics and tried to write some of them into the rules governing the army.[26]

The systematic teaching of skirmishing was the beginning of the US military's evolution from a militia structure to a professional army. Years later, after the Civil War, John Watts de Peyster, a New York militia member in the Mexican War and military scholar, advocated in the *Army and Navy Journal* that the US Army adopt skirmishing tactics as the standard tactical *modus operandi*. This was a revolutionary proposal. According to him, the unwarranted death toll during the Civil War proved

> the old Napoleonic conception of infantry tactics in columns of brigades was doomed to pass away with the use of better arms and field works of modern warfare … he maintained that the infantry fighting of the future would be by means of single lines of men following one another at some distance – a succession of skirmish lines. These ideas were adopted by the armies of the civilized world.[27]

Scott took the first step in that transition by recognizing the efficacy of skirmishing tactics and codifying them into US military training. In the 1830 *Infantry Tactics* exercises 'covering light-infantry and riflemen', the updated rules allowed individual soldiers considerable leeway when engaging an enemy. For a soldier traditionally required to stand in a column and hope not to be hit by incoming projectiles, the adoption of skirmishing tactics, although not yet standard, was welcome news. Furthermore, as in guerrilla warfare, the manual laid down the necessity to assess the terrain and react appropriately (italics added): 'In firing in extended order the skirmishers will be governed by circumstances, and fire *standing*, *kneeling*, or *lying*, as they may require, and take advantage of any object which presents itself.'[28]

The updated 1830 training manual covered skirmishing thoroughly and even took into consideration the 'very fatiguing' aspect of that mode of combat. Because of the nature of skirmishing, replacing soldiers engaged in combat had to be systematized. 'In relieving a line of skirmishers, the new line will extend in the rear, out of reach of the enemy's fire, and afterwards run up rapidly to the old line.' Covering aspects of both retreating and advancing, the manual advised:

Each file of the old skirmishers will run straight to the rear, the instant that a file of new skirmishers reaches the line of defense; and, whenever the former is out of reach of the enemy's fire, they will close in upon their supports ... If the relief take[s] place while advancing, the new skirmishers will run up in the same way, and pass briskly in front of the others; the old skirmishers will lie down, until they are out of the enemy's fire, after which they close upon their support as before.[29]

Because Scott was creating order out of a mode of warfare dependent on individual action, the skirmishing tactics were accompanied by bugle signals used by a commanding officer to direct his soldiers. The instrument most associated with nineteenth-century cavalry charges, the bugle was usually loud enough to pierce the noise of both galloping horses and gunfire. The nineteen 'Simple Signals' were: 1. to extend, 2. to close, 3. to advance, 4. to halt, 5. to retire, 6. to fire, 7. to cease, 8. to annul, 9. to relieve skirmishers, 10. to recall, 11. to assemble, 12. too fast, 13. too slow, 14. to incline, 15. right, 16. left, 17. centre, 18. double quick march, and 19. alternative ranks. In addition, these signals could be doubled up to create more complex orders 'under various circumstances'. For example, a bugle call using orders 15 and 3 would mean to 'throw forward the right', while a combination of 7 and 3 would mean to 'cease firing and advance'.[30]

Because large troop formations were still the dominant military unit, skirmishing was Scott's tactical response to guerrilla warfare without directly acknowledging it. Changes over time and advances in weaponry, as de Peyster later believed, made adopting more complex forms of combat necessary. However, hidebound as Scott was, he did not recognize the evolutionary trajectory of skirmishing as the future mode of warfare – even though he ushered the process along. A disciplinarian who respected and admired Napoleon and the French Army, Scott rarely mentioned Mexican guerrillas in his *Memoirs*. He dealt with them and used the terms *banditti* (emulating Napoleon) and *guerrilla* in correspondence, but believed with tactical training and preparation the efficacy of guerrillas could be blunted with both enemy-centric and population-centric approaches to warfare. Essentially, Scott himself was learning from the mistakes of his predecessor. To acknowledge guerrillas would be to respect them and their mode of warfare, and Scott could not do that. On the other hand, Scott was proud of the role skirmishing played in Mexico. We know this because he included it (using possessive phraseology) in the opening line of the most important chapter of his life story – the siege of Veracruz. To include skirmishing in a short litany of successes meant it was a focal point of his thinking (italics added): 'Successful was every prediction, plan, siege, battle, and skirmish *of mine* in the Mexican war.'[31]

Nevertheless, in 1830 Scott had some trials to endure before invading Mexico. He continued to absorb recent publications on military matters, many of which related to the Peninsular War. In fact, the 1830s saw a renaissance in military studies, as many prominent works of military education were published. Most similar to O'Conner's 1817 *Summary* was the 1831 release of *The Officer's Manual: Military Maxims of Napoleon*. The *Maxims* were ostensibly written by Napoleon (although they were probably compiled from various sources) and 'translated' by Sir George Charles D'Aguilar, an officer with a colourful career who was present when Wellington took Paris in 1815. *Napoleon's Military Maxims* would go through several editions, published before, during and after the Mexican War.[32]

Comprising seventy-eight maxims illustrated in a second 'notes' section using historical examples that included Napoleon, Frederick the Great, Gustavus Adolphus, Caesar and Hannibal, among others, D'Aguilar's compilation presented conventional tactics expressed in platitudes. For example, Maxim 5 stated, 'Wars should be governed by certain principles, for every war should have a definite object and be conducted according to the rules of art.' Other topics included maintaining an army's morale, the importance of having one line of operation, and avoiding confrontations with a superior army. Regarding the occupation of enemy territory, *Napoleon's Maxims* mimicked O'Conner's vague prescriptions. If a general was too 'severe, he irritates and increases the number of enemies. If lenient, he gives birth to expectations which only render the abuses and vexations inseparable from war.' The ambiguous advice for a general in this regard was to 'know how to employ severity, justice, and mildness by turns, if he would allay sedition or prevent it'.[33]

Like O'Conner's work informed by Jomini, the *Maxims* omitted guerrilla warfare. There was a single reference in the notes section based on Maxim 76, which called for certain actions to be taken when operating within an occupied country, such as: reconnoitring the surrounding area, employing dependable guides and acquiring information from the local '*curé* and postmaster'. Other recommendations included establishing cordial relations with locals, sending out spies and intercepting 'public and private' correspondence to gain intelligence. Maxim 76, according to D'Aguilar, amounted to a tacit recognition of insurgent warfare in occupied country: 'A chief of partisans is to a certain degree independent of the army. He receives neither pay nor provisions from it, and rarely succor, and is abandoned during the whole campaign to his own resources.' In this type of warfare, the partisan leader needed to sustain himself 'on his own resources'.[34]

Had Scott not been a Francophile he might have been more receptive to the Prussian school of military studies epitomized by Napoleonic war veteran Carl von Clausewitz. It was Clausewitz, rather than his counterpart Jomini, who first took guerrilla war seriously and subjected it to military analysis. However, we know Scott did not study Clausewitz's pioneering work on small wars (*Kleiner Krieg*), because the notes from the 156 lectures Clausewitz gave at the Prussian War Academy over a nine-month period beginning in 1810 were not compiled until 1816 – nor published until the modern era. Nevertheless, from a military perspective, they are worth noting since they discussed many of the problems the French faced from guerrilla units in Spain.[35]

The prescriptions Clausewitz embraced to carry on successful partisan operations may seem obvious in a modern context, but at the time the idea of formalizing guerrilla warfare was unheard of. These principles included collaborating with mounted units, night marching and camping during the day under cover in small units. Other recommendations were to 'move forward on concealed roads' and to treat the native population kindly. The Prussian 'emphasized that secrecy was of paramount importance', and thus information regarding raids should only be shared with a few people. Since ambush was one of the key tactics of partisan warfare, such attacks were most successful in the evening 'or at midday, when those in the camps would be cooking and least prepared to face the enemy'. Clausewitz drew his recommendations from an insurgent perspective, noting that inducing 'false alarms' the evening prior to attacking 'was always advisable, since this would result in less vigilance the day after'. Besides collecting intelligence, other partisan assignments included: intercepting enemy communications, kidnapping enemy officers (particularly generals), destroying infrastructure such as roads and bridges, and capturing enemy money and materiel'.[36]

Assuming that Scott read *On War* (1832), we know that Jomini's *The Art of War* (1838) was written in part as a response to Clausewitz. Jomini stated that Clausewitz's 'logic is frequently defective' – which was the sole reference by name to the Prussian in his book. *The Art of War* was required reading for officers at West Point in the years leading up to the Mexican War, and was most assuredly studied by Scott, who was known to travel with a bulky military library. Jomini stated that the 'art of war, independently of its political and moral relations, consisted of five principal parts, viz: strategy, grand tactics, logistics, tactics of the different arms, and the art of the engineer.' By 'grand tactics' Jomini meant the operational level (or operational art) of war, and he expounded on traditional 'maxims on lines of operations', which (like Napoleon) he believed were of paramount importance. 'If the art of war consists in bringing into action upon the decisive point of the theater of operations the greatest possible force, the choice of operations ... may be regarded as the fundamental idea in a good plan of campaign.' Here again, the focus was on maxims and truisms related to strategy.[37]

Jomini agreed with Clausewitz that 'the morale of armies, as well as of nations', were important to victory, but drew distinctions between *tactics* and *battles*, noting that tactics 'is the art of making good combinations preliminary to battles, as well as during their progress'. Without mentioning Spain or Russia, Jomini referenced 'some writers' who believed that battles were 'the chief and deciding features of war. This assertion is not strictly true, as armies have been destroyed by strategic operations without the occurrence of pitched battles.' In other words, once things went wrong for an army over a prolonged period, the momentum necessary for victory was lost: 'No system of tactics can lead to victory when the morale of an army is bad.'[38]

One area in which the Frenchman excelled was addressing the importance of logistics. The word is derived 'from the title of the *major général des logis* (translated in German by *Quartermeister*), an officer whose duty it formerly was to lodge and camp troops' and to maintain order among marching columns. Jomini noted that these duties required a competent chief of staff, adding that it was a difficult job because 'it became in this way necessary that a man should be acquainted with all the various branches of the art of war'. The responsibilities of the logistics division were innumerable. Duties of staff officers working under the chief of staff included: moving material, ensuring 'proper composition to advanced guards, rearguards, flankers, and all detached bodies', organizing and 'superintending the march of trains of baggage, munitions, provisions, and ambulances', and administration of supplies and lines 'as well as lines of communication with lines of detached bodies'. In other words, in addition to locating, building, supplying and policing the camps required to sustain large (and sometimes scattered) armies, logistics officers had to ensure that whatever orders a general gave under a strategic plan could be implemented with reasonable flexibility. Essentially, logisticians were (and remain) the interconnecting sinews of an army's body of operations. Jomini generally avoided discussing guerrilla operations, but he did maintain that 'great changes in army organization' had taken place since the French Revolution.[39]

One of the areas of military evolution which Jomini specifically contrasted with the 'old system' was skirmishing. Here he asserted that Napoleon's 'system of modern strategy' employed for the first time in 1800 and utilized in Italy in 1805 and 1806 'marked a new era in the conception of plans of campaigns and lines'. Despite Jomini's assertions, there was a notable lack attention given in *The Art of War* to the rough and ready mode of warfare that led to Napoleon's demise in Spain. 'It may now be a question,' Jomini wrote triumphantly, 'whether the system of Napoleon is adapted to all capacities, epochs, and armies, or ... there can be any return, in the light of events in 1800 and 1809, to the old system of wars of position.'[40]

Even when Jomini came close to describing guerrilla warfare he still did not specifically mention the debacle in Spain but concentrated on the Russian campaign: 'We must by no means conclude it possible for a body of light cavalry deployed as skirmishers to accomplish as much as the Cossacks or other irregular cavalry.' Even in 1838, the Peninsular War veteran avoided addressing the question of Spanish partisans:

> The history of the wars between 1812 and 1815 has renewed the old disputes upon the question whether regular cavalry will in the end get the better over an irregular cavalry which will avoid all serious encounters, will retreat with the speed of the Parthians and return to combat with the same rapidity, wearing out the strength of its enemy by continual skirmishing.[41]

To Jomini's credit, he posed important questions concerning potential changes in warfare on the horizon. 'Will the adoption of the rifled small-arms and improved balls bring about any important changes in the formation for battle and the now recognized principles of tactics?' It was a serious question that ultimately played no small role in the Mexican War when revolutionary rifle technology was introduced. Another question was one that Scott (and later de Peyster) were in the process of addressing. 'Will whole armies be deployed as skirmishers,' he asked, 'or will it not still be necessary to preserve either the formation lines deployed in two or three ranks, or lines of battalions in columns?' The ever-changing and evolving military technology, especially during a period of rapid scientific development, was altering the equations used by strategists to formulate their tactics and theories. 'Will battles become mere duels with the rifle, where the parties will fire upon each other, without maneuvering, until one or the other shall retreat or be destroyed?' All these were pertinent questions concerning the changing nature of warfare in the first half of the nineteenth century.[42]

Failing the Florida Test

Even if Scott did read Jomini's 1838 work, he could not have applied any of its precepts to the Second Seminole War (1835–1842) in Florida when he was sent there in 1836. Nor could he have relied on Clausewitz's small war theories prior to organizing the campaign to oust unruly Floridian tribes and their escaped-slave allies from the former Spanish domain. The point is somewhat moot, since the Seminoles were not white, and thus considerations granted to other European states were not applied to native tribes. This, ironically, was a major advantage to the Seminoles: white Americans continually underestimated the military capabilities of tribes – particularly their skill in using traditional Native American guerrilla-like tactics.

Schooled in Napoleonic military studies based on 'civilized' European warfare, Scott was dumbfounded by the tactics used by the Seminoles. In an interesting contrast to his military predecessor, Andrew Jackson, Scott attempted to apply conventional tactical thinking to a military problem nearly impossible to solve by conventional means. This was another aspect of the Europeanization of American military jurisprudence in relation to the Native Americans. White Americans applied European norms to the rules and laws of war when it came to facing European enemies in the Americas, but were entirely flummoxed when trying to apply those norms and conventions to tribes who had no recognition of such conventions beyond their own local and regional traditions.[43]

When General Jackson entered Florida during the First Seminole War (1817–1818) he employed a scorched-earth strategy of burning Seminole villages that Scott had no desire to follow – even though Jackson advised him to. Having grown up on the frontier, Jackson in many ways personified the lawless nature of frontier warfare, beyond the borders of states and outside presumed international norms. In that regard, the Texas frontier was not much different to Florida, and Jackson was merely the product of his environment and times. Scott, on the other hand, was an elitist unwilling to discard the accumulated formal military knowledge he had spent most of his life absorbing. In other words, in 1836 Scott was not ready to deviate from the established rules of warfare in order to achieve victory.[44]

Myer Cohen, an officer during Scott's campaign, wrote a book on the US Army's experiences tracking elusive Seminoles in the swamps of Florida. He was 'baffled in his effort to find and subdue the foe,' Cohen wrote of Scott. When the Americans entered an abandoned Seminole village they usually 'discovered a trail by which they could proceed much more rapidly'. The Seminoles, however, were almost impossible to find, because they had the advantage of operating on well-known territory: 'The Indians must have entered the wood by this secret pass, and thus were enabled to flee so quickly … In a word, they are on their own familiar grounds – we are strangers in a very strange land.'[45]

Despite long drawn-out preparations, Scott's war in Florida was a failure. Cohen drew parallels between the over-meticulousness of his commanding officer and the situation the French faced in Spain. 'We are not inaptly compared to a prize ox,' he wrote, 'stung by hornets, unable to avoid, or catch, his annoyers; or are we justly likened to men harpooning minnows, or shooting sandpipers with artillery?' Cohen shuddered at the thought that the Seminoles had bested the US Army. In addition to the shortage of transport, ignorance among Washington politicians, and the humid climate causing widespread illness, Cohen claimed, 'The most prominent cause of failure was to be found in the face of the country, so well adapted to the guerilla warfare which the Indians carry on, affording ambushes and fastnesses to them, and retardation to us.' The Second Seminole War was a hard lesson for Scott: that bringing 10,000 men to fight fewer than 2,000 Seminole warriors did not guarantee victory. Cohen wrote, 'In such a region, their strength was in their fewness, our weakness in the number, of our respective forces.'[46]

Although Scott had been beaten by the Seminoles, his reputation suffered no damage, because in early 1836 the US press turned its focus to the rebellion in Texas and the siege of the Alamo. Nor did they refer to the Seminoles in the context of guerrilla warfare. Such references to native tribes only came *after* the Mexican War – particularly to describe the Apaches, who fought the US Army for decades. On the other hand, accounts of guerrilla warfare reaching the American public in the 1830s trickled in from Spain, which between 1833 and 1840 was roiled by the first of a series of civil conflicts known as the Carlist Wars. Therefore, even by the 1840s, the term *guerrilla* was still exclusively used in reference to Spanish fighters or insurgents in former Spanish-American dominions. A *Times-Picayune* analogy illustrated the semantic (but not tactical) distinction Americans drew between Native Americans and Spanish guerrillas prior to the Mexican War:

We heard a young man yesterday pay a very high compliment to New Orleans mosquitoes, as contradistinguished from their fellows over the lake. Here, he says, like an honorable enemy, they sound the tocsin of war – you hear the note of preparation before the advance to attack; but *there*, they act as treacherously as an Indian, or a Spanish guerrilla – they lie in ambush and pounce on their victim before he is aware of their offensive intention; their weapons are imbued in his blood before he discovers their presence.[47]

Planning for Occupation. Halleck, Scott and the New Strategy

For years Americans had seen a conflict with Mexico approaching. In 1836 Texas declared itself an independent republic and defeated Santa Anna's forces at the Battle of Jacinto. The Mexicans, bitter over the loss of their northern state, continued to hope they might someday reassert control over the breakaway province and even used ethnic arguments to draw comparisons between the Texas revolt and the Vendée in France. 'Many say it is better to continue the war ... for were a truly Mexican province to revolt we could recover it, as France recovered La Vendée, because the people would be of our race.' Adding to their difficulties was the short-lived establishment of the unrecognized Republic of the Rio Grande in 1840 and the re-emergence of the second Republic of Yucatán in 1841 – the latter survived throughout US-Mexican War. The existence of these republics demonstrated the lack of Mexican unity prior to the conflict.[48]

Once it became apparent to observers during the US presidential election of 1844 that annexation of the Republic of Texas meant the US was likely to inherit the breakaway state's conflict with Mexico, prudent military planners like Scott began a more formal study of comparable wars. That study is reflected in Henry Wager Halleck's 1846 publication of *Military Art and Science; or Course of Instruction in Strategy, Fortification, Tactics of Battles*. Sent to Europe by Scott, Halleck – who was among the top cadets of his West Point class – returned to the United States on the eve of the war with increased insights into the critical mistakes made by Napoleon in Spain. Halleck was so inspired by the Iberian conflict that many of the 'best works' he recommended on military history were authored by notable French generals of the Peninsular War, such as General Maximilien Foy's *History of the War in the Peninsula* (1827), Suchet's *Memoirs of the War in Spain* (1829) and Marshal St Cyr's *Memoirs* (1831). With an acute understanding of the Peninsular conflict in mind, one of the main conclusions Halleck reached regarding the failed French occupation – which is reflected in the novel counter-insurgency policies articulated in Winfield Scott's 1864 *Memoirs* – was the counterproductive employment by Napoleon of the ancient military maxim *bellum se ipsum alet*: war will support war:

> In this connection the war in the Spanish peninsula is well worth a study. At the beginning of this war Napoleon had to choose between methodical operations with provisions carried in the train of his army, or purchased of the inhabitants and regularly paid for; and regular warfare, with forced requisitions – war being made to support war. The question was thoroughly discussed.[49]

Where did Halleck acquire his inspiration to reject the long-held tradition of supplying an invading army through forced requisitions? The answer was not entirely apparent in 1846, but Halleck left clues pointing to Henri Jomini's 1827 biography of Napoleon. Halleck, fluent in French, was probably familiar with Jomini's *Vie politique et militaire de Napoléon* (*Political and military life of Napoleon*) before going to Europe, but he certainly came back inspired by what Jomini had failed to fully articulate in his better-known 1838 work, *Art of War*. Halleck's excerpts from Jomini's biography – related enigmatically by Jomini in the first person, as though Napoleon was defending his actions from the grave – are scattered throughout the section of *Military Art and Science* as it related to rethinking the military maxim first invoked in Spain by Cato the Elder:

> In forming my plans for subjugating Spain, I [Napoleon] had to choose between regular and methodical operations and a war of a more irregular character. By the first system, provisions must be carried in the suite of the army, or be regularly purchased and paid for from the inhabitants. No great detachments could be made to regulate the administration of the provinces, or to pursue the insurgent corps to the fastnesses of the mountains. In fine, effecting a military occupation of Spain without its subjugation. By the second, war would be made to support war.[50]

After Halleck returned to the United States in the spring of 1846 he consulted with Scott concerning his dislike of forced requisitions and discussed strategy in the upcoming campaign to seize the Mexican capital via Veracruz. Accommodating their opinions about Napoleon's mistake in seizing too much territory, it was decided the campaign would have 'no great detachments to regulate the administration of the provinces' but consist of a small and disciplined force purchasing all the supplies it could not carry from the Mexican population between Veracruz and Mexico City. Soon afterwards, Halleck was sent to California on an important mission to ensure that this critical piece of territory ended up in American hands. Like Scott's *Memoirs*, it was only in 1864, towards the end of the Civil War, that Halleck informed the public that during the seven months aboard an ocean-going ship en route to the west coast he had translated Jomini's 1827 biography of Napoleon. In essence, Halleck was admitting in 1864 that his inspiration for repudiating the Roman and Napoleonic military maxim came from Jomini, who had represented Napoleon in a 'clumsy' first-person posthumous perspective. In an 1864 review of Halleck's translation of Jomini's biography, the *North American Review* noted it had 'not received in England and America that study and attention it deserves' because 'until the translation by Major-General Halleck … there had been no English version of the work'.[51]

As noted, Halleck was extremely critical of the time, money, and resources the French spent in besieging major cities throughout Spain; he believed that the best approach was to avoid sieges, while focusing on the main objective of seizing the capital in the hope that the Mexican authorities would then concede defeat. Halleck asserted that one of Napoleon's most successful strategies (before the war in Spain) was seizing an enemy's capital, which 'is almost always a decisive strategic point, and its capture is therefore frequently the object of the entire campaign'. Halleck referenced Napoleon's conquests of Venice and Rome (1797), Vienna (1805, 1809), Berlin (1806) and Madrid (1808) as examples, while arguing that the 'taking of Washington, in 1814, had little or no influence on the war, for the place was then of no importance in itself, and was a mere nominal capital'. Like Napoleon, Halleck advised against changing lines of operations in the middle of a campaign and recommended employing 'the shortest and most direct line of operations, which should either pierce the enemy's line of defense, or cut off his communications with his base'.[52]

Like his famous predecessors, Halleck advocated keeping 'forces concentrated' but noted certain exceptions existed, such as when foraging or intercepting an enemy's convoys. Using the American Revolutionary War as an example, he criticized the British for having ignored 'leading maxims' by scattering 'their forces over an immense country', thus becoming 'too weak to act with decision and affect any one point'. He also recited one of Napoleon's sacred rules about keeping forces 'fully employed'. The belief was that soldiers with too much free time would grow lazy, engage in licentious activities and be unprepared for action.[53]

Halleck warned that wars of invasion have their downsides. One of these problems, which reflected the strategy used by the Americans in Mexico, was how to prevent lines of operation from becoming 'too deep, which is always hazardous in an enemy's country'. As had been the case in Spain, Halleck referred to the importance of perception among the population of an invaded country. When 'local authorities and inhabitants oppose, instead of facilitating his operations … and if patriotism animate the defensive army to fight for the independence of its threatened country, the war may become long and bloody.' Halleck asserted that such a situation could be avoided by a scrupulous general 'if a political diversion be made in favor of the invading force, and its operations be attended with success'.[54] The best way to maintain relatively harmonious relations with an occupied people was to ensure that soldiers did not engage in reckless activities – particularly if these involved the local citizenry. Therefore, ensuring the strictest discipline, especially among volunteer soldiers, became the other chief pillar of the US Army's strategy to preventing insurgency in the heart of Mexico.

Maxim of Discipline

General George Meade was one of the most vocal critics of volunteer soldiers during the Mexican War. An 1835 West Point graduate who passed out third in a class of fifty-six cadets, Meade served with distinction during the Second Seminole War before taking a break from military life. In 1842 he re-enlisted as a lieutenant and was promoted to first lieutenant following the Battle of Monterrey. Meade's observations on volunteer soldiers reflected the divergent attitudes of Americans towards the military and its increasing professionalization during the period. In his *Life and Letters*, Meade wrote that while in northern Mexico, 'regular officers, being disciplined' were more 'restrained, kept in subjugation, and the war made a war against the army and government of Mexico, and not against the people'. In contrast, soon after arriving in theatre, volunteers 'commenced to excite feelings of indignation and hatred in the bosom of the people, by their outrages on them'.[55]

The undisciplined nature of volunteer soldiers, who often disobeyed orders and drank far more than regulars, was a concern for Meade and exactly what Halleck had warned about, especially their foraging (theft) of property from civilians during the occupation:

> Everyday complaints are made of this man's cornfield being destroyed by the volunteers' horses put into it, or another man's fences being torn down by them for firewood, or an outrage committed on some inoffensive person by some drunken volunteer, and above all volunteers, those from Texas are the most outrageous, for they come here with sores and recollections of wrongs done, which have been festering for years, and under the guise of the entering the United States service, they cloak a thirst to gratify personal revenge.[56]

Meade warned that if such conduct by volunteers continued, Mexicans would eventually support an uprising. On the Mexican side of the Rio Grande at Matamoros, Meade described the volunteers as 'perfectly ignorant of discipline, and most restive under restraint. They are in consequence, a most disorderly mass, who will give us, I fear, more trouble than the enemy.' As the soldiers settled into their new role of military occupiers in the river city, even policing the volunteers became burdensome. 'Already are our guardhouses filled daily with drunken officers and men, who go to town, get drunk and commit outrages on the citizens.' The city, he wrote, 'has become a mass of grogshops and gambling houses.' Meade criticized the commanding officer General Zachary Taylor, who was popular among the volunteer soldiers and traded on his common-man image to win the presidency after the war. 'Now it is impossible for General Taylor to restrain these men; he has neither the moral nor physical force to do it,' he wrote, 'and my apprehensions are that if we advance with them into the interior, they will exasperate the people against us, causing them to rise *en masse*, and if so there is no telling when the war will end.'[57]

The result of volunteer excesses in Matamoros and elsewhere was an order limiting the liquor trade at the mouth of the Rio Grande: 'No spirituous liquors will be permitted to enter the river or the city for the purpose of barter or traffic on account of any person whatever, whether sutler in the army or private dealer.' Violators were warned that confiscated goods would be sent to New Orleans and resold for the benefit of the army hospital department. Informants were offered incentives, but Matamoros merchants were still allowed to sell liquor they already had 'on hand but to receive no new supplies'.[58]

George Ballentine, an English soldier in the US Army, gave a colourful description of volunteer soldiers, whose presence caused the locals of Tampico to stay locked in their houses 'as if in a state of siege'. Ballentine was not surprised that Mexicans 'should be a little shy of the strange, wild-looking, hairy-faced savages of the half horse and half alligator breed', as they were variously 'armed with sabres, bowies, and revolvers, and in every uncouth variety of costume peculiar to the backwoodsman'. The intimidating and foreign appearance of these wild-looking invaders forced the inhabitants to deal diplomatically with them:

> The señors or caballeros, masters or gentlemen, the Mexicans called them when addressing them, but when speaking of them in their absence, it was 'Malditos Volunteros', which they enunciated with a bitterness in tone, that showed the intensity of their dislike … the volunteers seemed to be objects of their special detestation; and I imagine today they looked upon us all with similar complacency, to that which the Spaniards looked upon the army of France, during its usurpation of the Peninsula.[59]

The duty of preventing violence and indiscriminate acts against civilians or their property rested on the shoulders of the officers. To effectively carry out this task Scott demanded absolute discipline and severely punished anyone who violated his orders. In his *Memoirs* he elaborated on his novel programme of martial law and its application to Mexican civilians, US military personnel and anyone else affiliated with the army's logistics system. Promulgated for the first time in Tampico before arriving in Veracruz, Scott wrote, 'Without it, I could not have maintained the honor and the discipline of the army, or have reached the capital of Mexico.'[60]

What was military justice like in Mexico? In short, 'disciplinary' is the word commonly used by historians. The justice meted out by courts martial in Mexico was strict, and this generally had the intended deterrent effect. From the period of the occupation of Puebla – where the main US Army headquarters was based between early May and August 1847 – sentences and punishments were carried out with expedition. In the first issue (1 July) of the US newspaper in Puebla, *American Star No. 2*, the entire first two pages were devoted to thirty-four recent court-martial proceedings.[61]

Of the thirty-four cases heard in Puebla twelve concerned desertion. Most soldiers pleaded 'not guilty', and seven were acquitted of the more serious charge but found guilty of being absent without leave (AWOL) and forced to pay five dollars a month as restitution for either five or six months. Private John W. Blair of the mounted riflemen fell into that category and was discharged from service due to 'the manner and appearance of the prisoner, that he is unsound in mind and body, and totally unfit for military duty'. Those found guilty of desertion had to 'refund the United States' thirty dollars for being arrested and usually received fifty lashes on the back – some 'well laid on' – before being restored to duty. Others were confined for the restitution period when not on duty. Since the penalty for desertion could be death, this was considered lenient. In the case of Private John Bonecastle, who was in the habit of 'leaving his company in camp, and garrison, without permission, for days at a time, and totally disqualifying himself by drunkenness on duty', a second charge of 'utter worthlessness' was added. Before being drummed out of the service and forced to forfeit pay, Bonecastle was branded with a 'W' on his right hip.[62]

Other common charges against soldiers (mostly privates) were insubordination, drunkenness, mutinous conduct (including fighting), highly unsoldierlike conduct, neglect of duty, conduct prejudicial to good order and military discipline, and sleeping on guard. Punishments for most of the offences were reduction in rank (for sergeants or corporals), having stripes or chevrons cut off in front of one's battalion, public reprimand by a superior officer, forfeit of pay, and branding. One of the more unusual punishments carried out was being made to 'ride the wooden horse' (*cavaletto squarciapalle*). This was a torture device of some antiquity in Europe – the prisoner would straddle a V-shaped sawhorse with weights dangling from his legs – and could easily cripple an unfit prisoner. Private Robert Thompson was forced to ride it 'from reveille to retreat' for thirty days after being found guilty of conduct prejudicial to good order. The more serious charge was sleeping on post, since doing so put the lives of the company and army at risk. In the case of Private

John Quinn, the punishment was forfeit of pay and 'to wear an iron yoke weighing ten pounds, with three prongs, for three years'. Sleeping on duty or post could also potentially draw the death penalty.[63]

Sergeant James Bannan and Corporal Edward Hill of the 5th Infantry were convicted of 'drunkenness on guard' in Mexico City after the Americans took that city. Because tensions at the time were elevated, and insurrection or surprise attacks were considered imminently possible, both were found guilty and ordered to be shot the day after their court martial. Luckily for them, General Worth and 'all of the officers of the 5th Infantry signed a request for pardon', and the sentence was graciously suspended by Scott. Nevertheless, the episode was a deterrent to others who might engage in drinking or sleeping while on duty.[64]

In a public act of leniency directed at the Mexican people, Henrique Garcia, a Mexican soldier apprehended when 'found in arms in the city of Mexico' while threatening US soldiers, was acquitted by an American court. Although Garcia had violated the law by carrying a weapon, he was set free. He could have easily been found guilty by the military court and executed, but the acquittal reflected the humane nature of the occupation.[65]

'On Bended Knee'

In concert with the martial law codes enacted by Scott was an effort to assuage the concerns of the Catholic Church regarding US intentions in Mexico. This began at the war's onset, when Polk met with the influential Bishop John Hughes of New York in the Oval Office on 19 May 1846. According to Polk's account, the meeting was intended to 'procure his aid in disabusing the minds of the Catholic priests & people' during the war. As a result, Hughes agreed to extend these sentiments to the Archbishop of Mexico and pledged to send Spanish-speaking priests to Mexico with the US Army. The day after the White House meeting, the president met with Missouri Senator Thomas Hart Benton and the bishop of that state, and Polk came away believing that if the 'priests in Mexico can be satisfied that their churches and religion would be secure, the conquest of the northern provinces of Mexico will be easy'. The presidential meetings with church leaders were not kept secret, and reporting by the *New York Herald* indicated that 'correspondence between the Catholic hierarchy' in the United States and Mexico had preceded the Oval Office consultations by a year and increased after the war began: 'The American people have been much misrepresented in Mexico by the military despots of that country, and the Yankee heretics have been, no doubt, held up as hostile, in every respect, to the Catholic faith.'[66]

Other newspapers reported that two chaplains from Georgetown College and two St Louis (Missouri) Jesuits would be embedded in US forces, and that Polk took on 'the responsibility' for managing their placement. In this regard, four '*sine qua non*' stipulations were requested by the priests: that they 'be recognized and respected as clergymen in the army'; they be allowed to speak with Catholic soldiers; that Protestant soldiers be allowed to meet with them should they choose; and that they 'have the liberty to visit the Mexican camp, army, and people, at any and all times, except on the eve of an engagement, when their leaving the American camp might be fraught with danger to themselves, or lead to any breach of military discipline'.[67]

Dublin's *Freeman's Journal* acknowledged the benign nature of the occupation as Scott's small army slowly made its way towards the capital. 'The policy pursued by the Americans is in the highest degree conciliatory,' their New York correspondent wrote. 'Not only is the course of paying for everything and repressing all military violence rigidly continued, but the utmost respect is paid to the religion of the people.' Reports from Mexico indicated conciliation was working: '"Los Yankis" were denounced beforehand as "heretics and infidels"; the religious prejudices of the people were most strongly aroused against them; now they have come, they appear determined to show that they are almost as good Catholics as the Mexicans themselves.' The *Journal* also described how Colonel Thomas Childs, the military governor of Jalapa, together with Scott, attended 'with uncovered heads, presented arms and on bended knee, the procession of the host there. General Scott himself joins in the procession, carrying a lighted candle in his hand.' Attending mass was 'but an instance of a system of policy ... producing at least in measure, its intended effect'.[68]

The contrast with French behaviour in Spain was stark. The US Army did not intentionally requisition church-owned buildings, churches, convents, or monasteries – even though such buildings were generally the sturdiest and most easily defensible structures (which is why the French used them). There were occasions when such buildings were seized out of military necessity, such as during the siege of Puebla, or after the *ayuntamiento* (city corporation) of Mexico City recommended some religious buildings be used to house soldiers, but there were no requisitions on the scale of the Peninsular War. Scott wrote that while 'occupying the capital and other cities, strict orders were given that no officer or man should be billeted, without consent, upon any inhabitant; that troops should only be quartered in the established barracks' and other government buildings.[69]

Nevertheless, despite overtures to the Catholic Church by US political and military leaders, the need to enforce discipline superseded diplomatic niceties. When more than seventy Irish-American military deserters, known as the St

Patrick's Brigade (*San Patricios*), were captured by US forces following the Battle of Churubusco on the outskirts of Mexico City, they were summarily court-martialled. These former soldiers had been induced by Mexican handbills offering incentives in the shape of land and money to desert and fight for Mexico. Eventually, their numbers reached a few hundred.

Scott made an example of the San Patricios' desertion by conducting two court-martial proceedings in late August while the army threatened the gates of the capital. Fifty soldiers were sentenced to death by hanging, thirty of whom symbolically received their punishment on 13 September at Chapultepec Castle as the US Army rode into Mexico City. 'I sincerely pitied these poor fellows,' George Ballentine wrote, and he surmised that the young men had made their fatal decision as a result of suffering harsh discipline, noting that at the Chapultepec battle the deserters had specifically targeted US officers: 'The large number of officers killed in the affair was also ascribed to them, as for the gratification of their revenge they aimed at no other objects during the engagement.' In a symbolic gesture of American anger, most *San Patricios* were hanged at the moment the US flag was raised over Chapultepec's walls. Scott reminded his 'Protestant and Catholic' soldiers soon afterwards to 'remember the fate of the deserters at Churubusco'.[70]

Occupation Open for Business

Another important strategy designed to appease Mexicans was the abolition of the unpopular *alcabala*, a sixteenth-century colonial tax on transactions particularly hated by poor peasants and Indians. While some historians have argued that Scott's efforts to collect taxes from compliant provincial governments during the occupation fell short of expectations, the truth is that tax collection was intentionally neglected by Scott because his main source of revenue came from payments he drew from representatives of London banking interests in Mexico City. When the *alcabala* initiative is viewed in a counter-insurgency context, it becomes obvious that Scott was not dependent on Mexican tax revenue but was using military-administrative leverage to further his social-strategic goals.[71]

The *American Star* reported that the *alcabala* was rescinded at an early stage of the occupation. 'In Veracruz, Jalapa, Perote, and Puebla we gave liberty to the laboring and productive classes, by abolishing the odious system of the *alcabala*, or tax on labor, by which both the producer and consumer are benefitted.' Mexico City was especially reliant on the tax and enforced it on visiting merchants vending goods in the city. The *Star* explained that any 'poor Indian who presents himself at the gates of the city with a basket of fruit ... is obliged to pay a tax before he enters, and if he has not the money with him, he is made to deposit with the guard either a part of his produce ... [or] to redeem the article pledged.'[72]

However, unlike the cities along the corridor in which the Americans banned the tax, there was pressure to maintain the *alcabala* in Mexico City. Not only did it bring in much-needed municipal revenue, it also acted as a security measure justifying inspection of those arriving at the city's gates. The *American Star*'s editors lamented 'the temporary continuation of this most unrighteous (*alcabala*) tax on labor' and addressed the visible wealth disparities in a city where 'twelve thousand' landowners ruled over some 200,000 residents. The *Star* noted, 'They are in possession of all the wealth, and power, by which they have managed to keep in force the monarchical custom of *alcabala* or tax on the poor labor ... The injustice of this mode of taxation must be obvious to everyone.'[73] It was not until 31 December that Scott issued a directive eliminating the tax in the capital. In one of his final acts as commander in Mexico, he wrote, 'All transit duties (*alcabalas y derechos de internacion*) heretofore payable at the gates of the cities and ... between States have been abolished, together with the national lotteries.'[74] Few outside observers recognized the significance of abolishing the *alcabala*. London's *Morning Post*, however, discerned the impact it would have:

> People in general expect benefit from this occupation. It will do away with the military and the *empleados* (bureaucrats), the two greatest plagues of the nation. The interior customs and *alcabalas* are also abolished where the Americans pass the property, and persons are well protected by them. Trade is promoted, and everything receives new life. All these material improvements strike the eye of the lower classes, and this again accounts for the want of *patriotism*, and for the country not rising against the invaders.[75]

Nor was the Mexican capital entirely dreary under occupation. For soldiers who adhered to the rules, Mexico City under US control offered numerous venues where men could congregate in their free time. The Lone Star House, at the corner of Refugio and La Palma, was officially (like many establishments) a coffee house 'supplied with the best wines and liquors to be obtained in Mexico'. The Eagle Coffee House boasted of 'procuring wines, liquors, and segars [*sic*] of the choicest brand'. The Theatre Coffee House and Restaurant, run by US Army matron Sarah Foyle, claimed to be open 'all hours' of the day to cater to American soldiers. The Orleans House advertised 'new cider' made at their establishment. Other locales included the Mansion House, The

Anglo Saxon House, the United States Hotel and the Olive Branch Coffee House. For officers inclined to learn either Spanish of French, lessons were provided by a Harvard graduate in the National Palace 'for the benefit of such gentlemen of the army ... to cultivate either of said languages'.[76]

For officers there was also the popular Aztec Club. Established a month after the US Army entered the gates of the city, the club – a precursor to other veterans' groups – was originally intended for officers who took part in Scott's central Mexico campaign. General John A. Quitman, the Military Governor of Mexico City, was the club's first president, and Scott was made an honorary member. The club was located in a palace built in the 1700s for the viceroy of New Spain near the Zocalo (main square) and now Scott's headquarters. According to its history, the 'original home of the Club was the handsome residence of Señor [José] Bocanegra, who had been formerly Minister to the United States' and briefly President of Mexico. The original 160 members form a veritable list of US military legends.[77]

In addition to bullfights and balls, there were other sorts of entertainment. Madame Armand and Madame Turin performed at the Olympic Circus – which usually hosted European talent. The National Theatre put on many performances, including a 'beautiful comedy' in the shape of the two-act historical drama *Napoleon lo Manda* by a Spanish company. The Principal Theatre offered a crusade romance based on the Sophie Ristaud Cottin work *The Saracen, Or Maltida and Malek Adhel* (1805). Cottin's romantic martial themes in *Matilda* undoubtedly spoke to the Yankee attendees, who 'abandon their vast and flourishing states, and, through the perils of a stormy sea, come to meet their death in a foreign clime'.[78]

After the initial chaos following the capture of Mexico City, life returned to relative normality. US soldiers fell back into the routine of drilling daily and relaxing in their free time. The Alameda Central, the oldest public park in the Americas, became a popular place for morning and afternoon strolls; it was 'a favorite place of resort for recreation, and there are few spots in the world where one can take a more pleasant promenade'.[79] Violations of Scott's Martial Law Orders did occur, but nothing compared to the scenes at the time of the initial occupation. The city was generally shut down at night. Early twentieth-century Mexican War scholar Justin Smith cited one soldier's account that 'if the patrol finds you in the street after eight o'clock in the evening you are taken to the guardhouse, and if noisy you are handcuffed'. Indeed, one month after taking the city, the editors of the *American Star* noted a considerable change in attitude among the citizens:

The women too ... have ceased to flash the fire of indignant scorn from their beautiful eyes, and now stand upon their balconies and walk the streets, viewing us with mild serenity ... The city has changed, indeed; the crack of the rifle or *escopeta* [shotgun] is heard no more in the streets, the roar of artillery no more startles the ears of the timid, and all walk the streets in quiet without looking for a shot from this or that house top ... who would have believed in so short a time so palpable a change could have come over the place?[80]

Lieutenant William H. Davis told his sister Elizabeth of a pending lunch date with a Mexican girl who had spent several years in New York, asking whether a 'Mexican sister-in-law' was a possibility. He wrote that the city had undergone a rapid change once it was learned an armistice had been signed – noting it had 'become much gayer'. True, the large metropolis remained dangerous at night, as straggling and intoxicated soldiers were often picked on or even killed by opportunists. Daytime, however, was another matter:

Ladies who before confined themselves closely to their houses now show themselves, radiant in smiles and beauty. They are very pretty, and even hardened soldiers cannot altogether withstand their fine black eyes and winning manners. They now come out to the theatres, and upon the public drives, and are not the least afraid of the American officers. I am going into a Mexican family to live during the rest of my stay in Mexico, for the purpose of learning the Spanish language, and hope to acquire a tolerable knowledge of it.[81]

Others decried the dubious behaviour often accompanying the extended occupation: the crowds of officers and enlisted soldiers who filled the 'ball rooms' and gambling houses every day of the week, including Sundays; and the unmarried and married men of both high and low rank who spent their free time drinking and carrying on intimate relationships with Mexican women in public and private. Mexico City during the US occupation was certainly a place where an American with money to spend could easily indulge in the vices found in large cities; and although Scott was not a drinker, he turned a blind eye to activities considered immoral because (in a way) they complemented his efforts to conciliate the lowest and highest classes of a conquered country.[82]

The Mexican Army did not try to retake the capital. Instead, they immediately cut off the main American force from its connection to the coast by laying siege to Puebla – the largest city between Veracruz and the capital. It was the last chance for Santa Anna to muster a significant conventional resistance to the invasion. If the Mexicans retook Puebla, the critical logistics lifeline would be severed and Scott's army isolated from the coast.

Despite fielding an army twice the size of the Americans, the Mexicans' attempts to stop Scott's advance at Veracruz, Cerro Gordo, Contreras, Churubusco, Molina del Rey and Chapultepec were all to no avail. These defeats were frustrating. Some Mexican leaders had always believed that defeat in conventional battle was inevitable, and therefore, even before the Americans landed at Veracruz, influential leaders attuned to the capabilities and weaknesses of the Mexican army were promoting a different military approach to halt what appeared to be an otherwise unstoppable army.

Winfield Scott had effectively spent an entire lifetime making his way to Mexico City. It was the summit of his long military career. The life of the 'rules man' whose first profession was the law ultimately came full circle in his professionalization of the US military and enaction of codes of conduct for US soldiers in foreign wars. As Henry Halleck advised, this was done to prevent the emergence of an insurrection like the one that plagued the French in Spain. The general who best embodied the profound changes in the US military during the antebellum period later noted in his *Memoirs* that his martial law regime 'worked like a charm; it conciliated the Mexicans, intimidated the vicious of several races, and being executed with impartial rigor, gave the highest moral deportment and discipline ever known in an invading army.'[83] The pupil of Napoleonic maxims, tactics and ancient rules of war outgrew the master. However, whether or not his efforts to placate the Mexicans through conciliatory measures were enough choke a guerrilla resistance remained to be seen.

Chapter 5

Mexico Invokes the Spanish System

Mexico is ... alone. Spain received help from England, and the Duke of Wellington, with a powerful army, threw into Napoleon's ranks. The United States had General Lafayette and the French fleets and armaments. To destroy Napoleon, the most powerful nations in Europe were allied. Mexico is alone; but this is not important, nor the setbacks that she has suffered, as long as we have perseverance.[1]

Carlos María Bustamante, *The New Bernal Diaz del Castillo* (1847)

The guerrilla war set in motion against the Americans was not Mexico's first, and many of the features of the insurgency against the Spanish beginning in 1810 and ending in 1821 informed the guerrilla campaign against the US Army. In essence, the Mexicans had an insurgent strategy based on historical precedent and hinged on isolating the occupying army in Mexico City by attacking and severing its logistics line from Veracruz. While the initial revolt in 1810 against Spanish rule was put down by Peninsular War veterans supported by the Catholic Church, attrition had eventually taken its toll. With this in mind, many Mexicans believed a protracted guerrilla war based on the lessons of the independence movement and the Peninsular War would result in victory. The Mexicans looked to both the martyred heroes of their revolution and the guerrilla campaign waged by the Spanish against Napoleon. Spiritually they paid reverence to the initiator of Mexican independence, Father Miguel Hidalgo, but tactically they invoked the Spanish. The most intense guerrilla activity of the war occurred after the Battle of Cerro Gordo in April of 1847, when Scott's army routed Santa Anna's larger force. Prior to that turning point, the authorities in Mexico still believed the regular army (a powerful political institution) could defeat the invaders, and early calls to employ guerrilla tactics were pushed aside during a crucial period of the war.[2]

From the beginning of hostilities many Mexican observers asserted that the Spanish system was their only chance of victory. Six months after fighting began, the *New York Tribune* published an excerpt from *El Republicano* outlining a previously disseminated opinion piece advocating guerrilla warfare: 'We shall, on this occasion, repeat what we have already said: the war must be carried on against the Americans as the Spaniards of this country warred against the French, by the system of guerrillas, capable of destroying the most numerous and best organized army.' *El Republicano* called for national unity and urged its readers to establish a 'National Guard ... devoted to the practice of this system. In any other way the Republic is lost.' The excerpt further explained that the US Army's artillery was better, but that Mexicans should 'counteract that powerful element by calling into play all the resources of which history, experience, or reason has taught us ... Shall those lessons be lost on Mexico?'[3] General Anastasio Parrodi, the commander of the Department of Tamaulipas and an old foe of Texan independence, issued a call to arms once hostilities commenced, framing the conflict in epic terms and depicting the Mexicans as righteous underdogs:

> Soldiers! If we have lost some of our brothers, the glory will be greater, there will be fewer conquerors; it is not the number which gives victory. There were but three hundred Spartans, and the powerful Xerxes did not cross the pass of Thermopylae. The celebrated army of the great Napoleon perished in Spain at the hands of a defenceless people, but they were free and intrepid, and were fighting for their liberty.[4]

Many observers saw the potential for a long drawn-out partisan conflict like the Seminole Wars. 'The Florida war is being acted over here again,' reported a correspondent for Baltimore's popular *Niles' Register* in September 1846. 'The "hawks of the chapparal", like the Seminoles of the hammock, now infest every road and path to cut off the unwary.' Indeed, many US soldiers who wandered away from their bases subsequently disappeared. 'The "Guerrilla" system of old Spain is commenced in the new world. The only consolation we have is that at this kind of warfare the Texans are equally good with the Rancheros, and we can put Capt. Walker against Roman Falcon.' Nevertheless, the Mexicans had not yet adopted insurgent warfare on a national scale. The question in 1846 was whether they would do so.[5]

Since the outbreak of war Americans had been actively monitoring the Mexican press for signs of a shift in military strategy. One anti-war newspaper wondered if Santa Anna would stay back and fortify the mining state of San Luis Potosi, or move to attack Zachary Taylor's northern army. If Santa Anna employed 'the guerrilla mode of warfare ... Taylor will fare hard and suffer great loss.' The paper included advice to the Mexicans that 'a guerrilla system of warfare upon Taylor and a poor supply of provisions would melt off his army and conquer him, when all Mexico could not do it in one or two engagements'.

In the second year of the war, the question kept returning: would the Mexicans resort to guerrilla warfare?[6]

The *Louisville Morning Courier*'s editors, citing the same October *El Republicano* excerpt calling for Spanish-style resistance, claimed they had 'seen the same idea in some of our own papers'. However, the newspaper dismissed the idea of a Mexican insurgency as coming from 'closet warriors – a very good theory; but when examined, and tested practically, it will turn out a mere historical fancy – a delusion – a hasty dash of the pen.' The article added sceptically that 'Mexico may be good country for guerrilla warfare, but the Mexicans will make very poor guerrillas; they have not the right sort of stuff for this character.' In the United States pro- and anti-war newspapers jousted over Mexican capabilities when compared to the Spanish. While there appeared to be similarities between the wars in Spain and Mexico, the Mexicans were facing a 'very different' army than the French, 'who were so often cut off by the Spanish guerrillas in the Peninsular War'. In other words, the Americans were different because they had their own way of war:

> This is just the kind of fighting, this light skirmishing, bush-dodging – these hand to hand squad to squad encounters are the very cream of fighting for our boys. We will match the Americans against the whole world for irregular warfare – for the frontier, rough, roll and tumble fighting. Indian wars have afforded a constant exercise of these qualities, and developed them to the highest degree of skill and sagacity. If this guerrilla system is your only hope, Mr. *Republicano*, then you may as well 'come down' and surrender, it is a settled question, and your republic, as you call it, 'is' already 'lost'.[7]

Despite boastful taunts from the pro-war press, the question was not settled. More prescient voices indicated 'the fullest expectation of the most active guerrilla war' with the insurgents holding the advantage in their own territory. 'Move where we will, the mountains and passes afford every facility to carry it on successfully and most disastrously for us. Our army, as now situated, can be compared to the French in Spain, when Joseph was driven out.' The theme of the Spanish war against Napoleon was repeatedly used because it was the most obvious example of the type of war into which the US invasion and occupation of Mexico could potentially devolve.[8]

Regardless of their political affiliations, most American observers agreed that Mexico's geography was well suited to guerrilla warfare. Indeed, Mexico and Spain share geographic similarities, and insurgent movements have been a constant in Mexican history – including in the twentieth century. Large parts of Mexico are quite dry and, like Spain, cannot sustain massive armies because they lack adequate supplies of water. Furthermore, Mexico City, like Madrid, is situated in a basin surrounded by mountains with access points from all directions. Complicating an invasion from Veracruz (as opposed to Texas) was the logistical difficulty of escorting troop reinforcements from Veracruz to replace men whose enlistments had expired. Since Veracruz was not adjacent to US territory, troops and other essentials needed to cross the interior from the port city. The frontier from Texas to Mexico City was simply too inhospitable to attempt a large-scale invasion.

Santa Anna demonstrated as much in early 1847, when he led a desperate march from San Luis Potosi to Saltillo to confront the US Army, and only 15,000 soldiers arrived out of the 21,000 who had departed. After that disaster, it was the opinion of General Andrés Terrés that the Mexicans should 'follow the example of Spain, and never send back to these lands more than small batches of troops, who can carry with them the elements of life'. Equally important was General Julián Juvera's observation that 'the cavalry troops had no grain for the horses'. In other words, the northern region was not conducive to supporting large armies, but it was ideal for guerrilla warfare. In addition, central Mexico, the most populous part of the country, was dotted with small towns and villages where partisans could rest and re-supply themselves before or after striking the US logistics line. Even today, this region contains isolated communities of indigenous Mexicans who only speak Spanish as a second language.[9]

Complicating the campaign in Mexico was the dreaded sickness known as *el vomito* (yellow fever), which afflicted thousands of unacclimatized US soldiers not only in Veracruz, but in New Orleans and other Gulf states. Including deaths from other afflictions such as malaria, typhoid, diarrhoea and dysentery, approximately seven times more soldiers died of disease than in battle. At the time, it was believed that northern soldiers could not acclimatize quickly enough to the subtropical weather in the Gulf of Mexico. The Mexican Central Valley was hot, but its elevation meant diseases such as yellow fever and malaria could not survive there. Although it was believed that summer months in the lowlands of the gulf were too much to endure for thousands of dough-faced Americans from northern states, the reality was that these soldiers – unlike veterans of the Florida Wars, southerners and Texans – had never been in a climate that favoured yellow fever or malaria. Rules on maintaining proper hygiene (including abstinence from heavy drinking and sex) gave West Pointers and other formally trained soldiers an advantage over their peers when it came to preventable ailments, but yellow fever and other tropical diseases represented an uncontrollable factor which would favour the guerrillas, and the Mexicans knew it.

Santa Anna and 'the only means left'

Some observers had demanded that Mexicans utilize the Spanish system even before the advent of the 'North American' invasion. One of them was Juan de la Granja, a wealthy merchant-diplomat who emigrated to New Spain in 1814 before founding the first Spanish language magazine (*Noticioso de Ambos Mundos*) in New York City in the late 1820s. Mexican officials took notice of La Granja's advocacy of their new republic, and after being appointed Vice Consul in New York he was promoted to Consul General when the position fell vacant in 1842. Having spent nearly twenty years living in the United States, La Granja was ideally placed to observe the gathering clouds of war and gauge American sentiment. He believed that to understand the United States 'it is necessary to be here many years, study it well in all its aspects, undergo many vicissitudes, and experience difficulties'.[10]

Some time after arriving in Mexico La Granja befriended Santa Anna and in the spring of 1844 wrote to him warning the *generalissimo* that Mexico would have to teach the Americans (who were 'ambitious without bounds') some 'hard lessons' in the looming conflict: 'To do this, it is only necessary to prepare yourself to maintain an endless war against this country.' Like other advocates of resistance, La Granja noted how the 'Russians burnt Moscow, and saved the empire. Moscow is now flourishing, and Napoleon terminated his days sadly at St Helena.' La Granja claimed that Americans had 'the greatest contempt' for the Spanish race, and advised Santa Anna that a guerrilla conflict would need to be protracted:

> Let the people retire from the coasts with all their cattle and effects; and let them guard the mountain passes, continually surprising from thence those who land on the shores, and the climate will do the rest... . let an army of 20,000 regular troops be planted in Texas ... who will act as guerrillas; let both these forces retire to safe positions whenever the enemy advance in large numbers, merely endeavouring to fatigue them by continual marches and countermarches ... we can imitate the example of Fabius ... so that the Mexican army may be preserved intact, and the war may last as long as the one between the Spaniards and the Moors.[11]

Much to La Granja's dismay, however, Santa Anna was a conventional military officer who did not approve of guerrilla warfare, much less the idea of promoting it so long as a formal army existed. Santa Anna was the figurehead upon whom all Mexicans placed their hopes of beating the Americans. Although controversial because he was politically unpredictable, he seemed to be the only leader capable of uniting the fractured Mexican polity during a critical period. For this reason, his political opponents hoped a united opposition would supersede the centrifugal tendencies which had plagued Mexico in the period prior to the invasion.[12]

For years following independence monarchism remained a viable third option among certain circles of the elite in Mexico. For the two main political factions – the centralists (*Moderados*) and federalists (*Puros*) – the persistence of these elites with Old World proclivities represented a dangerous and ever-present factor undermining their various efforts to unify the nation against foreign and domestic enemies. Monarchists, on the other hand, believed Mexico was incapable of the unity shown by its more powerful northern neighbour and spoke out against republicanism in favour of a strong European ruler who might act as a deterrent to US expansion. When fighting broke out between US and Mexican soldiers in southern Texas in the spring of 1846, political debates among Mexicans became increasingly heated, until President Mariano Paredes (a royalist revanchist) was ousted in a coup by federalists José Mariano Salas and Valentine Gómez Farías. On 4 August President Salas and Vice President Farías published a declaration (*Pronunciamiento*) accusing monarchists of being 'traitors' and proposed a plan to fortify the nation. Their solution to the infighting in the face of the invasion, which turned into a two-front conflict after General Winfield Scott landed a massive force at Veracruz in April of 1847, was to allow the return of General Antonio López de Santa Anna from exile in Havana, Cuba.[13]

A pragmatic leader capable of changing political affiliations to meet the moment, Santa Anna was not necessarily a friend of either Salas or Farías, but he was an ardent republican and competent military strategist and therefore the best man available to lead the Mexican Army. Santa Anna's seminal biographer William Fowler notes that the general's 'devotion to army life, his sense of belonging to and respect for the army as an institution, together with his love of combat' were essential aspects of his character. However, his devotion to military and republican ideals made Santa Anna an opponent of monarchy and an officer unlikely to turn to guerrilla war when conventional victory appeared out of reach. That moment came after the Mexican Army was routed at the Battle of Cerro Gordo on 18 April 1847. In essence, by bringing in Santa Anna, the Mexican leadership frustrated calls by others during a critical period to transform the conflict into a guerrilla war.[14]

The 'Plan of the Citadel' (*Plan de Ciudadela*) was declared to a country eager for action and ready to unite. Considered a 'national movement' by its federalist proponents, the plan recognized Santa Anna as 'general in chief of all the forces committed and determined to fight for the nation'. The plan was supported in a series of separate pronouncements from the key states of Puebla (6 August), Guanajuato (8 August) and San Luis Potosi (9 August). Article 5 was especially important because it referred to efforts to confront US forces conventionally: 'The existence of the army is guaranteed, assuring that it will be attended and protected as befits the meritorious military class of a free people.' The plan therefore expressly protected the established system the new government needed for political support. San Luis Potosi's leaders were in agreement with Salas – an important endorsement because the Mexican Army's long march north to confront Taylor's army in 1846 began from that city:

> The garrison of San Luis Potosi supports ... the plan of freedom and regeneration that the Honourable Mr General in Chief, Mr Mariano Salas and the other chiefs and officers and citizens proclaimed in the Citadel of Mexico on the 4th ... so that the Mexican Republic is saved, both from the imminent dangers of foreign invasion and the anarchy and dissolution that brings with it fierce civil discord.[15]

Talk of launching an insurgency was therefore shelved. In mid-August, after his arrival, Santa Anna issued his own manifesto denouncing both foreign enemies and domestic ones who might attempt to 'fortify the nation by means of a monarchy with a foreign prince'. Although he did not abide by La Granja's advice on employing guerrilla warfare, he invoked 'the great Hispanic-American family' to appeal to Mexico's disparate social and political factions. Lastly, Santa Anna vowed to continue the revolution begun in 1810 by referring to Hidalgo and Morelos – the martyrs of the independence movement against Spain.[16]

Anti-war sceptics in the American press aware of Santa Anna's manifesto would have known about his preference for confronting US forces in pitched battle. The first major battle, however, took place without him after General Pedro de Ampudia disobeyed Santa Anna's orders and engaged the Americans at Monterrey on 21 September. Measured in casualty figures, the fight was technically a draw, but the inability of the Mexicans to hold the city shattered their morale. As a result, many soldiers deserted and resorted to guerrilla warfare. Santa Anna's own chance of victory came on 22 February near Saltillo, but after a gruelling march north from San Luis Potosi beginning in late January, a severely weakened army of roughly 15,000 men was defeated by a force led by Taylor that never amounted to more than 5,000 soldiers. The battle of Buena Vista was a stunning defeat and further contributed to the demoralization of the Mexican Army. According to Ulysses S. Grant, Taylor's surprise victory at Buena Vista made Scott's approach to Mexico City much easier, because Santa Anna re-crossed the desert to 'get back in time to meet General Scott in the mountain pass west of Vera Cruz'. Grant believed this long march constituted 'a distance not much short of a thousand miles'. With roughly fifty-five days between engagements, the march from Saltillo to Cerro Gordo required nearly 30km of marching per day – an extremely arduous pace in a tough environment for a fatigued and beaten force.[17]

As Grant noted, Cerro Gordo was an important position west of Jalapa in the foothills of the Sierra Madre Oriental and essential to Scott's advance into the interior. Although the amphibious landing at Veracruz had been a success, many Mexicans pinned their hopes on stopping the Americans before they could leave the coastal area. Less than two weeks after the battle, *El Monitor* asked its readers if Mexico would 'continue this mode of defending our country in preference to selecting innumerable mountains, the passes, the cliffs, which the invaders must traverse before they reach the capital of this great republic?' To many observers, Cerro Gordo was good place to cut off the invaders, but Mexicans were asking themselves if the successive defeats justified 'keeping up this disastrous system' of conventional warfare.[18]

Although the US Army had numerically superior forces, the approach to Cerro Gordo was uphill, which gave the defenders an obvious edge. That edge was blunted, however, by some astute reconnaissance and flanking under the direction of Captain Robert E. Lee. Together with the element of surprise, skilful skirmishing quickly undermined the Mexican positions. As a result, Santa Anna's army fled. Only a few hundred American soldiers were killed, but 3,000 Mexicans too exhausted to run became prisoners. With the pass into the Sierra Madre cleared, Puebla and the gates to the Mexican capital were now open. A couple of days after the rout, former President (and recently appointed General) Salas called for enlistments to launch a guerrilla war against the Americans:

I have obtained permission to raise a guerrilla corps, with which to attack and destroy the invaders, in every manner imaginable. The conduct of the enemy, contrary both to humanity and natural rights, authorizes us to pursue him without pity ... *War without pity, unto death!* will be the motto of the guerrilla warfare of *vengeance*.[19]

According to historian Irving Levinson, a fleeting federal effort led by Pedro María de Anaya accompanied the call by Salas to foster a guerrilla campaign in the final days of April in 1847 using 'National Guard' soldiers and volunteers; the Mexican government laid down codes regulating their establishment, but the effort was hamstrung by 'enduring elitist' restrictions in the organization of groups. The *Louisville Morning Courier* explained that Anaya had 'been appointed temporary President (*presidente sustituto*)' and that Salas, 'who was elected President *ad interim*, before the arrival of Santa Anna ... issued a proclamation announcing that he is empowered to raise a guerrilla corps, and calls upon all good Mexicans to join his standard'. If reports were accurate, it was 'President Anaya' who 'issued a grand proclamation to the Mexican nation, calling upon one and all to turn out to the rescue'. In his 2005 work, *Wars within War*, Levinson explains how the Mexican government issued authorizations (*patentes*) for the formation of guerrilla units, but rapid changes of leadership (especially the presidency), class differences and provincialism undermined efforts to achieve unity and momentum against the Americans.[20]

Talk of Zaragoza-like resistance aside, many Mexicans had had enough of pinning their hopes on Santa Anna. In early May, Puebla's *Regenerador Republicano* printed an article entitled 'The Guerrilla System'. They lamented the 'disasters suffered' while adding that 'no one doubts' the US Army could make its way to Mexico City. That Puebla would soon become the next city to fall under foreign control was on the minds of Mexicans. That 'sad and desolate' reality, they asserted, 'under the iron rod of the conqueror', had caused widespread demoralization. According to them there was only one mode of warfare remaining to challenge the Americans. '[T]he guerrilla system ... is the only means left to us of salvation: this is the dominant thought, enunciated by the periodic press and adopted with general approval; consequently, it is undoubted that within a few days the insurrection will be established.'[21]

The newspaper admitted that 'guerrillas can cause harm to the natives of the country', which was an unfortunate but bearable effect of that system of warfare. However, taken in total, the article affirmed, 'The consequent evils of the guerrilla system can be avoided as far as possible, by regulating them, by making leaders capable of containing abuses and acting with prudence and order.' It was also argued that the achievement of victory was worth the negative aspects of unleashing a national insurgency. After all, what were these when compared to 'the immense evils that would weigh on us ... and [to] admitting treaties of a peace so disadvantageous, vile and humiliating for ourselves'.[22]

All sections of the population discussed the military situation. One article from Puebla argued the US Army of 10,000 soldiers was nothing more than a 'compact and momentary force' incapable of occupying all of Mexico. Therefore it could 'only dominate the ground that it covers, and not a span more'. This assertion was true. The small size of the American force was contrasted with the revolutionary-era insurgency, when 'the [Spaniards'] ... moral and physical strength extended to the darkest corners' of New Spain. Furthermore, the *Republicano* noted that the Americans had only two possible routes to reach the Mexican capital, and therefore the war would predictably be contained within these areas. In other words, 'the guerrillas have nothing to fear in the transit outside those roads where the enemy leads its force en masse'. With the aid of towns near these lines and the support of the populace, guerrilla fighters could 'form a fierce legion and make a decisive blow' against the invaders. To many Mexicans this approach made sense when examined in the historical context of the long drawn-out struggle for independence against Spain.[23]

'Let us imitate our fathers'

In early 1847 in the state of San Luis Potosi, Ramón Adame came to power as governor by criticizing the way national leaders had thus far conducted the war. Prior to Santa Anna's failed northern campaign, that state – a gold and silver mining hub strategically straddling both the northern and central theatres of war – had tacitly supported the Plan of the Citadel and conventional military efforts with supplies and reluctant conscripts. But after the defeat at Monterrey, the state's citizens elected Adame 'to save the national honour' by making 'San Luis an example of patriotism' for the rest of Mexico. The defeat at Buena Vista in February and disaster at Cerro Gordo in April crystallized the governor's view of the war and the manner in which he believed his state should contribute to the war effort. Essentially, Adame rejected the strategy of the ineffectual and squabbling national polity in favour of a more localized war designed to protect his state from a potential Yankee invasion.[24]

Governor Adame's promotion of guerrilla warfare was clearly informed by the Spanish war against Napoleon. Ten days after Cerro Gordo, he issued a decree calling for a '*levantamiento*' (uprising) of 'detached or free guerrilla bodies' of soldiers. Adame's outline of how an insurgency might be conducted contained forty-six articles divided into four sections. Dedicated to the welfare of his people, Adame ensured that enlistment in guerrilla bodies would be 'absolutely voluntary' and that those who served would be 'exempt from service in the army or national guard'. Article 5 guaranteed former deserters freedom from 'any or all penalties or prosecutions on behalf of the state if they enlisted in the guerrilla service for the permanent duration of the campaign'. This was important because multitudes of soldiers had deserted from the army after returning from the northern campaign.[25]

The size of insurgent units was also considered. The minimum was set at twenty-five men, with the option of enlisting with or without horses. Adame promised the state of San Luis Potosi would supply any missing or necessary materials, and incentives were issued to unit organizers – reflecting the merit-based system employed by the Spanish to reward effective guerrillas.

'A guerrilla leader who organizes a group of between eighty and one hundred men will be considered a captain', fifty- and seventy-man groups would be led by lieutenants, and groups of fewer than fifty men would be led by second lieutenants. Unit size and rank structure paralleled the federal efforts by Anaya and Salas to organize partisan units. Each unit leader was required to demonstrate 'political authority' over his subordinates, and each unit was required to have two horsemen for carrying communications to central authorities. Furthermore, the units had 'no limiting demarcation of territory' other than the state's borders, since the governor's political authority was limited to San Luis Potosi. The regulations also allowed guerrilla leaders leeway to grant holidays, and units were subject to monthly inspections.[26]

Moreover, Adame embraced key aspects of the Spanish Junta's *Corso Terrestre*. For example, 'intercepting correspondence' and handing it over to authorities was one of the 'objectives of the guerrillas' outlined in Article 18. The interception of correspondence was not rewarded financially, as the Spanish had done, but Article 33 outlined incentives for seizing the enemy's goods: 'whether it be money, effects, food, horses, beast of burden or cargo, weapons or armaments … munitions will be considered war booty and distributed among the victims, guerrilla leaders, officials and soldiers'. The regulations also offered some practical tactical advice, including 'not rushing an invading army while on its main lines, never charging organized masses or columns' and always ensuring a safe retreat. The units were encouraged to 'confuse the enemy with false movements', to 'sow discord', 'foment desertion' and 'strike fear with surprise attacks'. Article 23 expressly forbade the killing of prisoners, one of several offences mentioned. American prisoners were required to be handed over to regional authorities.[27]

One of the local leaders in San Luis Potosi who answered Adame's call was Paulo Verástegui. He was the son of Basque immigrants who had settled the hacienda of San Diego outside of Rioverde shortly after war broke out with France on the Peninsula. The family-owned hacienda, located on the road between the coastal city of Tampico and the capital, San Luis Potosi, became the focal point of the community. In May of 1847, Verástegui issued a public invitation to form a guerrilla *partida* at his expense:

The undersigned owner of the farm of San Diego and other farms in the district of Rioverde is organizing a guerrilla [unit] against the invader, and invites the tenants … to join with him to form a guerrilla of volunteers that, when the situation arrives, will harass and persecute the American army, and wage tenacious and continuous war in just defence.[28]

Verástegui´s paternalistic invitation consisted of seven articles written with the interests of the local community in mind. For example, the first article suspended all rents on homes and animals for the duration of the war; this was a major incentive for tenants to enlist. Verástegui also promised to compensate those who might lose their horses or weapons, and to reward soldiers' families from his personal holdings in case of death 'with a pension appropriate to the circumstances'. In addition, the hacienda owner noted that anyone 'distinguished for their valour' during the war would be rewarded with fertile land or animals. Verástegui reiterated Article 33 from Adame's decree on goods captured from the enemy: 'All the booty the guerrilla unit makes from the enemy will be faithfully and proportionately distributed between the individuals of that group by myself', in accordance with the regulations of the state. Verástegui´s call to arms explains why Mexican guerrillas were often called 'rancheros'. Winfield Scott used both terms. In one of his proclamations he cited the 'atrocious bands called guerrillas or rancheros', and complained that they continued 'to violate every rule of warfare observed by civilized nations' by menacing the roads between Mexico City and Veracruz.[29]

Haciendas were the economic backbone of small and scattered communities in northern Mexico and they were worked by men accustomed to weapons and horses. Like the Texans, the men who lived on the large estates spent most of their lives on horseback – sometimes covering long distances. The *criollo* (Spanish-descended) hacienda owners generally supported European rule in New Spain, which is why they were encouraged to carry weapons and patrol roads during the royalist counter-insurgency. During the US-Mexican War, however, like most Mexicans, Paulo Verástegui invoked Padre Hidalgo as the 'father of Mexican independence' in order to promote unity against the foreign invader. Verástegui was one of dozens of hacienda owners who answered the governor's call to mount an insurgency.[30]

The people of San Luis Potosi were aware that many Americans wished to seize their state and annex it to the United States. It contained the richest mines in North America, which were coveted by expansionists. Fortunately for both sides, US forces did not invade San Luis Potosi, but the US Army did provide escorts for a brief period to those carrying gold north to sell at Saltillo.[31] The preparations for guerrilla war made by Adame in the spring of 1847 following the defeat at Cerro Gordo were officially defensive in nature. However, many guerrillas operating around Tampico and peripheral points adjacent to the state undoubtedly used it as a base of operations, since the state's highest political officer had formally sanctioned the formation of guerrilla units and the targeting of US soldiers and supplies. Nevertheless, the efficacy of the public *levantamiento* was reduced because US forces rarely

crossed San Luis Potosi or attempted to occupy any of it. Located between Monterrey and Mexico City, the defiant state became an island unto itself during the war.

Another sharp critic of government conduct who called for guerrilla war was Melchor Ocampo, the governor of Michoacan. Ocampo, who studied at the Catholic seminary in Morelia (formerly Valladolid) and later took up the law, travelled to France in 1840, was influenced by the spirit of the revolution and came back harbouring liberal and anticlerical views. Ocampo was a staunch defender of Mexican rights and like other Mexican leaders would later vehemently reject the Treaty of Guadalupe Hidalgo which ended the war in 1848.[32]

Less than two weeks after Cerro Gordo, Ocampo published two circulars outlining his view of the war and his reasons for promoting an insurgency. The first, 'The War between Mexico and North America', was published 29 April. In it, Ocampo criticized the 'fools' who clamoured for peace as ignorant of its long-term consequences. Citing Cortez's imprisonment of Montezuma and the destruction of 'the gods of the country', Ocampo claimed Mexicans had a 'sacred social obligation to defend' their land, and that losing cities or 'ridiculous battles' was irrelevant to the larger military picture: '[I]f today we have not yet tried the only system that could be profitable, that of the guerrillas ... if today the enemy does nothing but threaten the capital of the republic, we already think about losing to him an opprobrious peace.'[33]

Ocampo was extremely critical of the way the Mexicans responded to the invasion; Mexicans were acting 'like timid and stupid sheep, to the insulting rapacity of our enemies'. He blamed Mexico City and its corruption for 'most of the ills that weigh on unhappy Mexico', and he implored his countrymen to 'preserve a principle of much more high importance, that of nationality'. The governor also warned of a possibility beginning to percolate among the Mexicans – the potential annihilation of their country. 'It has been said, sir, that nations do not die, that the history of man no longer presents examples like those of Troy, Babylon and Carthage, but this is not true.' Therefore, to sue for peace was to bring Mexico to the brink of destruction, since a 'peace destroys what we are today and what we could be, our dignity in history'. Michoacan would 'never, ever, ever, recognize any treaty of peace made with the United States' so long as US soldiers remained in Mexican territory.[34]

Ocampo's circular issued the following day, 'The Guerrilla System as a National Defence', was much more explicit about employing that mode of warfare. Although he continued with his general criticisms of his divided country, Ocampo admitted the Americans had a 'compact' and 'well-disciplined' army. He assessed Mexican capabilities by asking, 'How do we make war? Have we organized masses? Can we reunite them, improvise their discipline? ... Sad as it may be, it is necessary to say: we have nothing, and the enemy knows it.' Ocampo came to the same conclusion as Adame, Salas, and Anaya:

Let us then make war, but the only way that is possible. Let us organize a guerrilla system, since popular enthusiasm is in favour of it, which in other nations has been its origin: we abandon our big cities, retaining from the mountains what can be removed from them ... because the resistance would only irritate the enemy ... the Russians burned their sacred capital ... Let us imitate at least the tactics of our fathers in their glorious struggle against the brilliant tyrant of the nineteenth century.[35]

The American Response to Insurgency

As news of the Mexican response to Cerro Gordo trickled into the United States, the US press sensed an impending change in the conflict: 'With additional zeal would the triumph of Cerro Gordo be celebrated were it the general belief that it was the conclusion of the war.' Some were concerned the victory might alter the war's military landscape:

> But to conquer and disperse the Mexican forces will not necessarily lead to peace. War may cease for a time, because the fuel that supplies it may be exhausted. But we shall be obliged to hold military possession of the country, with a force large enough to keep up communications, and guard against the impending danger of a perpetual guerrilla warfare.[36]

Others were sombre about the potential for escalation. In an article entitled 'Guerrilla Warfare', the *Buffalo Commercial's* editors stated, 'We have before us a new mode of warfare, one that proposes not enmity against the army foe, a fair fight and full courtesy, but warfare against all, to the knife and the knife to the hilt.' The war was on the threshold of turning into a conflict like Spain. It would be a 'war of poisoning, assassination, measureless and merciless massacre. A guerrilla war has been commenced – a war in which every chief is a hero, and the avowed object of which is to meet the invasion by the worst desperation of animosity.' These opinions were echoed by newspapers throughout the anti-war sections of the United States, many of which were read by Mexicans seeking insight into how far Americans were willing to go to prosecute the war.[37]

The northern theatre also witnessed an outbreak of insurgent activity. The *Washington Telegraph* reported that 'the guerrilla mode of warfare has been adopted, clearly indicating a determination to resist to the last extremity'. The newspaper was responding to a proclamation by General Antonio Canales in early April 'calling upon all the inhabitants of the country bordering on the Rio Grande to arm themselves, and enter into the system of guerrilla war, which he is about to adopt'. The call by Canales, a former supporter of the failed Rio Grande Republic in 1840, was issued in response to an alleged massacre at Rancho Guadalupe by American volunteers. Canales declared martial law and wrote that in retaliation Mexicans were 'bound to give no quarter to any Americans whom you may meet or who may present himself to you, even though he be without arms'. According to the editors of the *Washington Telegraph*, Canales's proclamation was a stunning escalation of hostilities:

> Should the Mexicans adopt this mode of savage warfare pointed out by Canales, the war will necessarily become a war of extermination. They will give no quarter, and consequently can expect none. Our brave troops will spare only the weak and defenseless, and wreak their vengeance on all

armed bands of these relentless and bloodthirsty assassins. They will find it a fearful and terrible game to play.[38]

Iris Español represented Spain's perspective from the Mexican capital. The publication recommended that 'in order to have a good result from the guerrilla system' the Mexicans 'should be commanded by brave and determined soldiers, who will not fear any risk and be well acquainted with the topographical condition of the country'. They also advised, 'It is necessary that the government should not interfere in their operations, but allow them to act with perfect liberty, and not be subjected to orders of marching and countermarching.' The Spanish claimed that if the Mexicans organized an insurgency modelled after the Peninsular War, 'they will give the Americans more trouble than they have any idea of; Gen. Scott is aware of it, and consequently has addressed a proclamation to the Mexicans, adopting Marshal Soult's tactics in Spain.'[39]

The *Iris Español* was half correct. While it was true that Scott had published another proclamation to the Mexican people, he did not adopt, as the *Iris Español* claimed, the French general's tactics to 'punish with death every Mexican who should attack any American wandering out of the lines of the army'. Nevertheless, the Spanish encouraged the Mexicans to fight like they had against Napoleon: '[The] Spaniards did not lose courage, and they did not cease to attack the French until they exterminated them.' They also advised the Mexicans to

> follow the example of the Spaniards; that if General Taylor and Scott have declared all Mexican bands or guerrillas as outlaws, the Mexicans should likewise declare the Americans to be banditti, and as in Spain, decide that 'for every Mexican that should be treated as a land pirate by the Americans, three Americans will be hanged out of those falling into the hands of the Americans'.[40]

As reported, Scott heard the calls for guerrilla war by Mexican leaders and re-evaluated the situation. With the pass at Cerro Gordo cleared, he proceeded with his army to Puebla – the last major city before the capital. The 60-year-old general was in no rush and did need to ensure a viable logistics corridor remained behind him. On 24 April Scott informed Taylor, '[the] cavalry is already meagre, and, from escorting, daily becoming more so'. Although the army was short of a list of critical supplies (including ammunition, medicine, clothing and salt), the shortage of horses to cover and defend the line from attacks was the most pressing problem. He also told Taylor that 'depots, along the line of 275 miles, will be needed', and that he was continuing to pay for items rather than requisition them by force. Unaware that Taylor had not advanced to San Luis Potosi, as Scott and many others (including Governor Adame) believed he would, he wrote indicating that Taylor's occupation of that city in conjunction with 'advances on the capital might increase the chances of a peace or an armistice'. Lastly, he reiterated his opinion that occupying 'fifty other important points' would make things worse, because the Mexicans 'still hold out and operate against our trains, small parties and stragglers, with rancheros on the guerrilla plan'.[41]

Troop numbers were another issue for the Americans. Due to delays in organizing the assault on Veracruz, there were roughly 4,000 soldiers whose enlistment periods were set to expire in the approaching months. Scott could bring the men with him to Puebla, and perhaps even Mexico City, but then they would have to turn around and go back – which would complicate military operations. In addition, Scott had to factor in the approaching yellow fever season at Veracruz and the toll it might inflict on troops leaving the port city in the summer months. Rather than deal with a possible future problem, Scott discharged the soldiers and further reduced the size of his army.[42] On the face of it, the decision to voluntarily reduce his army's size seems illogical, but the decision helped to alleviate the mounting supply issues and went to the heart of his statement to Taylor that occupying 'fifty other important points' in Mexico was not the military objective. In essence, Scott adjusted his military decisions to maintain a compact but disciplined army not designed for the permanent occupation of Mexico. Spreading men out over the entire country was exactly what the French did in Spain – with disastrous results. By focusing on the single crucial line of operation Scott denied the Mexicans the advantage of geography while maintaining a relatively small area to patrol and defend. The major problem, however, was not the shortage of soldiers – particularly after Cerro Gordo – but the lack of horses. He needed cavalry to face the challenge of an impending guerrilla insurgency – a scenario that generally favours the defenders.

On 11 May, before leaving Jalapa for Puebla, Scott issued a new proclamation. He reiterated that the Americans were not at war with the Mexican people, but with their political and military leadership. Whether or not Scott's rhetoric was sincere did not matter; it was designed to drive a wedge between ordinary Mexicans and their leaders. The proclamation was similar to the one issued at Veracruz the month before, except that it addressed guerrilla war for the first time. It did not vow to summarily execute guerrillas *à la* Soult, as the *Iris Español* claimed, but it carried a dual message: the possibility of peace, and a warning about what would happen if the war was prolonged:

The system of forming guerrilla parties to annoy us, will … produce only evil to this country, and none to our army, which knows how to protect itself, and how to proceed against such cut-throats; and if … you try to irritate … you cannot blame us for the consequences which will fall upon yourselves. I shall march with this army upon Puebla and Mexico. I do not conceal this from you … We desire peace, friendship, and union; it is for you to choose whether you prefer continued hostilities. In either case, I will keep my word.[43]

Predictably, the Mexican military leadership did not heed Scott's warning to cease forming guerrilla units. Following Cerro Gordo, Santa Anna moved south to Orizaba, near Cordoba, where the Mexicans 'dedicated themselves to organizing infantry and cavalry of guerrillas' to attack Scott's main line. Apart from the road to Puebla from Veracruz (via Jalapa), Cordoba was the only viable route over the Sierra Madre Oriental and therefore a natural location to coordinate guerrilla attacks. On 9 May, Santa Anna informed the Ministry of War that he had organized 'three battalions of 1,460 men', or approximately 4,500 soldiers, for these operations. Despite these efforts, however, Santa Anna was not seriously interested in fomenting guerrilla war and made no public pronouncement that he would do so.[44]

By mid-May US forces had entered Puebla after encountering almost no resistance. General William J. Worth arrived before Scott and found that the commanding general's occupation policies and proclamations outlining the American intention to protect Mexican property had been well received by the locals. Worth informed Scott that travellers on the road between Jalapa and Puebla 'have been kept back by menaces' of guerrilla units; he estimated that between six and eight hundred mounted guerrillas occupied the line between the two generals, but that lesser numbers of 'men in compact order' could easily protect and escort trains coming into the city from the east. Lastly, he added that his spies reported Santa Anna had 'abandoned the project of making a stand' at Rio Frio and other points along the road west of Puebla leading to the capital, and that 'his badly armed force' was instead heading to fortify Mexico City. In fact, the Americans entered Puebla unopposed as the transition to guerrilla war was happening.[45]

Other Mexican states expecting a more robust invasion made their own preparations. On 26 May the *Diario del Gobierno* reported that Zacatecas was following in the footsteps of San Luis Potosi by launching an 'energetic plan to successfully defend the territory using the guerrilla system, and that in combination with the one in San Luis [it] will bother the enemy with good success'. The formation of ten to fifteen units consisting of eighty to one hundred men 'who know the terrain well' and can work with the light brigades of that state was also reported. The article asserted that the initiative taken by Adame in the formation of guerrilla bands had influenced the direction taken by Zacatecas. Located directly west of San Luis Potosi, Zacatecas was thus preparing to defend itself with a guerrilla insurgency if the US Army attempted to occupy it.[46]

By the summer of 1847 even news outlets in England had caught on to the change of tactics. *The Times* reported in mid-June that the 'character of the war is about to change. It is probable there will be no more field fights. The Mexicans hereafter adopt a guerrilla system of warfare.' The paper speculated on how the Americans would respond, and whether violence would escalate: 'Whether the Americans can be induced to retaliate, I pretend not to speak with certainty, but think they will not go further than to put to death captured Mexican officers.' Others noted, 'Mexicans were resorting in good earnest to guerrilla warfare, and the aspect of the country gives them great facilities for harassing detachments advancing from Vera Cruz to Puebla.' A month later, while American forces strolled along the relatively quiet streets of Puebla, the *American Star - No. 2* summed up the US Army's response:

> That system of guerrilla warfare is likely to produce some bitter fruits to the Mexicans themselves … We of the U.S may be slow in learning how to apply the system, but the Mexicans may teach us something on the subject, and possibly in due time, the scholars [students] may have something to teach the teacher. Those who live in glass houses, 'tis said, should not throw stones. There is something in Shakespeare on the subject of teaching bloody instruction, which being taught, returns to plague the inventor, and the government of Mexico would do well to ponder on the consequences of carrying on war against the laws of war, and in contempt of the civilized world.[47]

The word was out. The war's main theatre lay between Veracruz and Mexico City. Taylor's army did not push further into Mexico, which limited the range of operations for guerrillas in the north to areas adjacent to occupied cities in the region of Monterrey, Tampico, and Matamoros. The change was abrupt. On 16 June Taylor wrote to the Adjutant General in Washington that intelligence indicated an 'attempt has been made, or is now making, to operate the guerrilla plan in the states of Tamaulipas and New Leon; but it will, I think, prove abortive.' His hunch was correct. After the Mexicans became aware that Taylor had decided not to invade San Luis Potosi, insurgents moved south. On 23 June he reported, 'All is tranquil in this part of the country.' One week later, the region was 'entirely tranquil. The people who had abandoned their villages and ranchos are fast returning to them, and seem not at all disposed to engage in any warfare, guerrilla or other.'[48]

Royalists Return: Carlists and Monarchist Conspiracy

The most active guerrilla chieftain during the war was not Mexican, but Spanish. On 16 June the *Louisville Morning Courier* relayed reports from Veracruz's newspaper, *El Arco Iris*, confirming that 'the party of guerrilleros which is doing the most mischief on the road from Veracruz to Jalapa, is that of Padre Jarauta (a clergyman) with about 50 men'. The article described how Jarauta and his men detained a group of Mexicans on 22 May heading west near the National Bridge. As 'the Padre did not see any Americans among them, [he] confiscated the mules and horses because he needed them to mount about one hundred men that he had ready to join his party'. From there, Jarauta's unit headed to Medellin de Bravo, near Veracruz, where they 'were disposed to burn down all the houses, and take the curate and *alcade* [mayor] with them after reducing the town to ruins'. The report added, 'Padre Jarauta is a native of Spain, and was a partisan of Don Carlos during the last Peninsular War; he was sent to Cuba, and from there went to Mexico, where he formed his guerrilla corps.'[49]

The following day, news spread from Jalapa that a force of between 1,500 and 2,000 men had attacked a US convoy outside Veracruz. Fighters 'were principally commanded by three priests (Spanish Carlists) who had been banished from their own country for their ferocity, their fanaticism, and bigotry.' The origins of the Carlists were vague, but reports indicated the large insurgent group gave the Americans 'a great deal of trouble, and succeeded, during the entire route, in killing or wounding between forty and fifty of our men'.[50]

What were Spanish Carlists doing in Mexico fighting Americans and burning villages? Although it has never been confirmed, Jarauta was most likely the head of a cadre of refugees the French government refused to allow back into Spain after the start of the Second Carlist War in late 1846. In other words, they were exiles. An August report from Liverpool indicated that '*Cabecillas* [chieftains] in Catalonia have sworn to put to death every Frenchman that falls into their power, in revenge for the severity with which Louis Philippe's government treat the Carlist refugees in France'. The following month, another report mentioned naval vessels being sent 'to the coast of Spain to intercept the Count of Montemolin [Carlos VI], or his adherents, or the Progresista [progressive Liberal] refugees seeking to return', and stated that 'the French government is truly active in preventing the entry into Spain of Spanish refugees, Progresistas or Carlists'.[51]

As early as the fall of 1846, Spanish and French authorities worked together to prevent fighters from entering Catalonia, where the war began. The *Star of Freedom* of Leeds informed its readers: 'All the Spanish refugees, Carlists as well as Progressists, are being locked up in gaols and fortresses in the interior of the country.' The following month, the same newspaper noted the authorities were tightening the border:

> Seventy Carlist refugees are stated to have gone through Narbonne … with the intention of entering Spain. Seventeen of them were captured by the French authorities; most of them were officers. Forty-seven more Carlist refugees have been seized at Passas, who were likewise about to cross the frontier. They were dragged back to Perpignan, which town they passed through shouting 'Viva Carlos VI!'[52]

It is unclear whether Jarauta and his cadre received official permission from the French authorities to sail to Mexico. Although the origins of the Carlists remained unknown, a dispatch from Jacob L. Martin, the American Chargé d'Affaires in Paris, on 15 May 1847 to US Secretary of State James Buchanan mentioned the aid of one, or perhaps even two, European states. Jacob believed that sponsors had made plans for the 'deluded' fighters to embark from 'different ports with Mexican passports' to avoid detection. Relaying information he received from a Carlist officer, Jacob informed Buchanan that the soldiers were bound for Mexico and had perhaps even received the means to do so from the British:

> Since the failure of the contemplated expedition of the Count de Montemolin, the Mexican minister or consul in London had engaged about a hundred Carlist officers to enter the Mexican service. The same information has also reached me through another channel. The terms on which they are engaged are a free passage, ten pounds bounty, naturalization and certain boons upon arriving in Mexico; and a further inducement was held out that the course of events in that country might finally inure to the benefit of a prince of their party.[53]

Despite being a clergyman, José Celedonio Dómeco Jarauta was obviously accustomed to war. The Carlist Wars in Spain were marked by brutality on both sides. The clerical party in Spain (*apostolicos*) championed Don Carlos's claim to the throne, which received much support in the northern regions of

Spain skirting the Pyrenees, such as the Basque country, Aragon and Catalonia. Another theory to explain the emergence of the Carlists in Mexico was that they were working *with* France and the Bourbon King Louis Philippe under the direction of François Guizot – the influential Minister of Foreign Affairs from 1840 until he and King Philippe were ousted from power in the republican revolutionary movement that swept France and other European states in 1848. This possibility was raised in Congress by Senator John Dix of New York. Dix stated, in a speech on 26 January 1848 critical of Guizot's interventionist policies, that he had received 'a translation from a speech delivered in the Cortes of Spain on the 1st of December, 1847, by Señor [Salustino de] Olozoga' – a former Spanish Prime Minister and three-time ambassador to France. Dix asserted the existence of a 'close connection of the governments of France and Spain by the marriage of the Duke of Montpensier, the son of Louis Philippe, to the sister of Queen Isabella', in other words the opposition to the Carlists. Part of the translation of Olozoga's speech in the Cortes read: 'No one … can deny that the project has been entertained of establishing a monarchy in Mexico, and to place a Spanish prince on the throne. This project … would have saved our colonies from the sad fate they have suffered.'[54]

In any event, if the Spanish were clandestinely working with the French authorities, then Jarauta being a Carlist was a cover for combined Spanish and French efforts to intrigue in Mexican affairs. Jarauta was probably a Carlist but could have been persuaded to work with the French if he agreed to not re-enter Spain in exchange for his freedom. It is hard to argue that Jarauta was not a monarchist, and like fellow Spanish fighters, he favoured the reintroduction of a European monarch in Mexico. Nevertheless, Senator Dix was one of many US statesmen concerned about European interference in the war; he invoked the 'formal declarations of President Monroe in 1823' prohibiting European meddling in the Americas, and specifically called out Guizot by claiming that 'any attempt by a European power to interpose in the affairs of Mexico, either to establish a monarchy, or … in the language of M. Guizot, [to affect] "the equilibrium of the great political forces in America", would be the signal for a war far more important in its consequences.'[55]

Dix's public mention of François Guizot as the figurehead of a monarchist conspiracy was premised on the French official's widely publicized comments in 1845 concerning American annexation of Texas and combined Anglo-French interests in the region prior to the war. As the historian Frederick Merk pointed out in his 1966 work on the Monroe Doctrine, Guizot caused widespread anger among expansionist Democrats in the summer of 1845 when he was quoted in *Le Moniteur* as supporting a North American 'balance of power' between US, Spanish (i.e. Mexican) and British states. Merk explained the nuances of

Guizot's comments by indicating how 'carefully' the French statesman chose his words, using the term 'equilibrium of the several states' – which in Merk's words 'was the opposite in political affairs of domination by a single power over a continent or world'. Merk noted that the term "*équilibre européen*" was sparingly used by Guizot' and that he never used the term '*équilibre américain*'. Nevertheless, the fact that Guizot was addressing North American geopolitics was reason enough for Democrats to use the statesman as a lightning rod for perceived European opposition to US expansion. President's Polk's organ in the capital, the *Washington Union*, expressed exactly how the party in power felt towards Guizot:

> We cannot pass over, without much surprise, and some little indignation, the extraordinary declaration of the French minister … He considers England as one of 'the three great powers of the American continent' … and upon this position he seems to found the singular policy upon which we presume not only Great Britain but France herself, is next to act – that they 'should maintain their present balance of power'. How far Mr. Guizot is determined to go in supporting this new-fangled policy, we are not yet advised. The declaration itself is ominous and startling enough. We have long heard of the balance of power in Europe; and now, we presume, we are to have a balance of power in America. The old continent ought to be careful how she minds her own interests.[56]

Guizot's previous declarations supporting limiting American expansion, together with the recent arrival of Carlist guerrillas and the monarchist former Mexican President Paredes from France, was enough evidence for Dix to publicly accuse Guizot of interfering in the war. Furthermore, American observers noted that the disintegration of the *entente cordiale* between France and Great Britain meant the two most powerful European states would not act in unison to deny what American expansionists advocated. 'It will be remembered that M. Guizot deemed Mexico in her integrity an element in the political equilibrium of the new world,' the US Whig *National Intelligencer* reminded its readers. 'If the *entente cordiale* … had not been dissolved … there would probably have been co-operation and intervention in the quarrel between Mexico and the United States.'[57]

Regardless of who the guerrillas' European sponsors were, the introduction of Spanish fighters to the Mexican War added an extra level of intrigue. The *Louisville Morning Courier* reported that Padre Jarauta was from Aragon, and that he, along with a Veracruzan guerrilla leader named Juan Clímaco Rebolledo, had introduced partisans into Veracruz to undermine the occupation: 'The city has several emissaries within its walls from Jarauta and Rebolledo', some of whom were 'in the employ' of US authorities, it reported, and stated that the 'Spanish paper here daily teems with covert appeals to the sympathies of the foreigners, and the patriotism of the Mexicans'. At that point in time, Jarauta's ulterior motives in Mexico remained unclear, but the Mexicans initially seemed to appreciate that he and his imported Iberian partisans were adept at disrupting the invaders by utilizing the methods of war they promoted after Cerro Gordo. The article ended by indicating that all 'the leading men amongst the guerrillas now are Spaniards, and also many of the rank and file'.[58]

The American authorities attempted to track the movement of the Carlists from Europe. When Mariano Paredes was ousted from power in the summer of 1846, the ex-president fled to France to solicit aid for a scheme to introduce into Mexico a claimant to the Spanish throne. As would later be seen, the fact that many of the Spanish guerrillas came from that country soon after Paredes' arrival was no coincidence. The Spanish guerrillas and Paredes were working together. On 26 June, Secretary of War Marcy, thinking the Spanish were heading towards the Rio Grande, relayed information to General Taylor about 'seventy or eighty of them' along with their names, which had been provided to Buchanan by the US Minister in Paris:

A number of Carlist officers have left, or may soon leave France, with a view to join the Mexican army. Steps have been taken to prevent their entrance into Mexico. While on their way to that country we should not have a right to detain them as prisoners of war, but it is very clear that we may prevent them, if able to do so, from joining the enemy ... Should you have occasion to act in this matter, you will do what you can to intercept their passage into Mexico.[59]

The *American Star – No. 2* in Puebla gathered more information on Jarauta's mysterious background. Apparently, the padre 'was a guerrilla chief in Spain, but repenting of his cruelties and barbarities went to Havana, where he took holy orders'. According to the article, ecclesiastical life in Cuba did not suit him, 'and he left for Mexico'. Jarauta probably used his clerical position as a pretext to enter Mexico, and he wasted no time involving himself in the war after his arrival. The *Star* reported that Jarauta's base of operations was a town called Paso de Ovejas, 45km north of Veracruz, and issued a prediction: 'He may have been successful in Spain, but he is at war with the wrong sort of people to flourish long.'[60]

'As the Spaniards triumphed'

In the summer of 1847 Americans back home reading about Scott's movement towards Mexico City began making tangible connections between the unfolding guerrilla war and previous conflicts. One anti-war newspaper claimed, 'Guerrilla warfare has already commenced, and it is a means for the preservation of national independence, and of the confusion of the invading power' and stated that the insurgency was not dissimilar to previous independence movements, such as 'the British in America in our revolution':

> It was by means of the guerrilla, a little war of detachments under popular chieftains, that for centuries baffled all the efforts of the English kings to suppress the nationality of Scotland, and which in latter times resisted Napoleon in Spain, and finally rid the peninsula of the French.[61]

While many Americans acknowledged that insurgent warfare was waged to achieve independence, the most commonly recurring comparison was with the Peninsular War. This was especially true for Mexicans themselves. A long *Times-Picayune* article on 10 July written by an anonymous 'Mexican Citizen' claimed Mexicans 'were unanimous' for guerrilla war and warned the Americans not to implement 'a system of cruelty and war to the death'. In that event, the author asserted that Mexicans would 'rise *en masse*'. The author admitted that Puebla was 'pacific towards Americans' but warned that the situation could quickly change if the US authorities adopted harsher policies. Again, comparisons were drawn between Mexico and previous wars, but the article also highlighted the country's international isolation: 'Mexico in this contest stands absolutely alone. Spain was supported by England, and the Duke of Wellington with a powerful army drove out the hosts of Napoleon.' Despite lacking allies, the anonymous citizen asserted that Mexico would employ guerrilla warfare regardless of its bad reputation: 'It is true that the system is cruel, because every guerrilla chief, acting on his own account, will commit acts of inhumanity; but these are inevitable in all wars.' Guerrilla warfare was 'by no means new to Mexico,' the author said, 'and it is essentially adapted to people dwelling among mountains, or who are generally devoted to occupations in the field … Spain also adopted the system, and the war of the Spanish Americas was a war of guerrillas.' Near verbatim support for guerrilla warfare came from conservative statesman and historian Carlos María Bustamante, who in the middle of the war published a book with a title which likened the Americans to one of Cortez's soldiers and chroniclers, Bernal Díaz del Castillo. Comparing the two, it appears that the *Times-Picayune* article 'A Mexican View of the War' was copied directly from Bustamante's chronicle.[62]

There were additional motives for Bustamante's promotion of a long guerrilla war, since he believed the Americans did not have the stomach politically for such a conflict. Guerrilla warfare, he wrote, 'can have so much influence on the destiny of this country, that preparation under the tenacity of guerrillas … to destroy their trade can even produce a revolution in this country and force Polk to resign'. Bustamante cited the anti-war sentiment in the United States as a reason for Mexicans to continue the fight and sap the political will of the war party: 'At least if the war continues, it is positive that in the next elections … the new president will enter on the condition of making peace at all costs. Constancy, and nothing else, is what is necessary.' Bustamante's book in that sense advocated wearing down the Americans both politically and militarily.[63]

Not all Mexicans were confident a guerrilla war could be effectively waged, and pro-war advocates tried to assuage the fears of fellow Mexicans who harboured doubts. On 7 July, *El Diario* posted an article from Queretaro entitled, 'Can We Make War against the United States?' The authors lamented the pessimism of many Mexicans: 'Is there any doubt now that Mexico could make war on an unjust, perfidious and evil invader in the full extent of the word?' The article also invoked the original martyr of Mexican independence: 'Does the nation have fewer resources today than the immortal Hidalgo had in 1810?' Mexicans asked themselves, if they could oust a centuries-old entrenched Spanish ruling class using insurgent warfare, why would tackling the American invaders be any more difficult? Even among Mexicans the historical parallels between the Peninsular War, the Mexican Revolution and the current war were apparent:

> It is said that there is no army … that there is no public spirit for lack of a centre of union that would make the Mexicans triumph over their invaders, as the Spaniards triumphed over Napoleon … This was the way in 1810, when the *caudillos* [military leaders] of Dolores, with a handful of rancheros, attacked a large army, disciplined and led by good leaders, and independence was considered impossible … The Spanish government, absolute owner of New Spain, occupied all the towns, and was the owner of all.[64]

Michoacan agreed the war would end in 'a disastrous way for the enemy'. True, the US Army had entered Puebla unopposed, and it was no secret that Scott's ultimate destination was the capital. However, it was claimed that the occupation of Mexico City would be unimportant; when the 'capital is lost, only another population has been lost, which is certainly not the Republic'. Despite lacking weapons and money, the authors believed that if Mexicans had the spirit to fight, they could not lose, reminding them of 'a priest and a few children ... without other weapons, nor other resources, but only a firm will to save the country; thousands of warriors followed them, and ... they defeated a powerful enemy.'[65]

Ocampo matched Adame's efforts with concrete steps to foment guerrilla war. On July 5 he issued a decree in Morelia. Based on its contents, General Scott was not the only one having a difficult time getting horses. Ocampo's eight-point decree was expressly designed to supply the Mexican insurgency with badly needed mounted soldiers. Even though Ocampo sent out reinforcements, he admitted there had been 'great difficulty' in 'acquiring our own horses for the war'. He informed the public he was sending Michoacan state agents 'to look for them with enough money for immediate payment' – despite lacking the public funds to do so.[66]

Ocampo's July decree contained a basic plan. Farms and haciendas, where horses were essential to people's livelihoods, were required to contribute one mounted man for every 20,000 pesos of their net value. For example, if a farm was worth 60,000 pesos, it was required to contribute three men with horses. Ocampo also laid down a formula for smaller farms: 'The farms whose value does not reach ten thousand pesos will be united among themselves in the number that prudentially ... will be assigned by the prefects, and they will also contribute with a mounted man.' Horses, of course, were valued according to their size, age, breed and agility. Therefore, the decree contained a number of required specifications: 'The horses will be of sixty Mexican inches of height, from five to eight years old, healthy, meek, and if it is possible, of dark colours; their price will be agreed upon with the authority.'[67]

Ocampo's decree stated that certificates (or vouchers) given to the owner by the registered agent would 'be received as cash, in payment of the direct contributions that must be paid' by the owner of the farms. Ocampo implemented a fifteen-day time limit between the point at which the government agents assessed the required contribution and the arrival for enlistment of the mounted soldiers in Morelia, the capital. Although the governor did not outline penalties for non-compliance, the nature of the order required an obligatory contribution to the war effort backed by a financial guarantee from the state of Michoacan. It did not provide incentives for the individual guerrilla-entrepreneur to capture military communications or enemy supplies (like Adame's decree calling for a *levantamiento*) but was rather a war tax on farmers and ranch owners requiring compliance by administrative authorities. Nevertheless, the decree shows the pains Mexican leaders took following Cerro Gordo to foster an insurgency.[68]

By the summer of 1847 proponents of war in Mexico believed the insurgency was not picking up enough speed. 'What are you waiting for?' an article from *El Federalista* in Queretaro proclaimed. 'Let us rise en masse and annihilate these infamous adventurers, like the Israelites under the authority of God.'[69] *El Diario* lamented the delay: 'Fortune has turned its back on us in our meetings with the American troops.' The editors printed a Spanish poem relating to the Peninsular War that 'seems written for us'. The poem cited the 'immortal Zaragoza' and Joseph's 'flight from our Spain', among other themes, and was designed to provoke a sense of patriotism: 'Let us take the advice given by an ardent and inspired Spanish bard to a desecrated and vilified people like ours. This is how the invaluable benefits of independence and freedom are won and recovered.' A few days later, *El Diaro* claimed Mexico was reliving an old war:

> The peoples invaded by another more powerful nation, such as ours now, have suffered strong disasters at first, and without going any further, there we have Spain, in the early days of the French invasion, almost reduced to Cadiz and the Island of Leon; and Spain later rose up angry and powerful, and the laurels of Bailén and others and another thousand acquired in an unequal and glorious struggle, have come to illustrate the pages of their history.[70]

Despite such rallying cries, Mexico remained divided. Throughout the war, Mexicans argued about the roles and responsibilities of state and national governments in defending their country. These schisms had existed for generations and were in many ways the consequence of a long period of colonial administrative rule from afar. With independence achieved only in 1821, the 25-year period before the advent of war was not long enough for this ethnically, socially and geographically diverse country to develop the political foundations and mechanisms needed to respond effectively to a national crisis. In this context, it is no surprise that the editors of *El Diario* lauded the efforts made by Adame and Ocampo, while at the same time disparaging the inaction of other states: 'There are states that have exhausted their resources and have made heroic efforts … [such as] the generous efforts made by that of San Luis Potosi, Querétaro, Veracruz, Jalisco, and others.' The states opposing the Americans 'will occupy a very distinguished place in history', they noted, while pointing out that 'there have been states that, if they have done something, have not done it with the enthusiasm the terrible situation which the Republic is in demands'.[71]

Wedged between the northern and central theatres, San Luis Potosi was one of the most vocal states opposing the invader: 'Descendants of the heroes Hidalgo, Morelos and Iturbide, memorable for their courage, sagacity and patriotism call you to the battlefield to protect our valuable interests!'[72] The state of Michoacan, led by Melchor Ocampo, also pushed to continue the war, although it, too, lay outside the main theatres. Adding to the complexity of Mexico's problems, Ocampo opposed the machinations of Paredes and Jarauta to reinstitute a monarchy: 'Some people believe … the nation must be handed over to Europe through the establishment of a monarchy, others judge that under the same circumstances we must add ourselves to the northern states.' According to Michoacan authorities, such a move meant trading one corrupt system for another. Like *El Diario*'s editors, the declaration advised leaving internal quarrels for a later time, in order to focus on the pressing crisis caused by the invasion:

> If we were handed over to a monarchy, a few of the clergy and those who enjoy some comforts would be elevated to a bright position; But would this same fate do most for the nation? Surely not: perhaps those same privileged people would be the ones who will oppress and tyrannize the people! … Let us leave the monarchs for now, because the danger that most threatens us is the domination of the United States of the north.[73]

Republican suspicions of Paredes' royalist motives were slowly being confirmed both inside and outside Mexico. Although reporting on the monarchist movement was limited compared to reports of the military situation, some US newspapers made links between the former Mexican president's trip to Europe and the arrival of the Carlist fighters. In late August, a report from the *Picayune*'s correspondent in Veracruz noted Paredes' arrival from Havana 'in disguise', and his immediate departure from the port city. The correspondent reported that Paredes took a British 'royal mail steamer *Teviot*, under an assumed name, and [was] entirely unknown to the captain of the vessel'. The US Consul in Cuba tried to inform Colonel Henry Wilson, the commander at Veracruz, of Paredes' departure from Havana, 'but it came to hand too late to do any good'. The correspondent concluded that Paredes 'will no doubt make every effort to reach Mexico [City] before Gen. Scott', and it appeared that he was 'just the man the Mexicans have been wanting ever since the Battle of Cerro Gordo, and now that he is with them once more, there is no telling what mighty events may be the result of his return from exile'.[74]

Wilson's report from Veracruz to Marcy regarding Paredes' arrival painted a picture of British complicity. When Buchanan received it he informed the

US Minister in the United Kingdom, George Bancroft, that the captain of the *Teviot* was 'fully aware of the character of his passenger, brought General Paredes from Havana to Vera Cruz, and connived at, if he did not directly aid in, his landing at that port in a clandestine manner'. The accusation spread fast because the following day the *Morning Chronicle* – one of London's Whig mouthpieces for Palmerston's Foreign Office – denied any intentional wrongdoing by the *Teviot*'s captain when Paredes had embarked at Southampton. The British explained that 'England is a free country, and has no system of passports with which to fetter the motions of travellers'. They pointed the finger instead at the French: 'As for Paredes, if he carries with him the germs of any European intrigues, it is in the Tuileries, or the Rue de Courcelles, that they were concocted … How powerfully this dynastic mania rages in the bosoms even of the most degenerate branches of the house of Bourbon!'[75]

The *Public Ledger*'s Washington correspondent was doubtful that Paredes had been aided by the British, noting there were a few 'Carlist conspiracies fomenting in Spain', and reiterating that Paredes and Santa Anna were enemies. That the former Mexican president was a monarchist on a mission was apparent to everyone, but who exactly his European sponsors were remained a matter of speculation:

> That Paredes has been applying to the different Courts of Europe for assistance, I do not doubt. That he was handsomely received by the Court of Tuileries [in Paris], demented on the subject of perpetuating dynasties, it is but reasonable to presume … Still, if any power in Europe meditate such a foolish design, it is much more likely to be France than England … Agents of Paredes, previous and after he became President of the mis-called Republic of Mexico were known to be busy in Madrid, but that power has spent its last pistareens [silver coins in Spanish America].[76]

'Pray to God to deliver us'

Ocampo and others believed the monarchist movement was not the immediate problem. More pressing was the presence of a foreign army on Mexican soil. As US forces marched into the central valley, time to prepare the defence of the capital was slipping away. Tasked with defending the city, on 9 August Santa Anna made an appeal for unity. The *caudillo*-president cited slavery and American aggression in the Seminole Wars, and called on familiar themes of resistance in a last-ditch effort to bolster flagging morale: 'Mexicans! … you belong to a noble and generous race which honours the memory of Numantia and Saguntum,' he proclaimed, while invoking 'the defences of Zaragoza and Gerona'. It was a desperate and final plea for unity. 'The time has come for you to declare that the descendants of those heroes are also heroes under the beautiful sky of the New World.'[77]

In addition to the epic language, Santa Anna proffered a last minute '*Plan de Hacienda*' designed to unite Mexico's disparate social groups by implementing 'beneficial laws' based on promoting equality. The plan outlined reforms in fourteen points to 'free the taxpayer from the cruel and unfair exactions that are generally victims of distant capitals'. The thirteenth point – the one Santa Anna elaborated on the most – was directed at the *alcabala* tax: 'Experience has proved how hateful the system of *alcabalas* is to the people, both for the severity with which they are charged by the exactors and for the delays, obstacles and damages suffered.'[78]

Santa Anna's eleventh-hour proposal to abolish the *alcabala* is proof of the effectiveness of the US initiative in rescinding it. The Mexicans noticed the success of the policy, the indifference of the poor and the indigenous peoples to the US invasion, and the way Scott exploited class differences to divide and conquer. Mexican leaders condemned the lack of support for a *levantamiento* among the lower classes – especially among victims of the tax system. The propertied classes and the Church were sufficiently placated by Scott's directives respecting property, but it was the lower classes who would form the backbone of any insurgency. Santa Anna wrote that 'the system of *alcabalas* gravitates on a half of the society' and described how 'people see with disgust, at the same time, that the exactors handle with more hardness and excess in the collection of the rights'. He called the persistent colonial tax the 'hacienda system' and advocated 'ceasing all the *alcabalas* and contributions' connected to it.[79]

Although *El Diario*'s editors believed Santa Anna's plan was an 'historical document, written with the eloquence of the heart', it was too little too late.[80] After basing US forces at Puebla for much of the spring and summer, Scott left the city with most of the army in early August. It was the final leg of the march to the capital. Even as the US Army came within striking distance of the city, calls for peace by Mexican doves were shouted down and their authors looked upon with suspicion. The Americans were the ones who had provoked the war, critics argued, and to sue for peace was an injustice worse than being conquered. Mexico 'will not degrade its noble cause', San Luis Potosi proclaimed in *El Diario*. A Michoacan circular appearing on the same day stated that Mexico 'was under attack by a grave and violent sickness, whose symptoms could get worse' so long as the US Army continued unobstructed on its path to Mexico City.[81]

Roughly three weeks before US forces set foot in Mexico City, *El Diario* printed a long poem entitled 'Zaragoza'. Written by Spanish statesman Francisco Martinez de la Rosa, the poem hailed that city's resistance to the French. Sprinkled with footnotes added by *El Diario*'s editors explaining the historical events of the siege of Aragon's sacred city, the Mexican authorities tried to use the verses to muster a spirit of defiance.[82]

However, invoking the spirit of Zaragoza proved futile, and supporters of the national army watched as the Americans defeated the Mexicans at each decisive engagement before the gates of Mexico City. 'We are in a bad way,' one distraught resident wrote to his brothers from Mexico City. 'We lost the battle on the hills of Contreras, and that of Churubusco, and tomorrow or the next day the Yankees will be in the capital.' What was equally frustrating was that, although Scott had a smaller force due to the discharge of men at Jalapa, the numerically superior Mexicans still appeared helpless. 'The Yankees have lost 4,000 men out of the 10,000 they had, and with 6,000 men they undertake to occupy the capital, which is almost incredible.' Another Mexican writing to his friend lamented that 'the bridge of Churubusco was lost almost without resistance, and at great sacrifice'. Superior American skirmishing played no small part in these successes. The result of the final rout outside the capital was disorder on a massive scale. There were 'soldiers running into the city, dispersing in all directions, filled with terror, and crying that the enemy was coming in immediately after them'.[83]

Others directed their anger at their leaders. One young lawyer asked his father, 'Who is to be punished for these disasters? The public accuses Santa Anna.' He added that the 'end has proved ... the correctness of our prophecies'. Another wrote, 'Fear and consternation pervade the whole city ... I have no confidence in our dispersed soldiers, who are all of them robbers, most of them drunk.' Still others viewed the disaster as God's retribution and asked for divine intervention. 'Pray to God to deliver us', wrote one man to his mother. 'His Divine Majesty has sent these devils to punish us for our sins. These are the fruits of our domestic quarrels, for only by this could these devils have so scorned a nation.' Demoralization of the Mexican military and people had set in. Another man wrote his family, 'My blood boils at witnessing so much cowardice, so much ineptitude and infamy, and one must either die, or fly from this country, which is stamped with the seal of Divine reprobation.'[84]

As Scott's conventional campaign ended with the seizure of the capital, the guerrilla war behind him intensified. Reports emanating from Jalapa's *El Boletin* noted that on the evening of 19 August 350 guerrillas attacked an American wagon train heading towards the city, and 'the road for near a mile was covered with men, women, and children, whom curiosity had attracted there'. US soldiers apparently tried to disperse the crowd with 'cannon and musketry', and 'the citizens succeeded in reaching their homes without receiving any injury'. After the convoy entered Jalapa it was again attacked, a few days later, by Jarauta on 'the other side of Jalapa, but ... driven back by our [US] troops, with loss on both sides'. The Americans wondered if they had to consider Jalapa's city leaders 'friends or foes', a question which would dramatically affect the army's position, considering the city's location on the road between Veracruz and Mexico City. The summer of 1847 thus marked the transition from conventional to unconventional warfare; the guerrilla war in central Mexico was now well underway.[85]

As guerrilla warfare intensified in the summer of 1847, the Americans were confronted with a dilemma. They needed to find a balance of effective conciliatory policies and a robust (but not oppressive) response to the insurgency. The trick – as Halleck had warned – was not to alienate the general population. For Scott, staying within the rule of law was an objective in itself, and he would maintain discipline and control over his soldiers at all costs. Adding to US Army's problems was a siege of Puebla by Mexican forces attempting to sever the only connection between Mexico City and the coast. A number of questions remained unanswered: what would be the American response to guerrilla warfare? Would Scott's counter-insurgency policies resemble the Viceroyalty during the Mexican Revolution, or the French during the Spanish War of Independence? Would captured guerrillas be summarily executed as bandits or outlaws? The war appeared far from over, with many predicting it would only escalate.

To all appearances, by taking the capital the Americans had won. Under the surface, however, there was nascent animosity to the victors that could easily surface as it had in Spain. Scott managed to neutralize that danger with a combination of lenient policies and strictness, deference to the Church, the rescinding of unfair taxes and occasional propaganda measures designed to divide the people from their leaders. However, the possibility of escalation remained real – especially after the occupiers' logistics line was severed. A violent incident or a massacre could easily change the whole atmosphere and provoke a mass uprising. The Mexican guerrillas and pro-war advocates hoped for such an incident, because it would confirm their belief in the worst intentions of the Americans. In essence, an escalation would result in previously indifferent Mexicans joining the fight against the invaders. Peace seemed far off indeed in the fall of 1847, and the conflict teetered on the edge of unravelling into a bitter and lawless war.

Chapter 6

Los Diablos Tejanos

The Mexican guerrilla bands, after the Texans take the field, will be shy of showing themselves within striking distance of any road where Americans may travel. A party of ten Texans will be equal to the task of catching and destroying any party of fifty Mexican guerrillas whom they may find in their road. The Texans made the Mexicans sick of the guerrilla warfare in the years preceding 1844.[1]

The American Star No. 2, Puebla, 8 July 1847

When General Winfield Scott asked General Zachary Taylor for mounted soldiers in late April of 1847 he did not specifically ask for Texans. He simply wrote that his cavalry was 'meagre' and he needed 'a competent fighting force' of mounted units to tackle the guerrillas and keep the logistics line between Mexico City and Veracruz open. Nevertheless, Texans were what he got. The Texas Rangers were formidable counter-insurgency soldiers, but their disregard for the laws of war and the novel pacification programme Scott was attempting to instate with US forces in Mexico meant there were great differences between the regular West Point warriors and these frontier fighters. Their involvement in the Mexican War is best described by historian Major Ian B. Lyles as a 'mixed blessing'. While the Texans helped keep the logistics corridor between Veracruz and Mexico City open after the siege of Puebla, they also undermined law and order in the new occupation regime.[2]

Just as Scott's army was entering Mexico City, on the night of 13 September, Santa Anna, in concert with General Joaquín Rea's guerrilla forces, laid siege to the small garrison left behind in Puebla. The Mexicans forced Colonel Thomas Childs and 500 soldiers stationed there to take up defensive positions inside the citadel of Fort Loreto and the San José barracks located atop a hill in the centre of the city. Communications between the beleaguered garrison and Scott's new command were so strained that it was not until 23 September that the *American Star* reported 'through one of Madame Rumor's numerous channels' on the occupation of the city by guerrillas. Despite this troubling news, the *Star*'s editors were confident Childs's garrison would be able to hold out until reinforcements arrived, since 'he can maintain himself against any force sent to oppose him, and he has four or five months' supplies with him'. However, the temporary recapture of Puebla essentially confirmed that the US logistics line to the capital had been severed.[3]

Almost no news of the siege of Puebla was printed in US newspapers until after its outcome. Whether or not this was intentional is questionable. News of the war was generally delayed by one month, information being relayed through Veracruz to New Orleans and sent eastwards from there. That being the case, there were virtually no reports of the one-month-long siege while it was ongoing; this means that either the Mexico City-Veracruz corridor was totally controlled by guerrillas from September to October, or that US military officials took pains to ensure that news of the siege was not printed. The most likely scenario, given that Scott was not keen on censoring news, was that guerrillas controlled most of the territory between Mexico City and Veracruz. In essence, the US campaign was in a more precarious position than historians have previously recognized. Had the Mexicans managed to take Puebla, American occupation of the capital would have been jeopardized. A retaken Puebla could have become a symbol of Mexican resistance, which in turn would have bolstered the cause of the guerrillas and encouraged those on both sides who sought to perpetuate, or even escalate the war. In this regard, the Texans' contribution towards eliminating the threat of the guerrillas was a positive development for the army of occupation.[4]

Los Diablos Tejanos and Horse Warfare

The Mexicans called them '*los diablos Tejanos*' or 'the Texas devils'. White settlers from the east were originally invited to the Texan borderlands by the Mexican government after achieving independence from Spain in the early 1820s. Ultimately, this vast area saw a confluence of three cultures: Native American, Mexican and Anglo-Saxon. The offspring of the first generation of settlers learned to fight in a style that had no name other than 'Indian warfare'. It was the way of war for a native and frontier culture that would later become known as 'guerrilla' warfare. Riding and shooting were the critical skills, learned by young and old alike, and there were few women in the Texas borderlands who did not know how to ride a horse or shoot a gun. Clashes in the region were marked by brutality on all sides.

According to Lyles, the Texas frontier fighting style embodied by the Rangers had 'evolved over time into a highly effective doctrine of mounted combat'. Texans were often outnumbered but compensated for this with tactical discipline: 'The Rangers initiated battle with well-aimed rifle fire usually against the enemy leadership or the most effective fighters, delivered from outside arrow or *escopeta* [shotgun] range.' Targeting the enemy leaders was an effective way of demoralizing enemy forces and causing confusion. 'After attempting to kill or disable the enemy's leaders, the Rangers followed up with a charge to disperse the enemy formation; each man using his pistol or pistols at close range.'[5]

The Colt revolver was another asset which gave the Rangers an edge in the Mexican War. Also known as the Walker Colt, the revolving six-cylinder pistol was the product of a collaborative effort between Ranger Captain Samuel H. Walker and gunmaker Samuel Colt of Hartford, Connecticut. It was designed at the start of the war in 1846 and saw action with the Texans in 1847. At the time, the Colt was the most powerful repeating handgun ever made, and 1,100 were manufactured expressly under military contract for use in Mexico. Heavy, sturdy and accurate, Colts were useful weapons even unloaded: 'If unable to break contact after expending their ammunition, the men used their bowie knives or swung the heavy Colt pistols by the barrels using them as clubs.' These weapons and tactics made the Rangers formidable and motivated fighters; in Lyles' words, the 'combination of audacity, fire discipline, target selection, firepower and shock effect proved a winning tactic on the frontier and served the Rangers well in combat in Mexico'.[6]

Next to the gun, the most important weapon in nineteenth-century warfare was the horse. During the conflict in Spain, the Junta, through the *Reglamentos* and *Corso Terrestre*, structured the *partidas* based on numbers of horses. Mexican governors Adame and Ocampo both factored horses into their proclamations promoting guerrilla war, and as in the Spanish conflict, both American and Mexican armies were in short supply of them. US cavalry soldiers and mounted rifleman generally did not bring their farm horses with them to war. So where did the US Army get theirs? They came from the Mexicans and the Tejanos.

To win the war the US needed to supply their cavalry with fresh horses. The journey from the northern states was long, and necessary supplies such as cannon, grain, forage, shelters and other essentials all required horses allotted to the US Army's undermanned logistics division. Draught horses were generally older animals assigned to transport duties in teams rather than to galloping into battle. Large numbers of horses therefore needed to be obtained in theatre. According to Ulysses S. Grant, the US Army was supplied with horses by opportunistic smugglers in the Rio Grande region: 'Wagons and harnesses could easily be supplied from the North; but mules and horses could not so readily be bought. The American traders and Mexican smugglers came to the relief.' The preferred method was buying and trading in bulk.

Contractors sold mules under contract at 'eight to ten dollars' and received payment 'in hard cash'. The animals came from Mexican and American smugglers, and Grant believed the US Army got the better of the deal: 'I doubt whether the Mexicans received in value from the traders five dollars per head for the animals they furnished … whether they paid anything but their own time in procuring them. Such is trade; such is war.'[7]

The future Civil War hero and President wrote that wild horses sold to the US Army were rounded up in the vast plains between the Nueces and Rio Grande Rivers. During the war, this region was almost entirely under US military control, and Mexicans traders would have had a difficult time marketing their horses further south in a cash-strapped Mexico. The grasslands of the region were well suited to wild horses. Near Corpus Christi, towards the mouth of the Rio Grande, Grant was impressed by the fact that wild horses were 'as numerous, probably, as the band of buffalo roaming further north before its rapid extermination commenced'. For the US Army it was the perfect solution to a difficult supply problem. 'A picked animal could be purchased at from eight to twelve dollars, but taken wholesale, they could be bought for thirty-six dollars a dozen.' Although the horses needed to be broken before being ridden, their quality was appreciated. 'The horses were generally strong,' Grant recalled, 'like the Norman horse … officers supplied themselves with these, and they generally rendered as useful service as the northern animal; in fact they were much better when grazing was their only means of supplying forage.'[8]

Catching Wild Horses on the Prairie.

Grant did not underestimate the importance of obtaining a substantial supply of animals in the borderlands. Northern horses had been domesticated for generations, and their 'descendants are easily, as a rule, subdued to the same uses'. Not so wild horse, and to meet the need, a system was quickly developed to break in thousands of animals. 'The process was slow but amusing. The animals sold to the government were all young and unbroken, even to the saddle, and were quite as wild as the wild horses of the prairie.' Mexicans working with US agents first corralled the animals into a stockade. This was Grant's first experience with Mexican *vaqueros* (cowboys), 'who were all experienced in throwing the lasso'. After the animal was brought to the ground, the teamsters seized it 'while the blacksmith put upon him, with hot irons, the initials 'U.S.' According to Grant this 'process was gone through with every mule and wild horse with the army of occupation'.[9]

As Grant recalled in his *Memoirs*, wild horses roaming the prairie between the Nueces and Rio Grande resembled in many ways the common Anglo-Norman horse in the United States. The Colonial Spanish horse, which was a cross between a North African Barb and an Andalusian, was first brought to North America by the Spanish conquistadors. These animals, known for their stamina and hardiness, eventually spread throughout the American South-West and were adopted by the tribal nations living in the region – most formidably by the Comanches. In the nineteenth century, thoroughbreds (a mix of English native mare, Arabian and Barb) were crossbred with western Mustangs and Spanish Colonials to create the American Quarter Horse – which was known for its speed and often used on ranches to herd cattle in the borderlands. Equestrian expert John Borneman notes that 'the Quarter Horse embodies more than any other breed the American West, and its origin is often expressed in a folksy Western manner'.[10]

Grant recalled that many officers liked the wild horses, and anecdotal evidence suggests Americans considered them better than the 'Mexican horses' found in the interior. Albert M. Gilliam, an Englishman travelling in Mexico immediately before the war, commented that a fellow English traveller referred to his hired horse as 'his "cattle", the gay, fiery, low-quartered, middling size Mexican horse, for they are all such in contrast with the American animal'. Gilliam wrote that the Mexican horse, 'a descendant of the barbed animals' from Spain, was generally smaller due to its natural diet. Its advantage, however, was that it was well adapted to the difficult terrain. 'He is more hardy than any other horse … and he never knows what it is to be fed on the luxury of grain, until his master has thrown the lasso over his neck, [and he] never fail[s] to raise his feet above all impediment … for he never stumbles.'[11]

Other descriptions of Mexican horses were less flattering. Captain William S. Henry, author of a popular history of the war during his time serving under Taylor, gave an account of his first ride on a Mustang: 'The animal was lively and frisky enough, but a mere rat compared to our northern horses.' Henry, like Grant, was stationed in the Corpus Christi area and recounted that a 'very capital mustang can be purchased for fifteen dollars, or from that to twenty-five, depending on the manner in which he is broken'. The price difference between accounts demonstrates the amount of money the US Army saved buying unbroken horses in bulk, as well as the price increase for a broken animal in good condition – regardless of its inferiority. It is unclear if Henry drew a distinction between the wild horses on the plains of Texas referred to by Grant, and Mustangs, which he considered Mexican. 'The mustang cannot compare, in either fleetness or endurance, with ours.' Nevertheless, if Henry was deliberately disparaging Mexican horses, he was equally capable of praising their riders. After the battle at Monterrey he recalled that the Mexican Lancers 'were as fine looking men as I ever saw. Their horses were inferior animals; *one* of ours could ride over *three* of them.'[12]

As Grant stated, one advantage of Mexican horses was their ability to subsist on the vegetation of their dry environment. Arid conditions had been a concern among US officials and war planners prior to the outbreak of hostilities, when Acting Secretary of War and historian George Bancroft wrote to Taylor in June 1845, prior to his departure to the Texas borderlands: 'It is understood that suitable forage for cavalry cannot be obtained in the region which the troops are to occupy. But it is possible that horses of the country, accustomed to subsist on meagre forage, may be procured, if it be found necessary.'[13]

John Salmon 'Rip' Ford, the adjutant who accompanied the Texas Mounted Rifles (Rangers) under John Coffee Hays when sent to Mexico, also believed northern horses were superior. To lose one's horse meant having to saddle a Mexican one for the remainder of the campaign. 'No one fancied losing his American horse,' Ford recalled, 'and then being mounted on a Mexican *caballo*. He was an animal of great endurance, but not as fleet as his American brother.' Speed was prized more than the ability to survive by grazing, and the solution to the problem of limited forage lay in the procurement of barley cultivated in the coastal region between Veracruz and Jalapa. According to Ford, barley was 'one of the best articles for horse feed ever', and he could not recall any horses foundering 'during our operations on General Scott's line in which the founder could be fairly attributed to barley'. Horses were essential to warfare and survival, and Ford and his fellow Texans devoted as much time to attending to their welfare as they did to their own. 'Our men were generally careful with their horses. They were well groomed and well fed.'[14]

After Cerro Gordo, Scott needed cavalry. Following his initial request to Taylor in April, on 6 May Scott informed Secretary Marcy he was busy 'sending off detachments of horse and foot, to meet and escort' convoys coming into Jalapa from Veracruz. Future supply trains needed to be large, because smaller ones were being ambushed by guerrillas. Scott wrote that he could not 'foresee that more than one other train, from want of escorts, may be expected up in many months'. In other words, Scott was denying the guerrillas easy targets by limiting the supply trains and increasing the size of their escorts.[15]

The following day, Scott was surprised to learn that Nicholas Trist– Polk's envoy sent to negotiate a peace treaty – had arrived at Veracruz and was inquiring about making his way to headquarters. Scott told him it would be difficult to provide a personal escort due to the 'rancheros and banditti who now infest the national road, all the way up to the capital'. Trist was asked to wait until a larger, heavily escorted convoy could be organized, or until the road was cleared by reinforcements. Scott also knew that Santa Anna ('the nominal president') was operating in the Orizaba area 'organizing bands of rancheros, banditti, and guerrillas, to cut off stragglers of this army'.[16]

While Scott strengthened his logistics line, Taylor organized mounted units for the campaign in central Mexico. He notified the Adjutant General in Washington that 'he had five companies of horse from Texas' ready for duty, which was more than enough: 'I beg that no more mounted troops may be sent me from Texas. With the regular dragoons and volunteer horse designed for this line,' he wrote, '[we have] a cavalry force abundantly large for our purposes, and indeed, too large to be conveniently foraged.' The request went unheeded, and scores of mounted Texans kept arriving for duty. The following week, Taylor informed his superiors that he was not planning to invade San Luis Potosi, and that instead he would assume a defensive posture. This was the week before the entire northern theatre went quiet and the guerrilla war moved to central Mexico. There was also another reason the future US President did not want the Texans. In his second letter Taylor asked again for them not to be sent, because he was having difficulty controlling their activities in northern Mexico: 'I deeply regret to report extensive depredation and outrages upon the peaceful inhabitants.' In other words, the Texans were not abiding by the laws of war:

There is scarcely a form of crime that has not been reported to me as committed by them … Were it possible to rouse the Mexican people to resistance, no more effectual plan could be devised than the one pursued by some of our volunteer regiments now about to be discharged … the mounted men from Texas have scarcely made one expedition without unwarrantedly killing a Mexican ... The constant recurrence of such atrocities, which I have been reluctant to report to the department, is my motive for requesting that no more troops may be sent to this column from the State of Texas.[17]

Numerous companies of Texans had shown up in the northern theatre in anticipation of an invasion of San Luis Potosi and points further south from where US forces were stationed. Taylor, not known for his attention to discipline, was overwhelmed. The unruly nature of the mounted units played a role in his decision not to advance further into Mexico, as did the task of supplying the army in an extensive region in which even the Mexicans found it difficult to operate. When Taylor decided to commit to a defensive line in northern Mexico, the guerrilla war in the north slowed to a standstill. It was Scott who needed mounted units to keep his line viable, but the problem was that Scott was running a conventional campaign with strict military discipline under the laws of war. Scott had not asked for Texans, but that is exactly what Washington sent him. Put another way, Scott was sent what he needed to fight the guerrillas but not what he wanted, because he believed that not alienating the population was more important as a counter-insurgency tool than the military efficacy of cavalry with years of experience skirmishing in Indian warfare. Scott was not out for revenge for wrongdoings committed against him by the Mexicans in years past – the Texans were, which is why they rode wholeheartedly into Mexico and into battle.

One newspaper was more positive about the reinforcements sent to fight guerrillas, saying, 'Gen. Scott will find himself at ease in the Halls of the Montezumas'. In the meantime, there even might be a 'virtual cessation of hostilities' interspersed with 'irregular throat-cutting here and there'. And once the Texans arrived, the guerrillas would be on the run:

> The communications of Gen. Scott will be opened and kept open, whenever the promise so long ago made to Gen. Scott to protect his 'rear,' shall be redeemed. It will be redeemed when Col. Jack Hays' battalion of Texan Rangers, now raised, shall take their destined position on the line between Vera Cruz and the city of Mexico ... They will be an overmatch for the guerrillas.[18]

The *American Star No. 2*, the organ of US forces in Puebla, got word of the impending deployment in July from a Washington correspondent. In an article entitled, 'An Opposition Force to the Guerrillas', the *Star* declared the Americans would fight fire with fire: 'It has been determined, it is said, by the government, to meet the Mexicans at their new game of guerrilla warfare.' The article claimed 'advance' initiatives were underway to counter the forces harassing the Veracruz-Puebla line: 'Major Hays' new battalion of rangers will be sent to Mexico on the guerrilla service.' The *Star* asserted that another unit being organized 'for the same purpose' was commanded by 'partisan officers, whose very name is a terror to the Mexican guerrillas'.[19]

The Rangers' reputation was warranted. They had existed since 1823 but were officially organized only in 1835. From their inception they were known throughout the region as effective fighters. When the *Daily American Star* in Mexico City learned of their deployment, the paper told its readers, 'The practice of taking prisoners appears to be entirely unknown to them.'[20] As *The American Star No. 2* noted, the Texas Rangers had played an important role in achieving and maintaining their state's independence from Mexico in 1836, and the region was plagued with violence prior to annexation in 1845. That violence not only emanated from forays by Mexican forces, but from native tribes such as the Comanches, whose territory extended throughout the northern and western borders of the entire country. Surprise attacks, raids and counter-raids were commonplace. Prisoners were an encumbrance to mounted men who needed to travel long distances and maintain speed and agility. Lyles notes that in frontier warfare 'neither the Comanches nor the Mexicans took prisoners (except for torture, slavery, mutilation and death), so the Rangers learned to shun taking prisoners in battle'.[21]

The problem for Scott was that killing prisoners was antithetical to the new kind of lawful war he was prosecuting. Therefore, once he found out Washington was sending him Rangers, it was his hope that their propensity to violence could be mitigated by mixing them with regular army units more conscious of his goals and more attuned to the laws of war. The last thing Scott wanted was to repeat Napoleon's policy of executing captured Spanish guerrillas, because the Mexicans were ready to begin doing the same to US soldiers. Nor did Scott support the random killing of civilians caught up in encounters between Mexicans and Rangers. The fearsome frontier cavalry had done their duty for the Republic of Texas, but in central Mexico they were representing the US and needed to restrain themselves. The reality was that their superb counter-insurgency skills were unmatched and sorely needed, but their involvement in the war generated a difficult balancing act for Scott.

'Clear the Route'

In mid-August Taylor received instructions sent by Marcy requiring Hays 'to proceed to Vera Cruz ... for the purpose of dispersing the guerrillas which infest the line between that place and the interior' of the country. Marcy reported he had not heard from Scott in a month, and Washington was 'without intelligence' concerning central Mexico.[22] For weeks on end, Washington officials were blind to what was occurring beyond the Sierra Madre Occidental. Two days later, Marcy informed Scott that he was sending more soldiers to the port city, adding that 'difficulties to be encountered on the route into the interior have rendered it necessary to detain the successive detachments at Vera Cruz', which is where they were held up. 'I need not, I am sure,' Marcy wrote, 'urge the advantages of having the line, from the coast to your column, kept open, and as free as possible' from guerrilla attacks. The urging was unnecessary, but the information was undoubtedly welcomed by the commanding general in Puebla. 'Efforts are in the making to raise several mounted companies of acclimated men, at New Orleans and in the region, principally for the purpose … to clear the route into the interior of the guerrillas who infest it and obstruct it.'[23]

It appeared that officials had attempted to avoid illegal acts of violence by placing the Texans under the command of Brigadier General Joseph Lane – a politician and commander of volunteer forces from Indiana who fought with the Texans at Buena Vista. The two groups blended well, and the Texans and Hoosiers became a cohesive unit. One report noted that on 22 August the group was ordered to 'proceed at once by sea to Vera Cruz to swell the ranks of General Scott'. Acting in concert with Lane was another unit led by Brigadier General Caleb Cushing of Massachusetts. Lane's group was a veritable mixed bag consisting of the Fourth Indiana under Colonel W.A. Corwin, an Ohioan regiment, a volunteer regiment from Illinois and the 'Texas Rangers, under the celebrated Jack Hays'.[24]

The Texans arrived as the guerrillas were ramping up their attacks. While Taylor and Marcy were communicating back and forth trying to drum up mounted units for Scott, Padre Jarauta was causing havoc between Veracruz and Jalapa. One dispatch reported that the 'American army, after much suffering on the road, has been attacked at Dos Rios by 700 guerrillas, and badly treated'. The dispatch also indicated that 'Father Jarauta will attack them tonight', but this could not be confirmed.[25] If rumours were to be believed, Jaurata's forces had grown significantly. A month later, the New Orleans *Delta* reported that Padre Jarauta had 'had an encounter' with US soldiers at the San Juan pass in mid-September, and that 'a new guerrillero, Father Martin, attacked with a unit composed of 500 infantry, with two pieces of artillery, and sixty cavalry'. Apparently, the Spanish priest led an ambush in conjunction with a Mexican colonel named Mariano Cenobio – another chieftain operating in the Veracruz vicinity. According to the report, the new Spanish warrior-priest had a similar past to Jarauta which further cemented suspicions concerning the Spaniards' motivation in fomenting guerrilla war. 'Father Juan Antonio Martin, formerly at Medellin, and more lately Tesechoacan [near Veracruz], is a native of Alcaniz, in the kingdom of Aragon, in Spain. As a Carlist, and commander of the battalion of "Guias de Aragon", he was decorated with various crosses for his warlike feats.' The *Delta* asserted that Martin was a 'faithful imitator of Father Jarauta in valor and intrepidity', and that he had personally led three separate attacks in early September near the National Bridge – a favourite location for insurgent ambushes.[26]

To observers, the introduction of foreign fighters complicated the war's potential outcomes. The *Buffalo Commercial*, like many northern newspapers, compared Mexico to the Spanish conflict. Spain had 'seemed subdued', they argued, but it was only then that Napoleon's unstoppable army 'was reduced more by the guerrillas than all else, to a flying, starving remnant of a refugee force'. They compared the wars strategically by claiming that Scott's victories were illusory, since as the US Army penetrated deeper into Mexico, the 'guerrillas are falling perpendicularly upon every line of communication, and cutting off supplies, and harassing expresses and trains'. The emergence of insurgents indicated 'most clearly the durable characteristics of the Spanish nation have not changed in the Mexicans', and the paper argued that the US Army was on the brink of disaster. Despite these dire predictions, the new troops pressed on until mid-October, when news of their impending arrival resulted in Santa Anna's forces abandoning the siege. On 12 October, Lane's brigade entered Puebla without opposition. The same day, the *Daily American Star* (changing its name on 12 October) reported that 'Col. Childs had quiet possession of the city of Puebla', and the Mexican troops had scattered through the surrounding region.[27]

Despite the road to Mexico City being clear, insurgents still operated freely in the coastal region. 'The guerrillas have full sway at Jalapa, making war upon their defenseless countrymen.' The Americans controlled Veracruz, but its environs were occupied by guerrillas trying to block the flow of goods into the city, and 'Padre Jarauta threatened to shoot all whom he found carrying provisions to Vera Cruz'. This tactic, reminiscent of Espoz y Mina's blockade of Pamplona, was undermined by ocean-going vessels reaching the city. In addition, the port was crucial to all Mexicans for import and export trade. That Jarauta was a foreigner probably caused resentment among state administrators accountable to merchants and business leaders who depended on a steady flow of commerce – despite the imposition of temporary import duties by the Americans. The report added, 'The Mexican government of the state of Vera Cruz talk of adopting measures to put them down.' In essence, the foreign guerrillas were beginning to wear out their welcome.[28]

A correspondent for the New Orleans *Times-Picayune* in Veracruz had his own take on Jarauta's attempt to control commerce from Veracruz: 'It is stated positively that the goods which are daily forwarded to the interior via Orizaba are no longer taxed by Mexican authorities.' This meant that the Mexican authorities rerouted goods coming into the country via Orizaba (instead of Jalapa) due to guerrilla activity, and that the interests of the Mexican government and the guerrillas were at odds with each other. The suspension of taxes was not only implemented to offset the temporary US duty on incoming goods, but also to redirect the flow of goods away from the guerrillas. That development, according to the correspondent, was because 'the guerrilla force is getting weaker, and hostile forces against the guerrilla tariff, composed entirely of those who are interested, is getting too strong for the guerrillas, who, if they persist in their old course, are in danger of being massacred by their own countrymen'.[29]

Changing Tone in Washington and Mexico

Reflecting a change in tone and war strategy by President Polk in late 1847, Marcy wrote on 6 October to Scott (from whom he had not heard since 4 June) about a new occupation policy. Marcy claimed, 'Our leniency has not been reciprocated, but ... repaid with bad faith and barbarity; and is only met by a blind obstinacy and a reckless determination to prolong the conflict.' The administration had been upset by the emergence of insurgents: 'The guerrilla system which has been resorted to is hardly recognized as a legitimate mode of warfare, and should be met with the utmost severity.' Essentially, Marcy blamed the Mexican people for the guerrilla action and pushed for a policy of retribution against 'not only those embodied for the purpose of carrying out that system, but those who at any time have been engaged in it, or who have sustained, sheltered, and protected them'. In sum, the general population was considered more responsible 'than the soldiers in the ranks of the Mexican army'. The new position of the US leadership echoed the Napoleonic occupation of Spain:

> However unwilling we may be to modify our humane policy, a change now seems to be required even by considerations of humanity. We must take the best measures within the clearly admitted course of civilized warfare, to beget a disposition in the people of Mexico to come to an adjustment upon fair and honorable terms. It should be borne in mind

that the people of Mexico, indulging … the most hostile feelings, are not less parties to the war than the Mexican army; and as a means of peace, they must be made to feel their evils.[30]

Due in part to apprehension created by the monarchist faction, the *Puros* – the party calling for protracted war – split along lines indicating that some of its members were in favour of the United States incorporating Mexico into a larger North American union. With this political faction in mind, Pedro Santoni notes in his 1996 work, *Mexicans at Arms*, that historian José Fuentes Mares 'casts doubts on the *Puros'* motives' by arguing that the faction 'presented themselves as champions of an armed struggle against the invaders, but only to obtain Mexico's final annexation to the United States'. This claim is followed by Santoni's assertion that there 'is no doubt that several *Puro* politicians advocated establishment of a United States protectorate'. Colonel Ethan Hitchcock, entrusted by Scott with recruiting local collaborators and establishing a native Mexican spy network, discussed this with *Puro* party representatives in the fall of 1847.[31]

Hitchcock received calls from *Puro* defectors and on 14 November wrote in his diary: 'They are all of one party – the *Puros*, so-called – and do not hesitate to express a wish that the troops of the U.S. may hold this country till the Mexican army is annihilated, in order that a proper civil government may be securely established.' Towards the end of that month, the colonel received a call from a doctor on his way to the ad hoc Mexican capital in Querétaro. 'Another proposition was discussed at great length … to ask the Mexican government to apply for admission into the United States. Before doing so, he would like to know what answer the American officers thought would make to such an application.'[32]

Scott believed that overtures by Mexicans to make him a dictator ruling with a political class of discharged US military officers was proof of the fairness of the military occupation. It had established a rule of law welcomed by many influential elites who would have furthered prospered in a political union with the United States. Scott wrote, 'Good order, or the protection of religion, persons, property, and industry were coexistive [*sic*] with the American rule.' In essence, the pacification policy had worked:

Everything consumed or used by our troops was as regularly paid for as if they had been at home. Hence Mexicans had never before known equal prosperity … The plan contemplated a *pronunciamento*, in which Scott should declare himself dictator of the Republic for a term of six or four years – to give time to politicians and agitators to recover pacific habits, and learn to govern themselves.[33]

Scott turned down the offer to become a Yankee *caudillo*, but the fact the offer was made demonstrates that Mexicans were fearful of the type of perpetual civil war that had consumed Spain after the French were driven out. Pundits of the anti-war party in Washington addressed similar concerns. 'Another dread that exists in Mexico is that this guerrilla system will result in a permanent and general organization of regular banditti throughout the country,' writers for DC's *National Intelligencer* surmised, 'which will be kept up long after the difficulties with the United States may be settled, and which it will be impossible to eradicate.' To many observers, it appeared that history was repeating itself: 'It was the same in Spain, where the guerrilla bands were not put down for years after the French were expelled, and only by the most vigorous and energetic measures, such as no government in Mexico will have in their power to employ.'[34]

Insurgent Hunters: Rangers and *Contra-guerrillas*

On 17 October, five days after Lane lifted the siege at Puebla, Hays and his 580 'cooped-up' Rangers landed at Veracruz. A correspondent with the *Washington Union* eagerly announced that the 'so-anxiously-looked-for Col. Jack Hays, the celebrated Texas ranger, has at last arrived'. The dispatch reported the Texans had already 'killed a guerrilla, dressed in a Mexican colonel's uniform, epaulets, cocked hat – and all'. The writer also claimed that 'the guerrillas will be rather scarce in a few days' because Hays was 'well-known to them by reputation; and ... the road from here to the city of Mexico would be as safe as the road from New Orleans to Carrollton [Texas]'.[35]

Lane managed to open much of the road between Veracruz and Mexico City, but guerrillas continued to attack US forces and small convoys. General Robert Patterson immediately informed the Rangers that Colonel Mariano Cenobio was launching raids from a nearby hacienda called San Juan, located about 50km from Veracruz. Rip Ford surmised from the conversation that Cenobio and his group 'were fighting more for plunder', and Patterson inquired whether the Rangers were up to the task. The following morning, they located the hacienda and killed a few guards but found no trace of Cenobio. An after-action report of the assault cited the discovery of US goods as evidence that the hacienda was a guerrilla base. After interrogating two prisoners and burning everything 'except the church', the group returned to Veracruz.[36]

Losing his base for the launching of attacks was not Colonel Cenobio's only woe, since Mexican and Spanish guerrilla factions now began 'quarrelling among themselves'. This apparently resulted in Cenobio and Jarauta having a violent falling-out, which was publicized in numerous newspapers after being reported by *El Arco Iris* in Veracruz: 'Jarauta's band have declared Colonel Cenobio to be a traitor to them and to his country; that he is leagued with the Americans, and even supplied by them with arms and ammunition for the purpose of destroying his brother bandits.' There is no evidence supporting the claim that Cenobio was working with the US Army, but *El Arco Iris* claimed that a confrontation following 'much hard talking' resulted in thirty deaths on Cenobio's side, and the 'victorious' Jarauta was shot in the leg.[37]

The *Times-Picayune* correspondent in the port city weighed in on the effect of the occupation on the guerrillas: 'In truth, this city and the country around is getting wonderfully Americanized; as long as money is spent as freely here as it is now, it must remain so.' In essence, the policy of paying for goods was alienating the guerrillas from the people and especially the business class – this was a different scenario to Pamplona, despite Jarauta's efforts to implement an economic embargo of Veracruz. 'We pay for everything, as we ought', the paper claimed, 'while the guerrillas help themselves to what they want out of every poultry yard and garden that they come across.' According to this account, the outcome of such activity was predictably bad for the guerrillas: 'Any small guerrilla force from hereafter will … have a hard row to hoe, and the large ones cannot remain friends long, and in the end will, like Cenobio and Jarauta, cut one another's throats.'[38]

Infighting among Mexicans was obviously useful to the US cause, and Scott deepened these divisions when he arrived in Puebla and enlisted the services of Mexican *contra-guerrillas*. One article described them as 'a rough looking set of men'; their leader was an outlaw named Manuel Dominguez. Like the Spanish collaborators with the French in the Peninsula, Mexicans employed by the US Army understood they would be branded as traitors by their countrymen and executed if captured. 'They fight with ropes around their necks, as the saying is, and therefore fight gallantly.' The Mexican contra-guerrillas were a major asset to US forces, provided useful intelligence on routes and enemy positions, and were familiar with the country. Their main purpose was to aid US forces by gathering information and maintaining communications normally hindered by guerrilla activity. They also served as guides to help the Rangers track down insurgents. 'Col. Dominguez is thought to know the road intimately from long experience upon the line in a different capacity. We understand that we have altogether about 450 of their description of force in our pay.' One Alabama newspaper praised Scott's initiative 'to subsidize' the small force of Mexican outlaws: 'They are a match for four times their number of ordinary guerrillas, they have no attachments to their country … and they know every nook and cranny and private pass between Vera Cruz and the capital.'[39]

Colonel Hitchcock originally recruited Dominguez and gave a sympathetic account of the recruitment of the man he later brought to New Orleans after the war. According to the future Civil War general, Dominguez's career changes – from merchant to thief and smuggler, to US spy, to exile – were prompted years earlier by a Mexican soldier who 'waylaid and robbed' him somewhere between Mexico City and Veracruz. 'That like Lambo he has been "stung from a slave to an enslaver" is almost true.'[40]

Dominguez may have had personal reasons for fighting the Mexican military, but his services came at a price. The Americans essentially paid for passes to use the road between Veracruz and Mexico City, and allied themselves with an established network of black marketeers and smugglers. These connections were established in the early 1840s, when the Republic of Texas and Mexico were at war and Texan prisoners of war who escaped were smuggled to Veracruz. Hitchcock wrote in his diary, 'The robbers shall let our people pass without molestation and … they shall, for extra compensation, furnish us with guides, couriers, and spies.' The importance of the relationship should not be underestimated. When Hitchcock met Dominguez for the first time, both agreed that each agent under Dominguez would receive $2 a day and Dominguez would get $3. Eventually, they settled on a monthly fee of $20 per man – a good deal at that date. In Hitchcock's estimation, however, employing the contra-guerrillas was worth the cost. 'Each man counts, in fact, two for us,' he wrote, 'for if we did not employ them, the enemy would; so that one detached from the enemy and transferred to us makes a difference of two in our favor.'[41]

Another important aspect of these agents bears repeating. The most critical phase of the conflict occurred when Scott forsook the logistics line from Veracruz to Jalapa and marched to Puebla. It was a major gamble based on confidence in his army's capabilities. Even Wellington commented on the audacity of the move. 'Scott is lost,' exclaimed the Duke after the Americans left the line. 'He cannot capture the city and he cannot fall back upon his base.'[42] Indeed, abandoning a logistics line and venturing into the unknown with no means of escape was not what was taught at West Point, or any other military academy.

During this period Hitchcock wrote that Dominguez and his spies provided a critical communications network: 'To understand them one must imagine the American army entirely isolated within the enemy's country at Puebla when it was impossible for any of our men, except in large parties, to go safely beyond the limits of the city.' The inability to send out reliable couriers to provide (or receive) essential military information would have hamstrung the US Army, and the Spy Company thus provided vital intelligence. 'It was in this way that the General [Scott] communicated with his reinforcements while coming up from Vera Cruz. As these services were secret ... they have never been properly appreciated except by a very few persons.' Dominguez's network extended throughout the entire line and was useful even after the capital was seized. Hitchcock wrote, 'The road had become tolerably quiet, the Spy Company made several expeditions to Vera Cruz and back again to Mexico without ever losing one single dispatch committed to them.'[43] In essence, the alliance neutralized the effectiveness of the guerrilla action at a critical juncture in the war.

Dominguez, later identified as a colonel by Rip Ford, helped the Texans find their way around Mexico by assigning guides and scouts to the unit. Because they knew the country, the guides showed the Texans the location of Cenobio's headquarters at the San Juan hacienda and helped Lane track down Santa Anna's location. The Texans were exceptional fighters, bound together by a frontier tenacity, but without critical information on the whereabouts of insurgents they would have been left wandering through a thousand Mexican villages with little to go on.

'Neither regulars nor volunteers': the search for Jarauta

After burning the San Juan hacienda the Texas regiment headed into the interior. They encountered sporadic opposition but were relieved to learn that Lane's recent presence had made the road easier. Ford wrote that the 'guerrilla bands annoyed the troops less than previous to our arrival'. Nevertheless, there were rumours of incidents. One report surfaced from Veracruz that General Patterson had ordered the execution of 'two Mexican officers, Garcia and Alcalde ... who were taken prisoner commanding guerrillas, without having been exchanged'. The same report indicated the Aragonese guerrilla-priest Juan Antonio Martin had been captured. 'We have been informed that Padre Martin (the second Jarauta) has been made prisoner while sleeping in one of the *garitas* [guardhouses] of the city of Mexico.'[44]

Although Santa Anna's role in the war was over, General Joaquín Rea, who helped lay siege to Puebla, was still in the nearby town of Atlixco. A Spaniard who had fought on the side of the insurgents during the Mexican Revolution, Rea was well respected and commanded 'well drilled, well equipped and paid ... valiant guerrilleros'. According to Wilcox, Rea's force of 400 soldiers constituted 'the headquarters and temporary capital of the guerrillas, who had fitted out there many expeditions to attack American trains'. For that reason Atlixco was bombarded by the Americans. Although the decision to shell the town was criticized after the war, it was not enough to persuade Rea to cease operations. It took another month before most serious guerrilla activity against US forces in the region was stamped out.[45]

On 6 December the first of the brigade of 3,500 soldiers began to reach Mexico City. Ford was among them. The arrival 'produced a sensation among the inhabitants. They thronged the streets along which we passed. The greatest curiosity prevailed to get a sight at Los Diablos Tejanos – "the Texas Devils".' The *Baltimore Sun* reported the arrival scene:

> As the gallant Rangers filed through the streets, covered with mud and dust, accumulated on their long journey, it would have done you good to see the Mexicans stare, particularly when they were informed that these were the much dreaded Texans, or Tejanos.' To the mesmerized onlookers, Hays and his men appeared to be entirely different creatures to the US soldiers: Dressed as Rangers always are … some with blankets wrapped around them, and some in their shirt sleeves – but all well mounted and armed, they presented a sight never seen before in the streets of Mexico … *leperos* [the poor] were still as death while they were passing. The gallant Col. Jack Hays appeared to be an object of peculiar interest to all, and the better informed class of the Mexicans were particularly anxious to have pointed out to them the man whose name had been the terror of their nation for the last twelve years.[46]

Upon the Texans entering the ancient Zocalo, where the Metropolitan Cathedral and National Palace (Scott's headquarters) stood, an ominous event occurred. A Mexican with a basket on his head full of candy for sale was summoned by a Ranger, who proceeded to devour handfuls apparently without paying for it. Ford recalled that the Mexican thought 'he was being robbed, stooped down, got hold of a pebble, and threw it at the ranger with great force'. In return the Ranger shot him dead, causing thousands of 'desperately frightened' people on the plaza to stampede for safety.[47]

The *Baltimore Sun* reported the arrival scene: 'As the gallant Rangers filed through the streets, covered with mud and dust, accumulated on their long journey, it would have done you good to see the Mexicans stare, particularly when they were informed that these were the much dreaded Texans, or Tejanos.' To the mesmerized onlookers, Hays and his men appeared to be entirely different creatures to the US soldiers.

The hunt for Jarauta began shortly after the Rangers arrived. George Wilkens Kendall, a New Orleans *Times-Picayune* correspondent whose dispatches were some of the war's most regularly re-reported, noted the arrival of General Patterson and the Texans in the capital and informed his readers that *El Monitor* had recently revealed there had been a meeting between General Paredes and Jarauta in Tulancingo. Apparently the two were 'resolved upon calling in the aid and intervention of European powers in the affairs of Mexico'. Indeed, the arrival of Jarauta and the Spanish Carlist guerrillas after Paredes' short exile in France was no coincidence, as it became clearer that monarchists were hoping to take advantage of the chaos. The article further stated that 'Paredes has not abandoned his favorite project of placing a foreign prince on the throne of Mexico; in fact, it is the prevailing opinion here that it was for this purpose he returned' from France. Kendall also reported that Paredes was 'viewed with distrust by all parties … [but] is backed, however, by many foreigners'.[48]

Scott granted permission to Pennsylvanian Colonel Henry Wynkoop, with thirty-three Rangers and Mexican spies, to capture or kill the guerrillas, and the group set off to the north-west of the capital on 1 January. According to Rip Ford, after a few days they spent the night in the town of San Juan Teotihuacán in the largest building on the main plaza. In the morning, Jarauta attacked the group with cavalry and with infantry posted atop a few buildings. The Americans managed to repel the initial attack; as Ford wrote, 'saddles were emptied, and the *guerrilleros* began to evince respect for the six-shooters'. Jarauta then rallied his soldiers for a second assault, whereupon the Texans opened up again on the attackers. Ford recalled that Jarauta was shot and carried into a house by his men, which 'ended the fight'.[49]

Reports of Jarauta's death spread quickly, but the chieftain wanted the world to know they were false. By early 1848 the priest had achieved international notoriety based on a series of articles in Mexican and US newspapers. A week after the skirmish with Hays, Jarauta issued a circular entitled 'Viva la Republica Mexicana' from the city of Tula (in the state of Mexico), where he was convalescing. The guerrilla reaffirmed his commitment to defending the Mexican cause 'regardless of the comforts provided by private life'. He remained defiant:

I launched myself into war from the first days when the invader's filthy plant poked through the ground of the heroic Veracruz town. With some of its sons who joined me, I had the glory of exhausting the enemy in various encounters, inflicting damages, and constantly harassing them to the point of having attacked the same convoy seven times.[50]

Jarauta proclaimed that the wounds forcing him to temporarily 'abandon' the war were now 'restored', and that the governor of the state of Mexico had gave him 'all the necessary resources to sustain the strength' to carry on. Trying to rally the common people to the guerrilla war, he declared, 'I am pleased to return to the campaign … to fight for your just rights. Mexicans, won't you accompany me in such a glorious struggle?' The problem for the foreign fighter was how to convince (and recruit) non-Spanish Mexicans to fight for a Spanish priest with an agenda. 'Will you remain cold bystanders in view of the offences on your religion, which has scourged your fellow citizens? Do you expect the same affront to your own people, or perhaps even worse for those of your families?' Jarauta's defiant circular invoked 'the god of armies to manifest his power' to rid Mexico of its invaders. It was a rambling call to war addressed to a populace sceptical about the ulterior motives of Jarauta, Paredes and others conspiring to reintroduce monarchy to a dysfunctional republic. 'To arms, brave Mexicans, and without more party or currency, to war against the Yankees, do it until you repel them further than the Sabina [River]. These are the votes of your sincere friend who counts on your cooperation.'[51]

There were reports in early 1848 of an attempt by Jarauta to mount a national uprising, but it was obvious at that point that ordinary Mexicans – who would have constituted the backbone of any insurgency – would not support a foreigner with European allegiances.[52] Nevertheless, the Texans who were initially tasked with seeking out Jarauta were determined to do so before their enlistment period expired, and the search intensified until late February, when Rangers arrived at dawn in the mountain town of Sequalteplan (Zacualtipán) – surprising the guerrillas and gunning them down. According to an after-action report, more than 400 guerrillas were killed, but Jarauta 'effected his precipitate escape; thereby, for the present, saving his person from the treatment he so wisely dreaded'. Although they did not kill or capture Jarauta, the Action of Sequalteplan (as it was later called) did much to neutralize guerrilla attacks by foreign fighters against US forces between Mexico City and Veracruz.[53]

Peace seemed far off, however. Most people were led to believe Nicholas Trist, Polk's peace commissioner officially recalled to Washington in mid-November, had left the city 'with a strong and efficient' escort on or about 9 December, as reported in the *American Star*.[54] The reason for this piece of disinformation has never been ascertained, but it was assumed by almost everyone that he had failed in his mission, and that therefore the US Army (by all appearances) was expected to stay for the foreseeable future. The prospect of a prolonged occupation did not bode well when compared with Scott's previous proclamations outlining his desire for a brief conflict.

Time is the enemy of all occupying armies. The longer an army stays in an occupied country, the more the population begins to suspect that it has no intention of leaving. Although there were undoubtedly many Mexicans who enjoyed the benefits of American largesse, the American military presence was limited to a few northern, coastal and central Mexican cities. The Americans had not yet spread out over the entire country, as the French had done in Spain. This relatively small military footprint had three benefits: it helped to offset the general animosity the Mexicans harboured towards the Americans; it made them believe the Americans were not intent on seizing the entire country; and it eliminated the advantages which geography gave to the insurgents. Had the US Army attempted to occupy all of Mexico, the potential for a national insurrection would have been very real. As the reader will see, this is exactly what the US Commander-in-chief and his allies in Congress attempted. Had Polk had the powers of Napoleon, it is quite possible that Mexico would have ceased to exist after 1848.

Chapter 7

The Allure of Napoleonic Empire

Mr. President, let us take care that the disgraceful warfare of Spain be not renewed upon this continent! Is there to be no end to this state of things? I do not believe that the violated honor of the country requires such vindication. That honor is in much greater danger of being tarnished by our own conduct in the further prosecution of this war.[1]

James A. Pearce, US Senator from Maryland, 13 January 1848

In late 1847, with the US Army occupying the Mexican capital and insurgency ongoing between Veracruz and Mexico City, a major shift appeared in President James K. Polk's stance on the war. The conflict had become unpopular with half the country. In the midterm elections the anti-war Whig party had won control of the House of Representatives. The occupation was costing more than anticipated, and funding for it would now be more difficult to obtain. Polk notified Congress that he had recalled his peace envoy Nicholas Trist and that treaty negotiations were suspended. With these developments in mind, an effort was made to adopt the strategy used by Napoleon in Spain: *bellum se ipsum alet* – that the occupying army would henceforth supply itself from the revenues and resources of Mexico. In addition, Polk's supporters in the Senate acted to expand the war by introducing more troops. The contrast between benign and forceful styles of occupation was stark, the implication being that US soldiers would remain in Mexico indefinitely as an army of permanent conquest.

To many observers, the debate in the US capital over the future of Mexico marked a crossroads in the potential transition from American republic to military empire. The principal advocate for continental hegemony was the 1848 Democratic presidential candidate Senator Lewis Cass. Its main opponent was the powerful senator from South Carolina, John C. Calhoun. In tandem with General Scott's support for treaty negotiations in Mexico, despite Trist's recall, Calhoun played a critical role in preventing more troops from being sent to Mexico and delayed bills that would have expanded the occupation.

Informing the congressional debate over the future of Mexico was the ever-present history of the French in Spain and the slow blood letting that had undermined an overstretched army of occupation there. Concerned political leaders from both the South and North believed such an outcome was possible. In the end, opposition to escalation won, and the successful policy of paying for goods rather than taking them supplanted Napoleon's military maxim that 'war must support war'. The new doctrine, developed as a response to the dawn of guerrilla warfare, became the modus operandi for the US Army and for many other western nations.

The shift in war policy was announced in a much-anticipated annual address to Congress on 7 December. Polk stated that 'negotiations for peace have failed' and that a 'vanquished' Mexico was acting as if it had won the war. The president castigated the Mexicans for their intransigence, claiming they 'must have known that their ultimatum could never be accepted'. He said that he did 'not deem it proper to make any further overtures of peace' but preferred to wait for the Mexicans to reach out. Most alarmingly, Polk hinted that without a reliable negotiating partner the occupation would be extended indefinitely. He informed the country that new military forces on land and sea were being sent to occupy 'all the ports, towns, cities, and provinces now in our possession; that we should press forward ... and levy such military contributions on the enemy as may, as far as practicable, defray the future expenses of the war.'[2]

Polk called for an additional 50,000 soldiers and proclaimed, 'The Mexican people will be made to feel the burdens of the war.' The president specifically stated that the policy of paying for goods 'at fair and liberal prices' had failed, blamed the Mexicans, and told Congress the army needed to implement a more vigorous prosecution of the war. Polk also stunned his detractors by describing the limited guerrilla war in language which implied that it had escalated beyond redemption, and claimed that despite a 'spirit of liberality and conciliation' on the part of Americans, the Mexican people were supporting the insurgency:

> Not appreciating our forbearance, the Mexican people generally became hostile ... and availed themselves at every opportunity to commit the most savage excesses upon our troops. Large numbers of the population took up arms, and, engaging in guerrilla warfare, robbed and murdered in the most cruel manner individual soldiers, or small parties, whom accident or other causes had separated from the main body of our army; bands of guerrilleros and robbers infested the roads, harassed our trains, and, whenever it was in their power, cut off our supplies. The Mexicans having thus shown themselves to be wholly incapable of appreciating our forbearance and liberality, it was deemed proper to change the manner

in conducting the war, by making them feel its pressure according to the usages observed under similar circumstances by all other civilized nations.[3]

Aspects of the statement were accurate, but Polk used this portrait of chaos to outline a vague plan for more troops to subdue all of Mexico. Without knowing Polk's exact intentions, critics of the war were alarmed by his determination to 'prosecute it with increased energy and power in the vital parts of the country'. While denying that he advocated the annihilation of Mexico and 'her separate existence as an independent nation', Polk claimed that if 'we shall ultimately fail, then we shall have exhausted all honorable means in pursuit of peace, and must continue to occupy her country with our troops'.[4]

Adding to the grim prospect of a never-ending conflict, Polk stated that the army needed to remain in order to 'leave her [Mexico] with a republican government'. The United States had experience of establishing government in sparsely populated western territories, but the US Army had no prior experience of establishing, protecting and preserving government in an occupied country. Imposing a regime on a conquered state represented a previously uncrossed Rubicon. Polk stated that nation-building might become the goal of other European powers with interests in Mexico, and it would be imprudent to leave before peace was achieved. If the United States did not stay, Mexico might be 'inclined to yield to foreign influences, and to cast themselves into the arms of some European monarch for protection from the anarchy and suffering which would ensue'. That European states such as Great Britain were ready to enter and take possession of Mexico was a major argument used by expansionists.[5]

The most troubling aspect of the address was Polk's insistence on shifting the burden of war onto the Mexican people. He informed the legislative branch that through the Secretary of War he had ordered his generals to stop paying for goods and claimed that burdening the population would induce 'their rulers to accede to a just peace'. The Commander-in-Chief told Congress that he had sent instructions to General Taylor on 22 September to do so, but that Taylor had responded on 26 October that 'he did not adopt the policy' but instead 'continued to pay' for goods. The same orders were issued to Scott on 3 April following the Veracruz landing.[6] At the time, Marcy wrote to Scott:

[T]he President directs me again to call your attention to the dispatch to this department of the 3rd of April last ... the property holders of Mexico have no claim to find in the market afforded by sales to our army, and actual pecuniary benefit resulting from the war. They must be made to feel its evils, and it is earnestly hoped and expected that you will not

… adhere to your opinion … that a resort to forced contributions will exasperate and ruin the inhabitants, and starve the army.[7]

Forty-seven days later, Polk received a similar letter of refusal from Scott, who wrote to Marcy that any 'attempt to subsist it by living at free quarters, or on forced contributions, would be the end of military operations'.[8] Scott believed that acting as Napoleon had in Spain would fuel an insurgency and result in mass revolt, and he highlighted the exchange with Marcy in his *Memoirs* many years later: 'Early in the campaign I began to receive letters from Washington, urging me to support the army by forced contributions. Under the circumstances, this was an impossibility.' He also provided a few of his principal reasons for refusing to cooperate. Among them was the 'sparse' population, the lack of political allies within the country, and the issue of overcoming religious and racial differences. Under the occupation as regulated by Scott, any Mexican could assist the US Army and make money by selling supplies. If forced requisitioning was introduced, Mexicans could easily be turned into enemies:

Hence there was not among them a farmer, a miller, or dealer in subsistence, who would not have destroyed whatever property he could not remove beyond our reach sooner than allow it to be seized without compensation. For the first day or two we might, perhaps, have seized current subsistence within five miles of our route; but by the end of the week the whole army must have been broken up into detachments and scattered far and wide over the country, skirmishing with rancheros and regular troops, for the means of satisfying the hunger of the day. Could invaders, so occupied, have conquered Mexico?[9]

President Polk publicly acknowledged Scott's defiance in his address: 'General Scott, for reasons assigned to him, also continued to pay for the articles of supply which were drawn from the enemy.' Polk complained that his orders had been repeatedly ignored and castigated those who questioned his policy of forced requisitions, claiming that Mexicans were following the US debate on the war and receiving 'false impressions' that it might end on terms favourable to Mexico.[10]

'War must support war'

Plans to shift the burden of the war onto the Mexicans were made long before Veracruz. One South Carolinian newspaper noted in October 1846 'a very important change in the mode of conducting the Mexican war, which will likely soon give its decisive result, Napoleon's maxim was, that a war of conquest should support itself.' The historical context was further explained:

> Accordingly when he had overrun a district, his first care was to establish a government especially adapted to draw out it resources for the support of the army. We have been on very different maxims in the Mexican war … The consequences have been that the Mexicans have made a great bargain of our invasion. Losing nothing, they have gained the privilege of supplying our armies at enormous prices. This is to be amended hereafter.[11]

The context of the maxim as outlined was true to a certain extent, but the situation in the summer of 1810, when Napoleon required his generals to provide for themselves without aid from Paris, resulted from a lack of funds available to carry on the war. The French government had run out of money, and thus it was not a policy born of careful and considered planning, but rather initiated in haste after all other sources of revenue had been exhausted. Others reported that Polk was 'adopting the construction of the act of Congress authorizing him to employ 50,000 volunteers … [he] has a right to call out, [and] are to be called out'. The report was inaccurate, but it illuminates some of the wartime opinions floated by members of the executive concerning the powers of the Commander-in-Chief. 'The war now to be carried on against Mexico will be similar to that waged by Napoleon against Austria and Italy,' the *Times-Picayune* claimed in October 1847, 'by Sir Henry Pottinger against China, and by Sir Harry Smith against the Sikhs, i.e., it will support its own expenses and acquire territory besides – the right and lawful issue of all wars.'[12]

Since the military maxim's most recent adherent was Napoleon, pro-war advocates believed in its efficacy. The *Flag of Freedom* in Puebla caught wind of the proposal in July 1847: 'The first and most important item, if it be true, is that after a long cabinet council it was decided to change completely our system of warfare, if a treaty of peace is not immediately made.' The US Army-operated newspaper informed its readers, most of whom were soldiers, of the particulars of the new policy. The language was surprisingly neutral given the consequences involved:

> The property of the church is to be taken and used for the expenses of the war, and also 'particular property', so that the effects of the war shall be felt by all, and its original object be changed to that of conquest. Orders to this effect have been sent to Gen. Scott … the soothing system

might be advantageously changed, and that the world was preparing to acknowledge our right to pursue a more vigorous course.[13]

In the fall of 1847 and into early 1848, war advocates aligned with the Polk Administration pushed the military maxim into the public square. Three days before the presidential address to Congress, an article entitled 'On the Administration "Feelers"' was published in Washington's *Weekly National Intelligencer*, claiming the pro-war party was canvassing the Napoleonic idea and assessing its reception by the US public. 'It was a maxim of Napoleon that a "war ought always to support itself". In putting this principle into practice, Napoleon's troops, whenever they invaded a foreign country, began to levy contributions in money, provisions and forage.'[14] The *Buffalo Courier*'s editors claimed in an article, 'The Regiment Bill', that Americans had lost patience with 'making war upon that excessively philanthropic plan, which treats the invaded nation with the scrupulous exactness observed in marching through a friendly state, [and the US] is about to apply to Mexico, practically, the maxim of Napoleon that "war must support war".' The newspaper further explained its application in theatre:

> The taxes, imposts and levies of all descriptions, by which the Mexican government has heretofore been supported, are to constitute a fund for the maintenance of our troops. To collect them; to enforce order; to keep open communications, and to extirpate the robber bands which infest the roads – the principal and salient places of Mexico should be occupied, and moveable columns kept in motion between them. The capital, made the center of operations, should send out troops in all directions, to harass the enemy, and give him a realizing sense of the burdens of war.[15]

Despite Scott's refusal to exact contributions by force, Calhoun believed administration officials were 'resolved to go thoughtlessly forward, when it is clear, whether defeated or successful, the result will be unfortunate to the country'. Calhoun was sceptical about the war from the beginning and one of the few who abstained from voting to approve it because of its controversial start. To his way of thinking, the presidential address marked the moment when Napoleon's Roman-inspired military maxim was resurrected to justify an emerging era of military empire.[16]

The anti-war *Intelligencer* portrayed the policy from a grim historical perspective. The French Army's 'marches were accompanied by a host of commissaries, provided with wagon trains and horses. These locusts, attended by a proper escort, would diverge from the line of march to the right or left, or to any point where the spoils could be found.' This was what the administration was asking Scott to do in April 1847. Essentially, Polk was calling for Mexico to be plundered, as Spain had been:

> Grain was cut in the field; if green, it would answer for horses; if ripe, it was transported to a depot, and speedily ground in handmills to make bread for the soldiery. As the war went on supporting itself, the miserable were stripped of every article of food. Horses were seized to replace those of the cavalry which were swept off by the casualties of battle or fatigue … By this system of organized marauding the countries through which the French armies marched were completely ruined.[17]

The editors accurately claimed that 'the acts of oppression … were the principal causes of the general uprising against Napoleon', especially among the 'middling and lower classes in Europe', and asserted that to enact the maxim as policy would be disastrous for the occupation. 'To meet the exigency, feelers are put forth in [pro-war] newspaper organs, advocating the adoption of the Napoleonic maxim, "The war must support itself".' The editors of the DC Whig-run newspaper claimed, 'The scheme has proved a failure.'[18]

Inertia of Empire: Calhoun and the All-Mexico Movement

By mid-December Polk's allies in Congress were pushing for more troops, while his detractors questioned the wisdom of annexing Mexico. The dramatic debate as to whether the United States would absorb the entirety of Mexico unfolded in Congress over a three-month period from mid-December to late February. The first moves in the 'All-Mexico' movement, as it would later be called, came from Polk's Democrat-party proxies in the Senate. These included senators Lewis Cass, Daniel Dickinson, Edward Hannegan, Jefferson Davis and Henry Foote. What they were not counting on, however, was opposition from John C. Calhoun.[19]

Calhoun believed Polk's presidential address was 'undignified and full of false assumptions' and recognized what was at stake in the coming debate on the war. The 'cast-iron man', as he was nicknamed for his defence of slavery, had serious misgivings about Polk's intentions regarding Mexico and his moves either to reduce it to a US province or to annex it as an occupied state in a reconfigured empire. Writing to his son before the session began, he declared, 'Either [outcome] will overthrow our system of government … The country is in the most critical condition. It will be hard to save it.' A week after Polk's address, Calhoun cut off a move by Senator Daniel Dickinson to 'strengthen the political and commercial relations on this continent by the annexation of contiguous territory'. On the same day, the Senate deliberated on opening a new route to California, Calhoun warned against annexing Mexico, stating that 'you can hardly read a newspaper without finding it filled with speculation upon this subject'.[20]

His assertion was correct. Some newspapers had alluded to annexation since the beginning of the war, but more open discussion of it began in November 1847. Unlike the pro-war and anti-war sides of the debate, the annexation issue upended conventional thinking in every region of the United States and ripped apart traditional political alliances which had been in existence for decades. One pro-annexation New York paper wrote that anti-annexation opponents had 'as much reason as Don Quixote had to get excited against the windmill'. A centrist North Carolinian paper took a more 'dollars and cents' approach to what it called the 'huckstering' notion of annexation: 'The guerrillas are stigmatized as robbers for plundering our trains [convoys], and yet we would seize upon their whole country, and dignify the act by calling it an act of indemnity.' An editorial in the *New York Herald* appearing next to an article entitled 'The True Designs of the Administration with regard to Mexico', pleaded, 'Let Mr. Calhoun's policy be adopted, and the war is rendered interminable.' Calhoun's efforts were considered to offer a last chance of preventing the creation of a military empire. The editorial, however, noted, 'It is the opinion of some of the most far-seeing and prudent statesmen, that no efforts can now arrest the destiny of Mexico to be annexed to the United States.' Eventually, the *Herald* argued that there was money to be made in Mexican commerce and mines, and the paper came out in favour of 'holding on to Mexico, precisely as we have her at this moment'.[21]

In late December, Senator Lewis Cass, Chairman of the Committee of Military Affairs, introduced a bill requesting an additional ten regiments – or between 10,000 and 20,000 soldiers. A couple of days later, on New Year's Eve 1847, Polk met privately with Cass and Jefferson Davis and decided to dismiss Scott. The following morning, Secretary of War Marcy recommended that General William Butler replace Scott, and Polk's cabinet conferred. Polk believed that 'Gen'l Scott's bad temper, dictatorial spirit, & extreme jealousy' had led to the decision, but news of Scott's dismissal was kept secret from the Senate and the press.[22]

The following Monday, Cass returned to the Senate to argue again for an increase in troop numbers, citing the 'first conquerors of Mexico' and proclaiming that American success was the envy of the 'politicians of the Old World' who had 'denied our power to carry on a war' outside the country. The army had made him proud to know the 'war was the event of the day, and many a steadfast gaze was cast across the Atlantic to watch the prospects and progress of the pattern Republic'. Cass outlined the administration's new policies, sounding as if he had taken advice from French counter-insurgency veterans of the war in Spain. More troops were needed 'to strike an effective blow with concentrated forces at our detached posts … to hold these posts … and to prevent incursions into the territories which we might choose to appropriate to ourselves.' To hold territory already conquered, Cass advised 'the temporary establishment of civil government' and the creation of strongholds manned by numerous forces 'to secure the many and long lines of communication, to disperse and chastise the guerrilla bands which would obstruct them, and to suppress the more powerful aspirings of the people'.[23]

Only by sending more troops to Mexico, Cass reasoned, could peace be secured. 'By making them suffer the usual calamities of war, they must be made to desire peace.' He described what happened in Spain a generation before: 'All experience shows, that in this condition an invaded people will suddenly break out into insurrections, and sometimes display an energy and courage, which they failed to exhibit upon the battlefield.' A Spanish-style insurgency, however, could be prevented with the proper application of force to deter the enemy. Political divisions in the US would only embolden the opposition, whereas 'nothing would conduce more to impress upon the people of that country [Mexico] the necessity of a peace than a unanimous determination in Congress to put forth all the strength of the nation till it is obtained.' Cass and others then called for a quick vote, but it was rejected.[24]

The following day, Calhoun took to the podium in a much-anticipated speech. The senator criticized Polk and his allies and noted the bills under consideration would raise troop levels to about 70,000 men. He asked, 'Where will be the nationality of Mexico? Where her separate existence? … Gone!' He explained that escalation meant much more than soldiers; it would require an entire logistics network of armed immigrants paid by the federal government and accommodating 'those who live by the war – a large and powerful body'. Calhoun asserted that this military body would include the 'numerous contractors, the sutlers, the merchants, the speculators in the lands and mines of Mexico, and all engaged every way, directly or indirectly … in favor of continuing and extending conquest'. Overwhelmed with such military concerns, the legislature would become a mere tool of executive power:

> The conquest of Mexico would add so vast an amount of patronage of this government, that it would absorb the whole power of the States in the Union. This Union would become imperial, and the States mere subordinate corporations. But the evil will not end there. The process

will go on ... All the added power and added patronage which conquest will create, will pass to the Executive.[25]

According to Calhoun, one simply needed to look to Great Britain or Rome for examples of imperial overreach. Calhoun claimed that 'powerful armies' would be permanently required to occupy Mexico because the Mexicans were formidable and still had 'Castilian blood in their veins – the old Gothic, quite equal to the Anglo-Saxon in many respects – in some respects superior'. To avoid the fate of overextended empires, the US needed to abandon the war. 'You are tied at present ... to a corpse. My object is to get rid of it as soon as possible.'[26]

The following day, Cass introduced another bill asking for an additional 20,000 volunteers. Senator John Crittenden responded that if Mexico was 'without any army or government; with here and there only a body of guerrillas, instead of an army to oppose you; what, in the name of Heaven ... do you want with ten thousand more troops?' This, according to the Kentucky senator, would increase troop levels to 100,000 men. Opponents of the force bills believed war hawks were anticipating a protracted guerrilla war and making moves to ensure enough soldiers were on the ground to blanket the entire country. Crittenden understood this, admitting that there 'may be a few skirmishes here and there with parties of guerrillas' but claiming there was no large army to face US forces. Cass revived the legacy of the Peninsular War, noting that 'Portugal and Spain were full of lessons upon this subject'. It was that conflict that 'showed they might gain a battle and get possession of a country without being able to retain it'. He argued that taking the capital 'was one thing, and then to diffuse the forces over it, in various positions, in order to hold the people in subjugation, was another and quite different thing'. The bitter reality, to those listening to Cass's argument, was that he was advocating the same failed strategy the French had employed in Spain:

Our armies in Mexico ... were now to break up as a mass, to spread themselves into various detachments, else it would be impossible to hold the Mexican people in obedience. They would be now exposed to popular tumults, and liable to be cut down by detachments, and still the more, further they would be compelled to march. Besides, it was important that the Mexican people be convinced, by the exhibition of our overwhelming force, that resistance was out of the question. What we wanted was, to produce a moral effect upon the people of Mexico.[27]

Jefferson Davis concurred. The requirements included holding 'towns and posts in Mexico' in order 'to convince the Mexicans that resistance is idle ... [and to] afford protection to all the citizens of Mexico who are ready to recognize our authority and give us supplies'. In addition to confiscating supplies, Davis noted that 'large bodies of men' were needed to 'garrison our posts with forces adequate to make a sortie, if necessary, and not be shut up when any partisan chief chooses to come and sit down before their gates'. The future President of the Confederate States of America outlined plans to follow the Napoleonic maxim by seizing the lucrative Mexican mines. 'Then again, the resources of Mexico must contribute to the support of that army. We cannot afford to keep down anarchy in Mexico at the expense of our treasury.' Davis argued that the 'petty amount of property' held by the ranchers would not cover expenses, but that the 'richest mines' in Potosi would 'furnish a new source of revenue ... without touching private property, and the expenses of the war are borne by Mexico herself'.[28]

Press reports about reinforcements entering the Mexican capital also appeared to be in line with the administration's priorities. Rumours were flying that US soldiers were being positioned to invade San Luis Potosi, 'to open communication between there and Tampico' and possibly even invade Zacatecas – both of which were readying for guerrilla war. To onlookers it appeared the army was on the verge of being enlarged to occupy all of Mexico. 'The Mexicans here will soon begin to believe that we are about to occupy the country in real earnest.'[29]

'Scott's Evil Purposes'

Such were the developments in Washington DC in late 1847 and early 1848. The annual presidential address to Congress upended the entire political spectrum and widened the split in the Democrat Party. War sceptics, who until then had reluctantly passed multiple bills to supply the country's first foreign war with troops and treasure, had been led to believe peace negotiations were ongoing. After 6 December they were informed that not only were there no negotiations, but the administration and its allies in Congress were contemplating the absorption of Mexico by means of a Napoleonic military strategy. Soon afterwards, General Scott was fired. The fact that anti-slavery Whigs and staunch states'-rights pro-slavery Democrats were teaming up to deny Polk a military empire (and the possibility of a protracted guerrilla war in Mexico) demonstrates the precariousness of the situation. Opponents of the war were constantly reacting to the apparent inevitability of annexation, but that quickly changed when Nicholas Trist's letter to Polk arrived on 15

January. In it, Trist explained his decision to disobey orders and continue his efforts at Scott's behest to effect a treaty.

Polk was livid. Even before receiving the letter, Polk had feared that his peace negotiator had 'become the perfect tool of Scott'. The president believed Trist had been manipulated and 'entered into all Scott's hatred of the administration, and [was] lending himself to Scott's evil purposes'. The official report from Trist (dated 6 December) confirmed these suspicions. Polk wrote that it was 'the most extraordinary document I have ever heard from a diplomatic representative'. The normally cautious and circumspect president wrote in his diary that Trist 'admits he is acting without authority and in violation of the positive order recalling him. It is manifest to me that he has become the tool of Gen'l Scott and his menial instrument, and that the paper was written at Scott's insistence and dictation.' The president used terms such as 'indignant' and 'insulting' to describe the betrayal.[30]

News of Trist's insubordination was a blow to annexationists. By mid-January, relations between factions were wearing thin. At the same time as the House of Representatives contemplated the establishment of military posts on the road to Oregon, war opponents put forth two resolutions inquiring, 'Whether or not it is the object and design to subjugate the whole of the Mexican people, and to conquer and hold the whole of the Mexican territory?' On the other side of the Capitol building, the Senate deliberated on Polk's nebulous intentions. North Carolina Whig William P. Mangum, an All-Mexico opponent, asked whether Polk had consulted Scott over his plan to raise more troops. Mangum read part of an order (No. 376) from Scott: 'This army is about to spread itself over, and occupy the Republic of Mexico, until the latter shall sue for peace in terms acceptable to the government of the United States.' Magnum cited Polk's disavowals of conquest and added that Americans were 'not yet ripe for this scheme of wholesale rape and rapine'. Cass responded by saying the 'specific plan of the campaign' should be kept from the public so as to not inform the enemy of the army's movements, and confessed that if the United States 'should swallow Mexico tomorrow, I do not believe it would kill us'. The 1848 presidential candidate believed incorporating Mexico would result in 'one of the most magnificent empires that the world has yet seen – glorious in its prosperity'.[31]

On four separate occasions, South Carolina Democrat Andrew P. Butler called the bills introduced by Polk's allies and the forced contributions policy 'schemes' – arguing that holding Mexico would require at least 'two hundred thousand men'. Such a large army of occupation, Butler added, would not be organized for the business of soldiering, but rather become 'tax-gathers and jailers' for a new empire:

Bonaparte had not more, when he made his first campaign in Italy, than thirty-five or forty thousand men. And what is it that these troops are to be required to do? Not to fight battles. We are told they are not to fight battles. What are they to do? They are to overrun the Mexican states, to disarm the population.[32]

On the other side of the Capitol the same debate ensued. Although the expansion of slavery into newly acquired territories would later become an issue for many northerners, the more immediate concern was the drive towards military empire. Patrick W. Tompkins, a Mississippi Whig who moved to California the following year, invoked the unseen dangers entailed in Mexico's many connections with Spain:

How long was a portion of Spain occupied by the Moorish invader? Pent up in fortified positions for eight hundred years, without conciliating or subduing the neighboring Spaniard, in one prolonged unceasing struggle, unending war, he was at last expelled ... When we look again to their struggle with Spain for political independence, we saw the same implacable spirit displayed ... When every fortified position and stronghold throughout their land was in the occupancy of the royal forces of Spain, still the Mexicans, struggling for national independence, were unsubdued ... Judging from these facts, were we not led to believe, that to maintain our occupation of Mexico in the event of conquest, would require an armed force to be always kept there.[33]

A few days later, the Senate was officially informed of General Scott's dismissal, which led to inquiries demanding the details surrounding the decision. The administration stonewalled, and Cass lied by claiming he knew 'nothing upon this subject' before requesting a vote for more troops. Senator John H. Clarke said the 'veil has been partially lifted' and the All-Mexico scheme was 'unmistakably to view'. He pointed out the resolutions submitted by Polk's proxies: first Dickinson's bill to form governments from Mexican territories, then Hannegan's resolutions 'declaring constitutionality of territorial acquisitions'; after that came a mid-September report from Scott to Secretary Marcy requesting 50,000 more troops in order to execute Order No. 376, as outlined in the mid-December statement, 'the army is about to spread itself over and occupy the Republic of Mexico'. In addition, there was the Cass avowal to seize Mexico before changing his statement. The historical similarities to the Peninsular War were apparent, with the dire result portending imperial overstretch reminiscent of 'emperor Napoleon, in pride and plenitude of his power, impelled by his lust for conquest and glory'.[34]

Over in the House of Representatives, Caleb B. Smith pondered the 'concealed design' and 'wild schemes of conquest and annexation'. He provided his own historical perspective on the parallels between the wars while asking whether 'the history of Europe furnish[es] no precedents to deter us from this course'. The question was rhetorical:

> When Napoleon Bonaparte overran Spain to place his brother on the throne of that country, he placed armies there to retain the power he obtained; and while we imitated his conduct, we should profit by his example, and take warning from his fate. If we shall build up governments in Mexico, and attempt to keep them in power, we should require an army there of fifty thousand men for the next twenty years.[35]

Accompanying rumours of a treaty was unexpected support for Calhoun from influential anti-war newspapers. Denying the war more soldiers had been the original intention of the South Carolina senator. The result of Calhoun's resistance to the creation of a nascent imperial-military state resulted in unusual north-south partnerships which altered the political landscape of the country. In the congressional debates in early 1848, the threat of a protracted military occupation and guerrilla war superseded the concerns of a few anti-slavery northerners over the expansion of slavery. The real potential of that outcome resulted in unlikely alliances between pro-slavery Democrats like Calhoun and northern abolitionists like New Hampshire Senator John P. Hale. Centrists Whigs such as Senator Jacob Miller of New Jersey also voiced concerns about a 'blind destiny' portending potential annexation 'of all Mexico'. In his opinion, in accord with Calhoun's, such an outcome would have turned 'generals and colonels ... into tax collectors'.[36] Senator John Milton Niles, who left the Democrat Party in 1848 and was famous for casting the deciding vote admitting Texas into the Union, warned of the 'fatal step taken by Napoleon in making war with Spain'. That war, like the war they were considering expanding in Mexico, 'would be a war on the people'. The decision to occupy Spain, according to Niles, was Napoleon's 'first step in his fall'. Again and again, the concern was to avoid the fate of Napoleon's army.[37]

This concern was alleviated on 19 February, when the rumoured treaty from Mexico arrived on Polk's desk. After it was sent to the Senate, talk of annexation abruptly ceased. On 10 March that body agreed to incorporate one half of Mexico, with a two-thirds vote (38 to 14) required for ratification. On 30 May, the Treaty of Guadalupe Hidalgo – ratified by the Senate and sent back – was ratified in Mexico. On 1 June in Lagos, Jarauta proclaimed a plan to overthrow the Mexican government for 'betraying' the people by signing a treaty to end the war. Soon afterwards, the Paredes-Jarauta alliance was further revealed after Paredes seized control of Guanajuato in mid-June in a last-ditch attempt to foment an uprising. *El Monitor* asserted that the 'designs of Paredes are believed to be shadowed forth in the following plan … Jarauta promulgated it upon entering Lagos, and he is considered the "right hand man" of the ex-president'.[38] On 4 July 1848, just over two years after the outbreak of war and more than a year after US soldiers landed at Veracruz, the Treaty of Guadalupe Hidalgo was proclaimed in Mexico. For the Americans the war was over. Two weeks later, the Mexican Army quashed any lingering monarchist ambitions by destroying Paredes' insurrectionary forces at Guanajuato. On 19 July, Jarauta was captured and immediately executed for leading a rebellion against federal forces in defiance of the peace made between the US and Mexico. On 1 August, US forces lowered the American flag on their headquarters at the National Palace in Mexico City's central *zocalo*, and the Mexican flag was raised to replace it. A similar ceremony took place in Veracruz that morning.[39]

Lessons and Legacy

By the time US soldiers returned home there was no longer any romantic talk of Spanish conquistadors or the Halls of Montezuma. The American public was tired of such notions. The war had achieved its expansionist purpose and was over without having turned into an ugly and prolonged conflict like Napoleon's campaign in Spain. There were no Zaragozas in Mexico – they only existed in the minds of newspaper editors and columnists eager to sell the conflict. In 1848, republican revolutions in Europe quickly became the front page story in the eastern press; monarchies were out of fashion for the time being. In the American West, the war with Mexico was eclipsed by more pressing endeavours. Mexico remained divided, and American guns and equipment left behind were used by the government to suppress fresh insurrections.[40] It would be some time before stability in Mexico was achieved, but for US opponents of the war it was relief enough to know it would not be American soldiers fighting guerrillas and rancheros on far-flung and isolated roads south of the new border.

Although the laws of war predicated on international norms first established by Grotius and Vattel legally sanctioned the use of violent measures to suppress irregular warfare and non-combatant support of it, this course of action was deemed ill-advised by Winfield Scott and Henry Halleck on the eve of the campaign in Mexico. The right of occupying armies to requisition provisions and material in the theatre of war was long-established, but it was not invoked in Mexico because Scott believed it would not contribute to victory. The US-Mexican War therefore marks a transition in the way armies approached military occupation. The threat of guerrilla warfare forced invading armies to change their methods.

The word 'counter-insurgency' is a twentieth-century term, but the word 'contra-guerrilla' first appeared during the war with Mexico. The latter was most often used to refer to the band of Mexican collaborators aiding the US Army between Mexico City and Veracruz. More importantly, however, the new name showed that guerrilla warfare and formal efforts to confront its tactical efficacy were fast becoming an important facet of a new military paradigm, first prompted by Napoleon's defeat in Spain. By the time the Texas Rangers appeared in central Mexico, American newspapers were using the translated prefix to create the term 'counter-guerrilla' – one step closer to its twentieth-century descendant.

Nor did counter-insurgency itself originate in the Peninsular War. Since ancient times, invading armies have attempted to mitigate asymmetrical warfare by insurgents. Some of the precepts of those strategies, such as maintaining posts along strategic corridors, remain proven and viable methods used by armies today. Despite knowledge of the conflicts prior to the Peninsular War – the French and Indian Wars, the American Revolution, the Vendée and the invasion of Egypt – French officials did not develop a systematized counter-insurgency programme to accompany their invasion and occupation of Spain. Despite French military victories, the unproductive policy of violence and coercion directed at the Spanish people through pillaging, arrests, imprisonment, exile, executions and sieges, did little to benefit the occupier in the long term. Although those methods may have been legally justified, given that the Spanish were engaging in irregular warfare, they did not help to win the compliance of the populace which was necessary to achieve victory.

Since, in the mid-nineteenth century, the Napoleonic War in Spain was the most obvious parallel, Americans took note of what occurred there before invading central Mexico. The result of such study, which included the interwar years of scholarship under Jomini and other contemporary military strategists, was a policy of paying a fair price for goods in occupied areas and respecting the right of private property. This strategy, directly opposed to the military maxim 'war supports war', was essential to winning the compliance of Mexicans and assuaging the fears of the Catholic Church – a powerful institution in Mexico. Furthermore, the enactment of martial law and codes of conduct aimed *at the occupying soldiers* – itself a novel aspect of Scott's command – led to a perception of equal treatment under the law.

Coupled with these novel pacification initiatives was the evolving art of war. Over the interwar period, a professionalizing US Army stressed discipline and order on the Napoleonic model, together with developed tactical training – particularly skirmishing – which reduced the efficacy of both guerrilla fighters and conventional Mexican forces. The introduction of tactical skirmishing training, advocated by Scott during the interwar period, aided US forces in both large and small engagements. Other advantages included the superiority of American firepower, and the evidence that (northern) American horses were more effective in military operations.

Horsepower played an important role in both wars. Horse culture and horse warfare had permeated the Spanish insurgency. That conflict's defining document, the *Corso Terrestre*, is proof of the successful approach of the Spanish at an early point in the war. While it is true that the *Corso* allowed for the seizure of French supplies, the real significance of the document is that it was a blueprint for a cavalry-centric approach to asymmetrical warfare. The success of the Spanish method was so well known that Mexicans tried to mimic it, but they failed because of a lack of both equipment and horses. The French suffered from similar shortages, and the dozens of major sieges conducted deep within Spanish territory – along with the requirement to provide heavy escorts to mounted couriers relaying vital communications – meant that their counter-insurgency efforts were hamstrung. Despite improvements in weapon technology between the end of the Peninsular War and the beginning of the Mexican, horses remained a critical asset in warfare, and the abundant supply of fresh horses in the Texan borderlands offered a major advantage to the US Army.

Although the issue of the legal status of guerrillas continued to pose difficulties to the authorities in future conflicts, the war in Mexico set precedents in dealing with a form of warfare that first manifested itself in Spain. The novelty of guerrilla warfare was a shock to adherents of conventional warfare, and the French reacted to its implementation with stark and oppressive measures. Executions of guerrillas for violating the rules and laws of war resulted in reprisal executions of French soldiers. This widespread violence was studied in the post-war period by military scholars, who examined the social aspects of war waged in an occupied country. Lessons were learned, and a new approach was initiated. That approach, which included leaving the domestic judicial system intact, paying fairly for goods and prosecuting violators of martial law in the invading army, represented a turning point in the history of American warfare. Those lessons were carried into the Civil War by Halleck and other veterans. Some lessons were remembered, others forgotten, but the legacy and gradual systematization of a new military doctrine stemming from the Mexican conflict was a product of the revolutionary changes occurring in nineteenth-century warfare.

Despite attempts by the press to compare the Mexicans to the Spanish, by invoking Zaragoza, the Reconquista, Hernan Cortez or any number of historic Iberian scenarios, the Mexicans themselves were deeply divided at the beginning of the war. Obvious divisions were the political-provincial ones exemplified by breakaway republics like the Yucatán. Other internal divisions, such as the struggle between political factions, had disturbed the Mexican polity for years prior to the American landing at Veracruz. *Moderados*, *Puros* and monarchists were still at each other's throats when Mexico City fell. These divisions are often overlooked in histories lauding the victory of the US military, although their existence does not detract from the success of the small US Army but merely provides a reason why the war was not as violent as it could have been. Had the Mexicans mounted a united resistance, more US soldiers would have died from Mexican bullets than disease.

The Plan of the Citadel, issued by a new *Puro* government in the summer of 1846, explicitly supported the regular army and Santa Anna. Although there were cries for the implementation of organized guerrilla warfare at the beginning of the conflict, the insistence on using conventional forces stymied attempts to redirect the war strategy in its early phases. Politically, it was impossible for Mexicans to dismiss the army in 1846. After the Mexican defeat at Cerro Gordo in the spring of 1847, calls for guerrilla action became more prominent, but by that time demoralization had set in, and only regional efforts to mount guerrilla resistance occurred, in states the US Army wisely avoided. Once the Americans were ensconced in Mexico City, much of the Mexican Army's will to fight was sapped. The claim is not that the Americans won the hearts and minds of all the Mexicans, but only that the will to fight was reduced among an indifferent population by the conventional victories and the benevolent policies of the occupying army.

The emergence of experienced Carlist insurgents from Spain led by Padre Jarauta added to the complicated nature of the war. His appearance in 1847 may have contributed to the impression the guerrilla war was not being conducted for the benefit of common Mexicans, but to reinstate a foreign ruler. That the Europeans managed to do that in 1864 is evidence enough that the monarchists were indeed a powerful force within Mexico, and the arrival of the Carlists concerned both the Americans and Mexican republicans. Having undergone a long and bloody civil war to oust dynastic families from New Spain, Mexicans of various stripes were dubious about the motives of a cadre of foreign-born Spanish fighters. In that regard, it is important to remember that nineteenth-century Mexico was not a homogeneous society, but a large country with centrifugal political-provincial tendencies stemming from its colonial history and compounded by its multitude of indigenous societies with separate histories and languages.

Had the US Army stayed in central Mexico, it is likely that continuing divisions and social unrest within Mexico's diverse population would have been attributed to the conquerors, just as the Spanish were blamed in their administration of New Spain. The potential result of an American annexation of Mexico, however, is a matter of mere academic speculation, given that those machinations were stymied by opponents of military empire such as John C. Calhoun, and of course, Nicholas Trist. Ultimately, the fact that Mexicans did not revolt against the US Army in the manner they had against the Spanish royalists demonstrates the deep level of political divisions among them during the war. The efforts of the Carlists and former president Mariano Paredes to exploit those divisions and reintroduce monarchy ultimately contributed to a lack of support for the insurgency among more nationalist-minded Mexicans.

The emergence of the guerrilla system as a viable mode of warfare was a result of the war in Spain. The Americans, going back hundreds of years, had their own experience of fighting Native Americans who used similar tactics to the Spanish. To a certain extent, the Americans even recognized their own use of guerrilla tactics during the American Revolutionary War. Much of this historical reflection took place during the Mexican War. The Indian wars, then, had changed the way Americans viewed warfare – but in a racial and ideological context that manifested itself most intensely on the frontier. The advent of Spanish (i.e. European) guerrilla warfare legitimized it as a system, because only a system could have been responsible for crippling Napoleon's powerful army. In essence, Indian warfare only *became* guerrilla warfare after its efficacy was proved in Spain. Although it was denigrated as a method of fighting, military planners understood its potential and were forced to factor it into future war plans and military occupations. The war in Mexico, which set the precedent for the US military's counter-insurgency doctrine focused in part on winning the compliance of an occupied population, simultaneously ushered in an era of cavalry-oriented combat to fight tribes waging guerilla war in the newly acquired western territories. The Texans were the veterans of this style of warfare in the antebellum period, and their experience and fighting style was systematized into the developing military architecture of a modernizing US Army.

As much as any nineteenth-century general, Winfield Scott was well versed in military history and Napoleonic maxims. Both Napoleon and Scott believed guerrillas were violating the laws of war by using *irregular* warfare. However, an important difference between the two was that Scott understood guerrilla warfare in the post-Peninsular War era was a military reality and made efforts to mitigate its effectiveness in Mexico by implementing measures both on and off the battlefield. Perhaps the more important deviation from Napoleonic tactics was Scott's encouragement of a treaty of peace, and he more than likely ignored (or pretended not to receive) orders to the contrary. Because Scott disobeyed orders to stop paying for goods, the conclusion is that the general felt Polk and his allies were undermining the war – particularly as it related to annexationists' attempt to invoke the same military maxim that brought ruin to Napoleon's army in Spain. In the end, Scott believed the only way to win a Mesoamerican Peninsular War was to ensure it never started – just as the ancient Chinese military tactician Sun Tzu once wrote, 'The supreme art of war is to subdue the enemy without fighting.' Scott never articulated such a strategy, but the absence of a major guerrilla war in Mexico in the late 1840s is proof that Scott successfully managed to develop the American way of war by deviating from the maxims of the master.

After the advent and proliferation of guerrilla warfare, tactics changed. The US Civil War witnessed both Napoleonic-style battles and guerrilla operations. Improving weaponry, in conjunction with traditional troop formations, made that war particularly bloody. Military analysts prior to the Mexican War predicted the future trajectory of modern warfare, experts like Jomini and Clausewitz asking the pertinent questions. Warfare was becoming more systematized, technical and national. The rules of war, once exclusive to civilized European states, needed to be adapted to deal with the ancient aberration of insurgent warfare.

The contrast between frontier guerrilla warfare and scientific systematized warfare manifested itself most starkly in the Americas – although Napoleon was privy to the alien fighting style of both Cossack and Egyptian on the periphery of European civilization; just as the boundaries of the old Roman Empire stopped short where Parthian horses trod on Eurasian steppes. Guerrilla warfare had always been around – even before El Cid surprised his enemies in small encounters far removed from the sanguinary pitched battles of a later, more 'civilized' era. Educated nineteenth-century warriors understood as much, and they read the classics of earlier epochs to understand both past and present. Guerrilla warfare had indeed been around for a long time.

However, that form of warfare violated an otherwise inviolable law. It forced civilized people to engage in a form of detestable warfare most damaging to those who did not carry the sword but simply supported a just cause by whatever means they could, as non-combatants opposed to foreign occupation.

Napoleon was later admired not because he was brutal, power-hungry or maniacal, but because he was for a time invincible and laid waste to old kingdoms in a struggle which drew most of Europe into conflict with itself. It was only after Napoleon left the old borders of Charlemagne's Frankish empire that he discovered the accepted rules of war no longer applied; this left behind a legacy informing the way of war today, and the timeless warning that when empires stretch too far they succumb to the centrifugal forces acting on the periphery. The legacy prompted by Napoleon's unbridled and fatal ambition was the development of formal counter-insurgency methods – the doctrine created to win the quiet and essential compliance of invaded peoples through asymmetrical principles and policies. Scott's measures of conciliation – the olive branch accompanying the sword – represented the first formal benign counter-insurgency doctrine. It was implemented not only because it was just and civilized, but because it was effective. The advent of, or better yet, the re-emergence of guerrilla warfare in Spain torpedoed the old imperial paradigm that demanded war support war. It had come full circle from Suchet's invocation of ancient Roman wars in Spain. The efficacy of the novel and irregular system of war undermined all the conventional military maxims in two hemispheres, destroyed two empires and, despite evolving technologies, returned us to the asymmetrical age we live in now.

The year 1848 may have marked the demise of Cato the Elder's *bellum se ipsum alet* in the modern era, but it would not be the last time guerrilla warfare appeared to tackle larger and more formidable armies. That ancient system, resurrected in the late eighteenth century and formally unveiled in the hills and valleys of Spain, would continue its slow march into contemporary history by ignoring long-held tactical precepts and in the process undermine imperial forces that at one point seemed as invincible and awe-inspiring as Napoleon's mighty *Grande Armée*. The legacy of Napoleon may have been briefly usurped by attentive students of military history, but guerrilla warfare was not defeated. Its new dawn had just arrived.

Notes

Introduction

1. 'The Guerrilla System in Spain and Mexico,' Sunbury Gazette, Pennsylvania, 19 June 1847.
2. Ibid.
3. Evening Post, New York City, 29 May 1847; Times-Picayune, New Orleans, 10 July 1847; State Indiana Sentinel, Indianapolis, 14 Jan. 1847.
4. For British use of the term system see: Newcastle Weekly Courant, 12 Dec. 1778; Pennsylvania Gazette, 18 Sept. 1782.
5. Evening Mail, London, 4 Dec.1793 (French National Convention, Sitting of 25 Nov.)
6. For British descriptions of American 'insurgents' see: Derby Mercury, 20 Jan. 1775; Caledonian Mercury, 3 June 1775; Newcastle Weekly Courant, 17 Feb. 1776; Bath Chronicle, 22 Feb. 1781. In the 1780s the British also began using the term to describe Irish and Scottish insurrectionists. For British translations of French use of insurgents in the Vendée see: Evening Mail, London, 14 June 1793; The Times, London, 14 June 1793; Ipswich Journal, 3 Jan. 1795.
7. Major Charles W. Elliot, (ed.), 'Some Unpublished Letters of a Roving Soldier-Diplomat: General Winfield Scott's Reports to Secretary of State James Monroe, on conditions in France and England in 1815–1816.' The Journal of the American Military Foundation1, no. 4 (Winter 1937–8): pp. 172–3. Scott to Monroe, Liverpool, 19 March 1816.
8. Morning Chronicle, London, 28 Dec. 1819; Caledonian Mercury, Edinburgh, 1 Jan. 1820; The Examiner, London, 8 April 1821; National Gazette, Philadelphia, 19 April 1821; Buffalo Journal, 21 Aug. 1821; Morning Post, London, 14 Jan. 1822; Derby Mercury, 5 March 1823; Gettysburg Compiler, 25 June 1823; The Times, London, 21 July 1823; Morning Chronicle, 8 May 1823.
9. Louis-Gabriel Suchet, Memoirs of the War in Spain, from 1808 to 1814, vol. 2 (London: Henry Colburn, 1829), p. 196; Moyle Sherer,(ed.),The Duke of Wellington: Military Memoirs of Field Marshal, vol. 2, (Reprint from 1830: Philadelphia: Robert Desilver,1836), pp. iv, 55.
10. Ibid.
11. Newcastle Weekly Courant, 12 Dec. 1778. House of Commons 4 Dec. 1778.
12. Virginia Gazette, Williamsburg, 26 Aug. 1775.
13. Bath Chronicle, 28 June 1781.
14. Russel Weigley, The Partisan War: The South Carolina Campaign of 1780–1782 (Columbia: University of South Carolina Press, 1975); Walter Edgar, Partisans & Redcoats: The Southern Conflict That Turned the Tide of the American Revolution (New York: Harper Collins, 2001); Terry Golway, Washington's General: Nathanael Greene and the Triumph of the American Revolution (New York: Henry Holt and Company, 2006).

15. Pennsylvania Packet, Philadelphia, 12 September 1782. Excerpt cited from the New York Royal Gazette, 17 September 1782. House of Lords, 10 July 1782.
16. Evening Mail, London, 2 Oct. 1793.
17. Emer de Vattel, The Law of Nations, or, Principles of the Law of Nature, Applied to the Conduct and Affairs of Nations and Sovereigns (Philadelphia: T. & J.W. Johnson, Law Booksellers, 1852), pp. 62, 454–6.
18. Ibid. pp. 479–80.
19. Evan T. Sage, Livy with an English Translation in Fourteen Volumes, vol. 9 (London: William Heinemann, 1935), p. 445.
20. Ibid. p. 493.
21. The Times, London, 17 Oct. 1794.
22. Jonathan North, 'General Hoche and Counterinsurgency,' The Journal of Military History 67, no. 2 (April 2003), p. 530.
23. Howard G. Brown, Ending the French Revolution: Violence, Justice, Terror, and Repression from the Terror to Napoleon (Charlottesville: University of Virginia Press, 2006), p. 237.
24. O'Meara, Napoleon at St Helena, vol. 2, p. 37.
25. North,'General Hoche and Counterinsurgency,' JMH, pp. 530–1.
26. Ibid. pp. 532–5
27. Ibid. p. 534.
28. Ibid. p. 535–6
29. Ibid. p. 531. Thomas Auguste le Roy de Grandmaison, The small war or treaty of the service of the troops in campaigns, 1756; Armand-François de la Croix, Treaty of the small war in the French campaign, 1752. See: John Grenier, The First Way of War: American War Making on the Frontier, 1607-1814 (Cambridge University Press, 2005).
30. Walter Laqueur, 'The Origins of Guerrilla Doctrine.' Journal of Contemporary History 10, no. 3 (July 1975), pp. 341–5.
31. John Elting, Swords around the Throne: Napoleon's Grande Armée (London: Phoenix Giant, Reprint, 1997), p. 548.
32. Albert-Jean Rocca, Memoirs of the War of the French in Spain (London: John Murray, 1815), pp. 189–90.
33. The Black Legend (la leyenda negra española) traced its origins to anti-Catholic and anti-Spanish propaganda disseminated in the Spanish-ruled Netherlands in the sixteenth century, whence it spread to England. The English opposed Spain's dominance in European affairs during the Eighty Years' War (1568–1648) and were eager to perpetuate the belief that the Spanish were a corrupt and backward people. Such beliefs appeared during the Latin American wars of independence (1808–33) and reappeared in updated form on the eve of the Mexican War under the authorship of William H. Prescott (1796–1859). See: Richard L. Kagan, 'Prescott's Paradigm: American Historical Scholarship and Decline of Spain.' The American Historical Review 101, no. 2 (Apr. 1996): pp. 423–46; William H. Prescott, The History of the Conquest of Mexico (New York: The Modern Library, 1843). See also: See also: Christopher Schmidt-Nowara, 'The Broken Image: The Spanish Empire in the United States after 1898,' in Endless Empire: Spain's Retreat, Europe's Eclipse, America's Decline (Alfred W. McCoy, Josep M. Fradera, Stephen Jacobson, ed. Madison: University of Wisconsin Press, 2012): pp. 160–6.
34. Ibid. pp. 224–6.

35. Vivant Denon, Travels in Upper and Lower Egypt in Company with Several Divisions of the French Army, During the Campaigns of General Napoleon in that Country, vol. 1 (London: T.N. Longman and O. Rees, 1803), pp. 179–80, 339.

36. Denon, Travels in Upper and Lower Egypt, vol. 1, 209; Institut d'Égypte, Memoirs Relative to Egypt, Written in that Country During the Campaigns of General Bonaparte, In the Years 1798 and 1799 (London: T. Gillet, 1800), pp. 297–9.

37. W.S. Hendrix, 'Military Tactics in the "Poem of the Cid".' Modern Philology 20, no. 1 (Aug. 1922), p. 45.

38. Ibid. pp. 45–8.

39. Thomas Bourke, A Concise History of the Moors in Spain, From the Invasion of that Kingdom to the Final Expulsion from it (London: J. Rivington, 1811), pp. 215–16.

40. Ibid. pp. 141–3. One of the earliest English accounts of El Cid is Robert Southey's 1808 Chronicle of the Cid.

41. Francisco Luis Díaz Terrejón, 'El movimiento guerrillero en España durante la ocupación napoleónica (1808–1814)'. Iberoamericana (2001-) Nueva época, Año 8, no. 31 (Sept. 2008), p. 129. For a contemporary look at Iberian-African interaction, see: Geoffrey Jensen, 'Military consequences of cultural perceptions: The Spanish army in Morocco, 1912–1927,' The Journal of the Middle East and Africa 8, no. 2 (2017): pp. 135–50. The Spanish 'erroneously attributed a "native" quality to military practices that Europeans themselves had brought to the Maghreb, such as the razzia [raiding] in its modern, colonial form.'

42. Antoine-Henri Jomini, Life of Napoleon, with Notes by H.W. Halleck, vol. 3 (New York: D. Van Nostrand, 1864), p. 227.

Part I: The War in Spain

1. Vermont Aurora, Vergennes, 24 March 1825. 'Character of Bolivar and other South American Commanders'. From Gaspard Théodore Mollien's Travels in the Republic of Colombia: in the years 1822 and 1823 (London: C. Knight, 1824). See: Philip Matysak, Sertorius and the Struggle for Spain (Barnsley, UK: Pen and Sword, 2013); Daniel Varga, The Roman Wars in Spain: The Military Confrontation with Guerrilla Warfare (Barnsley, UK: Pen and Sword, 2015).

2. William F.P. Napier, History of the War in the Peninsula and in the South of France, vol.1 (London: Thomas and William Boone, 1828), p. 39; Faustino Casamayor, Zaragoza 1808, 1809 (Zaragoza: Editorial Comuniter: Institución Fernando el Católico (IFC), 2008), p. 51. 8 May 1808.

3. Napoleon Bonaparte, The Confidential Correspondence of Napoleon Bonaparte with His Brother Joseph, Sometime King of Spain, vol. 1 (New York: D. Appleton and Company, 1856), pp. 318–20. Napoleon to Joseph, 18 April 1808; Napoleon to Joseph, 6 May 1808; Napoleon to Joseph, 11 May 1808. Subsequently referred to as Correspondence.

4. Suchet, Memoirs of the War in Spain, from 1808 to 1814, vol. 1, pp. 44–5.

5. Ibid. p. 46.

6. Manuel Moreno Alonso, La batalla de Bailén: el surgimiento de una nación (Madrid: Silex, 2008), pp. 109–10.

7. Louise François Lejeune, Memorias del general Lejeune, 1792–1813 (Zaragoza: IFC, 2015), p. 67.

8. Correspondence, pp. 344, 351–2. Napoleon to Joseph, 1 Aug. 1808; Napoleon to Joseph. 1 Sept. 1808; Napoleon to Joseph, 8, 9 Sept. 1808.

9. Correspondence, pp. 354–64. Plan, 9 Sept.1808; Joseph to Napoleon, 14 Sept. 1808; Napoleon to Joseph, 16 Sept. 1808.
10. Correspondence, p. 365. Napoleon to Joseph, 13 Oct. 1808.
11. Correspondence, p. 326. Napoleon to Joseph. 13 July 1808; Gazeta de Zaragoza, 14 Aug. 1808.BNE.
12. Diego Saglia, 'O My Mother Spain!' The Peninsular War, Family Matters, and the Practice of Romantic Writing'. ELH 65, no. 2 (Summer 1998), p. 376; Herminio Lafoz Rabaza (ed.): Ramón Cadena: Los Sitios de Zaragoza (Zaragoza: IFC, 2017), p. 19.
13. Casamayor: Zaragoza (IFC), pp. 198, 224, 7 Jan., 10 Feb. (1809).
14. David A. Bell, The First Total War: Napoleon's Europe and the Birth of Warfare as We Know It (Boston: Houghton Mifflin, 2007), pp. 282–3.
15. Suchet, Memoirs, p. 7.
16. Adam Knobler, 'Holy Wars, Empires, and the Portability of the Past: The Modern Uses of Medieval Crusades', Comparative Studies in Society and History 48, no. 2 (April 2006), p. 297.
17. Bell, The First Total War, p. 287.
18. Saglia, 'O My Mother Spain!' ELH 65, no. 2 (Summer 1998), pp. 364-7.
19. Tone, The Fatal Knot, p. 70.
20. Quoted in: Ramón Guirao Larrañaga, Guerrilleros y Patriotas en el Altoaragón (1808–1814) (Huesca: Editorial Pirineo, 2000), p. 9. The full title of the Reglamento was: Regulation that the King Our Lord don Fernando VII and in his Real name the Central Supreme Board of government of the Kingdom has sent to send. The Supreme Central Junta (Junta Suprema Central) was established 25 September 1808.
21. Tone, The Fatal Knot, p. 71.
22. Bell, The First Total War, p. 287.
23. Esdaile, Fighting Napoleon, p. 106.
24. See: Alain Berouche, Pirates, flibustiers et corsaires de René Duguay-Troüin à Robert Surcouf; Le droit et les réalités de la guerre de Course (Saint-Malo: Éditions Pascal Galodé, 2010); Henning Hillmann, The Corsairs of Saint-Malo: Network Organization of a Merchant Elite under the Ancien Régime (New York: Columbia University Press, 2021). The French word corsaire derives from the Latin cursus, which means 'course', as in a journey.
25. Espoz y Mina wrote that the authority of the Corso Terrestre extended from July 1809 to late March 1810, after which the guerrillas were officially absorbed into the Spanish Army. He noted, 'There were no secretaries, no staff, nor any specific point where the reports of the events were deposited.' There were 'no documents with which to support them', and the only means of record was 'preserved in the memory of the country'. Francisco Espoz y Mina, Memorias del general Don Francisco Espoz y Mina, escritas por el mismo (Madrid: M. Rivadeneyra, 1851), vol. 1, pp. 9–16.
26. Thomask K. Heebøll-Holm, Ports, Piracy, and Maritime War: Piracy in the English Channel and the Atlantic, c. 1280–c. 1330 (Amsterdam: Brill, 2013), p. 137; Vattel, The Law of Nations, pp. 319–20.
27. Archivo Histórico Nacional (AHN), 'Órdenes, decretos, reglamentos, proclamas y manifiesto, Abril de 1809' ES.28079.AHN/1.1.19.4//ESTADO,9,D, Article #12. http://pares.culturaydeporte.gob.es/inicio.html
28. Bell, The First Total War, p. 287.
29. Larrañaga, Guerrilleros y Patriotas, p. 9.

30. Ibid.

31. AHN: 'Órdenes…, Abril de 1809' ES.28079.AHN/1.1.19.4//ESTADO,9,D, Articles 1, 2, 3.

32. Ibid. (AHN) Article 4.

33. Larrañaga, Guerrilleros y Patriotas, p. 13.

34. AHN: 'Órdenes…, Abril de 1809' ES.28079.AHN/1.1.19.4//ESTADO,9,D, Article 11.

35. Correspondence vol. 2, pp. 30–9. Napoleon to Joseph, 15, 16 Jan. 1809.

36. Don W. Alexander, 'French Military Problems in Counterinsurgent Warfare in Northeastern Spain, 1808–1813', Military Affairs 40, no. 3 (Oct. 1976), p. 118 (JMH).

37. Moyle Sherer (ed.), The Duke of Wellington: Military Memoirs of Field Marshal, vol. 1 (Philadelphia: Robert Desilver, 1836), pp. 157–8. Wellington cites 50,000 Spanish guerrillas. (Ibid. p. 159)

38. Florentino Hernández Girbal, Juan Martín, El Empecinado: Terror de los francese (Madrid: Ediciones Lira, 1985); Andrés Cassinello Pérez, Juan Martín, 'El Empecinado', o el amor a la libertad (Madrid: Editorial San Martín, 1995). The nom de guerre 'Empecinado' came from his home town, Castrillo de Duero, where nearby streams were filled with black and decomposing mud called pecina.

39. Girbal, Juan Martín, El Empecinado, p. 159; Sherer (ed.), Wellington Memoirs vol. 2, p. 56. See: Rocca, Memoirs of the War of the French in Spain, p. 324. 'Some Spanish partisans had been on the point of taking King Joseph prisoner in one of his country houses near Madrid.'; The Morning Post, London, 4 October 1810. An account of a July raid against King Joseph 'at his country seat near Madrid'.

40. Benito Pérez Galdós, Juan Martín el Empecinado (1874) (Madrid: Sucesores de Hernando, 1908), pp. 54–5.

41. Emilio Becerra de Becerra, Las hazañas de unos lanceros: Historia del Regimiento de Caballería I de Lanceros de Castilla, según los papeles de Don Julián Sánchez García, 'El Charro', (Salamanca: Diputación Provincial de Salamanca, 1999); Sherer (ed.), Wellington Memoirs, vol. 2, p. 56.

42. Rocca, Memoirs of the War of the French in Spain, p. 220.

43. Margaret, Duchess of Newcastle (Charles Harding Firth, ed.), The Life of William Cavendish, Duke of Newcastle, To which is added the true relation of my birth, breeding, and life (London: G. Routledge & Sons, 1890), pp. 60–2.

44. Francisco Espoz y Mina, Memorias del general Don Francisco Espoz y Mina, escritas por el mismo (Madrid: M. Rivadeneyra, 1851), vol. 2, p. 30, vol. 1, pp. 73, 90, 241.

45. Don. W. Alexander, 'French Replacement Methods during the Peninsular War, 1808–1814', Military Affairs 44, no. 4 (Dec. 1980), p. 193 (JMH).

46. Correspondence vol. 2, p. 69. Napoleon to Clarke, 15 Aug. 1809.

47. Rocca, Memoirs of the War of the French in Spain, p. 323.

48. Rocca, Memoirs of the War of the French in Spain, pp. 186–7.

49. Correspondence vol. 2, pp. 91–4. Napoleon to Berthier, 19, 20 Dec. 1809, 11 Jan. 1810; Michael Ross, The Reluctant King: Joseph Bonaparte, p. 171.

50. Correspondence vol. 2, p. 104. Napoleon to Berthier, 8 Feb. 1810. See: Ibid. pp. 114–16: Napoleon to Berthier 16 March 1810; Imperial Decree, 17 April 1810; 127: Decree, 29 May 1810.

51. The Military Exploits, pp. 61–2.

52. Sherer, Wellington Memoirs, vol. 2, p. 57.

53. Tone, The Fatal Knot, pp. 101–2.

54. Sherer, Wellington Memoirs, vol. 1, pp. 157–8.
55. Rocca, Memoirs of the War, pp. 193–4.
56. Rocca, Memoirs of the War, pp. 337–40.
57. Ibid. pp. 340–1.
58. Observer, London, 19 Aug. 1810.
59. Correspondence vol. 2, pp. 132–6. Napoleon to Berthier, 8 Aug1810; Napoleon to Berthier, 19 July 1810; Napoleon to Clarke, 6 Aug. 1810.
60. Caledonian Mercury, Edinburgh, 19 Dec. 1808. Translation of the French 'Tenth Bulletin of the Army of Spain'.
61. Tone, The Fatal Knot, pp. 84–5.
62. The Military Exploits, pp. 97–8.
63. Pérez, Juan Martín, 'El Empecinado', p. 117; Alexander, 'French Replacement Methods', pp. 193–4 (JMH).

Chapter 1: Pyrrhic Victories: Costly Sieges and Attrition

1. Henry Halleck, Military Art and Science; or Course of Instruction in Strategy, Fortification, Tactics of Battles, &c; Embracing the Duties of Staff Infantry, Cavalry, Artillery, and Engineers, Adapted to the Use of Volunteers and Militia (New York: D. Appleton & Company, 1846), pp. 62–3.
2. James Turner Johnson, 'Maintaining the Protection of Non-combatants', in (Syse and Reichburg) Ethics, Nationalism, and Just War: Medieval and Contemporary Perspectives (Washington DC: Catholic University of America Press, 2007), pp. 163, 179.
3. The Advocate of Peace 2, no. 14 (March 1839), p. 235.
4. Vattel, The Law of Nations, pp. 478–85.
5. Halleck, Military Art and Science, p. 311.
6. Ibid., p. 63.
7. Suchet, Memoirs, pp. 119–21.
8. Ibid., p. 116.
9. Alexander,'French Military Problems', p. 120, (JMH); Suchet, Memoirs, p.69.
10. Alexander, 'French Military Problems', p. 118. (JMH); Charles Oman, A History of the Peninsular War, vol. 3 (Oxford: Clarendon Press, 1908), pp. 13–14.
11. Correspondence vol. 2, pp.179, 164, Napoleon to Berthier, 15 April 1811; Napoleon to Berthier, 9 March 1811.
12. Suchet, Memoirs vol. 2, pp. 99–100.
13. Oman, A History of the Peninsular War, vol. 4, pp. 524–5.
14. The Times, London, 18 Sept. 1811.
15. Charles Francis Adams (ed.), Memoirs of John Quincy Adams, Comprising Portions of His Diary from 1795 to 1848, vol. 2 (Philadelphia: J.B. Lippincott & Co., 1874), pp. 299–300. 30 Aug. 1811.
16. Quoted in: Michael Glover, The Peninsular War, 1807–1814 (London: Penguin Books, 1974), p. 169.
17. Gazeta del Gobierno de México, 27 July 1811 (No. 89); 24 Sept. 1811 (No. 114). BNE.
18. Suchet, Memoirs, vol. 2, pp. 118–29, 141.
19. Glover, The Peninsular War, p. 120; The Times, London, 4 Dec. 1812.
20. David Gates, The Napoleonic Wars, 1803–1815 (London: Arnold, 1997), p. 184.
21. Halleck, Military Art and Science, pp. 83, 308–9.
22. Suchet, Memoirs, p. 51.

23. Espoz y Mina, Memorias del general Don Francisco Espoz y Mina, escritas por el mismo, vol. 2, p. 9.

24. Alexander, 'French Military Problems', p. 118. (JMH); Suchet, Memoirs, pp. 56–7.

25. Alexander, 'French Military Problems', p. 119. (JMH); Alexander, 'French Replacement Methods', p. 192.

26. Alexander, 'French Replacement Methods', pp. 192–3. (JMH).

27. Ibid.

28. Freeman's Journal, Dublin, 2 April 1812.

29. Morning Chronicle, London, 28 March 1812.

30. Espoz y Mina, Memorias, vol. 1, p. 122. The proclamation is dated 8 May 1811. Mina used blockades on a number of different towns and cities, such as Jaca, but his focus was Pamplona. See also: Rocca, Memoirs of the War, p. 197.

31. Morning Chronicle, London, 28 March 1812; Freeman's Journal, Dublin, 2 April 1812.

32. Correspondence vol. 2, pp. 185–8, 194 Napoleon to Berthier, 10 June 1811; Napoleon to Berthier, 19 Nov. 1811; Tone, The Fatal Knot, pp. 121–3.

33. Elting, Swords around the Throne, p. 514.

34. Correspondence vol. 2, pp. 194–5, 224, Napoleon to Berthier, 20 Nov. 1811; Napoleon to Berthier, 16 March 1812; Ross, The Reluctant King, p. 203; Rocca, Memoirs of the War of the French in Spain, pp. 105–6. Rocca's observations were verified by reports in London. See: Observer, London, 17 May 1812. Intelligence on troop numbers dated 22 April 1812.

35. Pérez, Juan Martín, 'El Empecinado', pp. 200–3. Letter to Joseph dated 25 May 1812.

36. Tone, The Fatal Knot, pp. 128–9; Bell: The First Total War, p. 289.

37. Alexander, 'French Military Problems', pp. 118–19. (JMH).

38. David Gates, The Spanish Ulcer: A History of the Peninsular War (London: George Allen & Unwin, 1986), p. 35. Elting states that guerrillas 'were Wellington's main source of military intelligence'. (Elting, Swords Around the Throne, p. 514).

39. Oman, A History of the Peninsular War, vol. 4, p. 593.

40. Lords Commissioners' Speech, Opening Ceremony of Parliament (House of Lords and House of Commons), 7 Jan. 1812, Hansard's Parliamentary Debates, vol. 21, columns 2–3.

41. Jean Hanoteau (ed.), Memoirs of General de Caulaincourt, Duke of Vicenza, 1812–1813 (London: Cassell and Company Limited, 1935), p. 441.

42. Espoz y Mina, Memorias del general Don Francisco Espoz y Mina, vol. 2, pp. 6–7.

43. Napoleon, Memoirs, vol. 3, pp. 277, 300.

44. Antoine-Henri Baron de Jomini, The Art of War (1838) (Reprint: Philadelphia: J.B. Lippincott & Co., 1862), p. 32. Antoine-Henri Baron de Jomini, Traité des Grandes Opérations Militaire (Paris: Giguet et Michaud, 1805); The Art of War (Précis de l'Art de la Guerre: Des Principales Combinaisons de la Stratégie, de la Grande Tactique et de la Politique Militaire) (Brussels: Meline, Cans et Compagnie, 1838).

45. Colonel J.J. Graham, On War: By General Carl von Clausewitz (London: N. Trübner & Co., 1873), pp. 12, 52. Carl von Clausewitz, On War (Vom Kriege) (Berlin: 1832–5); Clausewitz, The Russian Campaign of 1812, p. 1843.

46. Marquess Richard Wellesley, House of Lords, 12 March 1813, House of Lords, Hansard's Parliamentary Debates, vol. 25, column 47, pp. 30–2. 'Conduct of the War in the Peninsula'.

47. The Times, London, 12 Dec. 1840.

Chapter 2: The 'Second Saragossa'

1. New York Herald, New York City, 9 1847.
2. Green-Mountain Freeman, Montpelier, Vermont, 22 April 1847.
3. Wilmington Journal, North Carolina, 18 June 1847.
4. The Liberator, Boston, 15 Oct. 1847.
5. Buffalo Commercial, Buffalo, New York, 7 July 1846.
6. Mississippi Free Trader, Natchez, Mississippi, 10 June 1847.
7. New York Herald, 5 May 1847.
8. Robert A. Johannsen, To the Halls of the Montezumas: The Mexican War in the American Imagination (New York: Oxford University Press, 1985), pp. 74–6; Joel Tyler Headley, The Life of Winfield Scott (New York: Charles Scribner, 1861); Sir Archibald Alison (1792–1867), History of Europe from the Commencement of the French Revolution in 1789 to the Restoration of the Bourbons in 1815, 10 vols. (1833– 1843); Charles William Vane (1778–1854), Narrative of the Peninsular War (1828); William Francis Patrick Napier (1785–1860), History of the War in the Peninsula and the South of France, from the Year 1807 to the Year 1814, 6 vols. (1828–40).
9. Buffalo Commercial, 9 Oct. 1847. 'When Will the War End?'
10. Somerset Herald, Pennsylvania, 15 Dec. 1846; The Buffalo Commercial, 21 Nov. 1846. During the siege of Monterrey another Agustina-like female defending her city made its way into press accounts. Her name was Dos Amades, and she had apparently commanded a company of Mexican lancers. (Johannsen: To the Halls of the Montezumas, p. 137).
11. Natchez Weekly Courier, Mississippi, 14 Oct. 1846.
12. Washington Union, Washington DC, 6 Oct1847; Daily Picayune, New Orleans, Louisiana, 22 April 1847; The Tennessean, Nashville, 19 Feb1847. Santa Anna was also known as the 'Napoleon of the West', or the 'Napoleon of Mexico'.
13. Baltimore Commercial, Maryland, 26 June 1847; Portage Sentinel, Ravenna, Ohio, 14 July 1847; New York Post, 19 1847.
14. Vicksburg Whig, Mississippi, 17 Nov. 1847.
15. House Executive Document No. 60, US Congressional Documents: Library of Congress, (US Serial Set No. 520), p. 1223. Winfield Scott (Mexico City) to Secretary of War William L. Marcy (Washington DC), 24 Feb. 1848. Subsequently referred to as HED No. 60. (LOC).
16. Johannsen, To the Halls of the Montezumas, p. 245; William H. Prescott, The History of the Conquest of Mexico (New York: The Modern Library, 1843), p. 155.
17. Weekly National Intelligencer, 31 July 1847. Excerpt cited from De Bow's Commercial Review of the South and West vol. 3, no. 6 (June).
18. Hartford Courant, Connecticut, 5 Jan. 1847.
19. Weekly National Intelligencer, Washington DC, 6 Feb1847.
20. Ibid. (Often spelled 'Tlaxcalans').
21. Louisville Morning Courier, Kentucky, 25 Dec. 1846.
22. Free Soil Courier and Liberty Gazette, Burlington, 1 April 1847.
23. Green-Mountain Freeman, Montpelier, Vermont, 22 April 1847.
24. Louisville Morning Courier, Kentucky, 26 May 1847.
25. New York Herald, New York City, 2 June 1846.
26. Evening Post, New York City, 24 Dec.1847.
27. State Indiana Sentinel, Indianapolis, 25 March 1847.
28. New Orleans Weekly Delta, 4 Jan. 1847.

29. Kalida Venture, Ohio, 9 July 1847. (Quoting the Richmond Enquirer.)
30. Ibid.
31. New York Herald, New York City, 5 May 1847.
32. Mississippi Free Trader, Natchez, 10 June 1847.
33. Scott, Memoirs, pp. 423–4.
34. Ulysses S. Grant, Personal Memoirs of U.S. Grant, vol. 1 (New York: Charles L. Webster & Company, 1885), p. 130; John S.D. Eisenhower, Agent of Destiny: The Life and Times of General Winfield Scott (New York: The Free Press, 1997), p. 246; Scott, Memoirs, p. 429.
35. The Liberator, Boston, 15 Oct. 1847.
36. Weekly National Intelligencer, Washington DC, 15 May 1847.
37. Ibid. Also quoting excerpts from El Republicano, Diario del Gobierno de la Republica Mexicana and El Monitor.
38. Diario del Gobierno de la Republica Mexicana, Mexico City, 15 Aug. 1847 (No. 155). BNE.
39. Louisville Morning Courier, 25 Oct 1847; The Tennessean, Nashville, 30 April 1847.
40. Daily American Star, Mexico City, 24 Nov. 1847. BLAC. Quoted from 9 Aug. 1847.
41. Poughkeepsie Journal, New York, 8 May 1847.
42. Freeman's Journal, Dublin, 31 July 1847.

Chapter 3: Napoleon's Student: Winfield Scott
 1. Lieutenant General Winfield Scott, Memoirs (New York: Sheldon & Co., 1864), p. 404.
 2. Benjamin J. Swenson, '"Measures of Conciliation": Winfield Scott, Henry Halleck, and the Origins of US Army Counterinsurgency Doctrine', Journal of Military History 86, no. 4 (Oct. 2022): pp. 859–81. See also: Andrew James Birtle, U.S. Army Counterinsurgency and Contingency Operations, 1860–1941 (Washington DC: United States Army Center of Military History, 1998), p. 101.
 3. Scott, Memoirs, pp. 12-13.
 4. Johnson, Winfield Scott: The Quest for Military Glory (Lawrence: University Press of Kansas, 1998), pp. 31–3, 45.
 5. Major Charles W. Elliot (ed.), 'Some Unpublished Letters of a Roving Soldier-Diplomat: General Winfield Scott's Reports to Secretary of State James Monroe, on conditions in France and England in 1815–1816'. The Journal of the American Military Foundation 1, no. 4 (winter 1937/8), p. 165.
 6. Scott, Memoirs, pp. xx–xxi.
 7. Elliot, 'Some Unpublished Letters', pp. 166–8. Winfield Scott to James Monroe, Secretary of State. Paris, 28 September 1815; Scott, Memoirs, p. 157.
 8. Elliot, 'Some Unpublished Letters', pp. 170–1. Ney was executed by firing squad on 7 Dec. 1815.
 9. Ibid. pp. 172–3. Scott to Monroe, Liverpool, 19 March 1816.
10. See: Harris Gaylord Warren, 'The Origin of General Mina's Invasion of Mexico', The Southwestern Historical Quarterly 42, no. 1 (July 1938): pp. 1–20.
11. Thomas Auguste le Roy de Grandmaison, The small war or treaty of the service of the troops in campaigns, 1756; Armand-François de la Croix, Treaty of the small war in the French campaign, 1752. See John K. Mahon, 'Anglo-American Methods of Indian Warfare, 1676–1794', The Mississippi Valley Historical Review 45, no. 2 (Sept. 1958): pp. 254–75.

12. See: Todd W. Braisted, Grand Forage 1778: The Battleground Around New York City (Yardley, PA: Westholme Publishing, 2016); Walter Edgar, Partisans & Redcoats: The Southern Conflict That Turned the Tide of the American Revolution (New York: Harper Collins, 2001); Terry Golway, Washington's General: Nathanael Greene and the Triumph of the American Revolution (New York: Henry Holt and Company, 2006).
13. Johnson, Winfield Scott, pp. 67–8. 'The end result was a 360-page text, Rules and Regulations for the Field Exercise and Manoeuvres of Infantry (usually referred to simply as the 1815 Regulations).'
14. Ibid.p. 78. See: Eisenhower, Agent of Destiny, p. 124. Eisenhower called West Point 'the core of Scott's very being'.
15. Michael A. Bonura, 'A French-Inspired Way of War: French Influence on the U.S. Army from 1812 to the Mexican War', Army History, no. 90 (Winter 2014), pp. 6–7. See: Michael A. Bonura, Under the Shadow of Napoleon: French Influence on the American Way of Warfare from Independence to the Eve of World War II (New York: New York University Press, 2012).
16. Bonura, 'A French-Inspired Way of War', pp. 8, 17–18; Simon Gay de Vernon, A Treatise on the Science of War and Fortification Composed for the use of the Imperial Polytechnick School, and Military Schools; and Translated for the War Department, for the use of the United States: To Which is Added A Summary of the Principles and Maxims of Grand Tactics and Operations by John Michael O'Conner, vol. 2 (New York: J. Seymour,1817).
17. John Michael O'Conner, A Summary of the Principles and Maxims of Grand Tactics and Operations (found in de Vernon's Treatise, vol. 2) (New York: J. Seymour, 1817), pp. 386, 467.
18. O'Conner, A Summary of the Principles and Maxims, pp. 415, 428, 430.
19. Ibid. p. 447.
20. Ibid. pp. 449–50, 467.
21. Ibid. pp. 480–90.
22. Ibid. p. 490.
23. Johnson, Winfield Scott, pp. 75–6; Darrow Pierce and Winfield Scott, Scott's Militia Tactics; Comprising the Duty of the Infantry, Light-Infantry, and Riflemen (Second Edition) (Hartford: Oliver D. Cooke, 1821), p. iii.
24. Johnson, Winfield Scott, p. 79; Scott, Memoirs, p. 206.
25. Scott et al, Abstract of Infantry Tactics; Including Exercises and Manoeuvres of Light Infantry and Riflemen; for the Use of the Militia of the United States (Boston: Hilliard, Gray, Little, and Wilkens, 1830), p. 14. There are two numbering systems for the pages, but it appears the ones at the bottom are more accurate.
26. See: Bonura, 'A French-Inspired Way of War', pp. 14–16.
27. Frank Allaben, John Watts de Peyster, vol. 2 (New York: Frank Allaben Genealogical Society, 1908), p. 197.
28. Scott, Abstract of Infantry Tactics, p. 173. 'Intervals between Ranks' Nos 1752, 1753.
29. Ibid. pp. 195, 173. Nos 1754, 1755, 1756.
30. Ibid. pp. 175–6. The sheet music for the bugle appears on p. 175.
31. Scott, Memoirs, p. 415.
32. Sir George Charles D'Aguilar (ed./transl.), The Officer's Manual: Military Maxims of Napoleon (Dublin: Richard Milliken and Son, 1831). Napoleon's Maxims was often advertised next to Scott's Tactics during the war. See: New York Herald, 29 April 1847.

33. D'Aguilar(ed./transl.),The Officer's Manual, pp. 9–18, 56. Maxims 5, 12, 13, 16, 17, 70.

34. Ibid. pp. 247–8.

35. Laqueur, 'The Origins of Guerrilla Doctrine', Journal of Contemporary History, p. 350. See: Christopher Bassford, Clausewitz in English: The Reception of Clausewitz in Britain and America, 1815–1945 (New York: Oxford University Press, 1994).

36. Laqueur, 'The Origins of Guerrilla Doctrine', pp. 350–1.

37. Jomini, The Art of War, pp. 66, 114.

38. Ibid. pp. 178, 323.

39. Ibid. pp. 252–5.

40. Ibid. p. 137.

41. Ibid. pp. 313–14.

42. Ibid. p. 355.

43. William B. Skelton, 'Army Officers Attitudes toward Indians, 1830–1860', The Pacific Northwest Quarterly 67, no. 3 (July 1976), p. 114. See Robin F.A. Fabel, 'The Laws of War in the 1812 Conflict', Journal of American Studies 14, no. 2 (Aug. 1980): pp. 199–218.

44. Johnson, Winfield Scott, p. 113.

45. Myer M. Cohen, Notices of Florida and the Campaigns (Charleston: Burger & Honour, 1836), pp. 193, 214–15.

46. Ibid. p. 222.

47. Times-Picayune, New Orleans, 21 Aug. 1841.

48. Justin H. Smith, 'The Mexican Recognition of Texas', The American Historical Review 16, no. 1 (Oct. 1910), pp. 37–8. Smith quoted the Revista Económica y Comerical de la República Mexicana, 15 Jan. 1844; Justin H. Smith, 'La Republica de Rio Grande', *The American Historical Review* 25, no. 4 (July 1920): pp. 660–75.

49. Henry W. Halleck, Military Art and Science; or Course of Instruction in Strategy, Fortification, Tactics of Battles (New York: Appleton & Company, 1846), pp. 59–60, 91; Swenson, '"Measures of Conciliation": Winfield Scott, Henry Halleck, and the Origins of US Army Counterinsurgency Doctrine', Journal of Military History 86, no. 4 (Oct. 2022), pp. 859–61.

50. Jomini, Life of Napoleon, with Notes by H.W. Halleck, vol, 1 (New York: D. Van Nostrand, 1864), pp. 607–8. Antoine-Henri Jomini, Vie politique et militaire de Napoléon (Paris: Chez Anselin, 1827).

51. 'Reviewed Work(s): Life of Napoleon by Baron Jomini and H. W. Halleck', The North American Review 99, no. 205 (1864), p. 574. See: Swenson, 'Measures of Conciliation', JMH 86, no. 4 (Oct. 2022), pp. 874–81. Halleck's Mexican War experience with insurgents may have also informed his Civil War consultations with Francis Lieber when developing the Lieber Code. See: John D. Yates and Henry Halleck. 'Insurgents on the Baja Peninsula: Henry Halleck's Journal of the War in Lower California, 1847–1848', California Historical Quarterly 54, no. 3 (1975): pp. 221–44.

52. Halleck, Military Art and Science, pp. 47–8, 55, 229.

53. Ibid. Halleck, pp. 40–2.

54. Ibid. pp. 39–40.

55. George Meade, The Life and Letters of George Gordon Meade, vol. 1 (New York: Charles Scribner's Sons, 1913), p. 108. 14 June 1846.

56. Ibid.

57. Ibid. pp. 91, 108–10.

58. Niles' Register, 29 Aug. 1846.
59. George Ballentine, The Mexican War, By an English Soldier. Comprising incidents and adventures in the United States and Mexico with the American army (New York: W.A. Townsend & Company, 1860), p. 138.
60. Scott, Memoirs, p. 395; Swenson, 'Measures of Conciliation', JMH 86, no. 4 (Oct. 2022), pp. 865–8.
61. American Star – No. 2, Puebla, 1 July 1847. BLAC. See also: Johnson, A Gallant Little Army, pp. 134–5.
62. American Star – No. 2, Puebla, 1 July 1847. BLAC.
63. American Star, Mexico City, 20 Sept. 1847; American Star – No. 2, Puebla, 1 July 1847. BLAC; US Articles of War (Art. 46), Annals of Congress, 9th Congress, 1st Session, Appendix: 'Public Acts of Congress', Washington DC, Library of Congress (LOC), p. 1245.
64. American Star, Mexico City, 23 Sept. 1847. BLAC.
65. Ibid. 20 Sept. 1847. BLAC.
66. Quaife, (ed.), The Diary of James J. Polk during his Presidency, 1845–1849, vol. 1 (Chicago: A.C. McClurg & Co., 1910), pp. 408–11 (19 and 20 May 1846); New York Herald, 27 May 1846.
67. Louisville Morning Courier, Kentucky, 10 July 1846.
68. Freeman's Journal, Dublin, 31 July 1847.
69. Scott, Memoirs, p. 580; Daily American Star, Mexico City, 11 Dec. 1847. BLAC. 'The Ayuntamiento have furnished a list of buildings …'
70. George Ballentine, The Mexican War, By an English Soldier, pp. 255–6; American Star, Mexico City, 23 September 1847. BLAC. Many soldiers who defected prior to the congressional resolution beginning the war (13 May 1846) had their sentences commuted to fifty lashes. This included their leader, John Patrick Riley (O'Riley), who was branded with a 'D' on the cheek – a common punishment for desertion.
71. Thomas W. Spahr, 'Occupying For Peace, The U.S. Army in Mexico, 1846–1848' (PhD diss., The Ohio State University, 2011), pp. 294–6; See: HED No. 60, p. 1004. (LOC). Marcy (Washington DC) to Scott 6 Aug. 1847. Marcy informed Scott of an agreement with an agent (A. Belmont) of 'Rothschild & Sons' in London 'proposing to furnish funds for the use of the army in Mexico. British agents (Thomas W. Ward, Baring Brothers, Boston; Ewen C. MacKintosh, British Consul, Mexico City, 1839–1853) acted as middlemen between the US and Mexico and knew of the large incoming post-treaty indemnity payment. See: Barbara A. Tenenbaum, 'Merchants, Money, and Mischief: The British in Mexico, 1821–1862', The Americas 35, no. 3 (Jan. 1979): pp. 317–39. 'The war … provided marvelous opportunities for a banker… officially connected with the British Government.' (p. 322)
72. American Star, 20 September 1847.
73. American Star, 20, 25 September 1847. BLAC. See: Smith, The War with Mexico, vol. 2, p. 486. 'Transit dues on animals and goods, including the duties at city gates (alcabalas), were to be discontinued.' The alcabala originated in fourteenth-century Spain and became an important source of revenue for its overseas empire. See: Denis E. Berge, 'A Mexican Dilemma: The Mexico City Ayuntamiento and the Question of Loyalty, 1846–1848', The Hispanic American Historical Review 50, no. 2 (May 1970): p. 242. Working with the city council also contributed to lowering tensions during the occupation. Linda Arnold notes that Scott's relationship with Mexico City councillor Manuel Reyes y Veramendi was mostly productive, and Veramendi 'had

become quite well known among the people of the city for his fairness in handling disputes'. See: Linda Arnold, 'The U.S. Intervention in Mexico, 1846–1848', A Companion to Mexican History and Culture (Oxford: William H. Breezley, ed. Blackwell Publishing, 2011), pp. 266–9.

74. Baltimore Sun, 27 Jan. 1848. Winfield Scott, Army Headquarters, 31 Dec. 1847.

75. Morning Post, London, 9 July 1847.

76. American Star, Mexico City, 12 Oct. 1847. BLAC. Liquor was prohibited or severely restricted on holidays. On All Saints Day (1 Nov., Day of the Dead) 'all liquor stores, grog shops, pulque shops, bar-rooms, and other places where spiritous and intoxicating liquors are sold' were closed. (Ibid. 30 Oct. 1847).

77. The Constitution of the Aztec Club of 1847 and the List of Members, 1893 (Washington DC: Judd & Detweiler Printers, 1893), p. 3.

78. American Star, Mexico City, 12, 14 Oct. 1847 BLAC. Joseph Michaud (ed.), The Saracen, Or Matilda and Malek Adhel, A Crusade Romance from the French of Madame Cottin (New York: Isaac Riley, 1810), p. 95; Andrés de la Covert-Spring, Napoleon lo Manda, drama histórico-novelesco, en dos actos, D. Francisco Oliva, Barcelona, 1843.

79. Daily American Star, Mexico City, 15 Oct. 1847. BLAC.

80. Justin H. Smith, The War with Mexico, vol. 2 (New York: Macmillan, 1919), p. 226; Daily American Star, Mexico City, 15 Oct. 1847. BLAC.

81. George Winston Smith and Charles Judah (ed.), Chronicles of the Gringos: The U.S. Army in the Mexican War, 1846–1848 (Albuquerque: University of New Mexico Press, 1968), p. 400. Letter dated 14 March 1848.

82. John Franklin Jameson, ed., Correspondence of John C. Calhoun, vol. 2 (Washington: Government Printing Office, 1900), p. 1163.

83. Scott, Memoirs, p. 396.

Chapter 4: Mexico Invokes the Spanish System

1. Carlos María Bustamante, El Nuevo Bernal Díaz del Castillo, ó sea, Historia de la invasión de los Anglo-Americanos en México (Mexico City: Vicente García Torres, 1847), p. 16.

2. See: Hugh M. Hamill, Jr., 'Royalist Counterinsurgency in the Mexican War for Independence: The Lessons of 1811', The Hispanic American Historical Review 53, no. 3 (Aug. 1973): pp. 470–89.

3. New York Tribune, 11 Nov. 1846.

4. Quoted in: Nathan C. Brooks, A Complete History of the Mexican War: Its Causes, Conduct, and Consequences: Comprising an Account of the Various Military and Naval Operations, from Commencement to the Treaty of Peace (Philadelphia: Grigg, Elliot & Co., 1851), p. 157. 'The Commander-in-chief of the Department of Tamaulipas to the troops under his command.' 13 May 1846.

5. Niles' Register, Baltimore, 12 Sept. 1846. Report from Matamoros 18 Aug. 1846.

6. St Johnsbury Caledonian, Vermont, 14 Nov. 1846.

7. Louisville Morning Courier, Kentucky, 10 Dec. 1846.

8. American Citizen, Canton, Mississippi, 14 Nov. 1846.

9. D. Antonio López de Santa Anna, Apelación al buen criterio de los nacionales y estraneros (Mexico City: Imprenta Cumplido, 1849), p. 43. See: Peter Guardino, The Dead March: A history of the Mexican-American War (Harvard University Press, 2017).

10. Washington Union, 18 Oct. 1847. Letter from La Granja to Santa Anna, New York City, 7 May 1844.
11. Ibid.
12. See: William Fowler, Santa Anna of Mexico (Lincoln: University of Nebraska Press, 2007).
13. Salas and Farías pronouncement from Mexico City, 4 Aug. 1846. University of St Andrews Pronunciamiento Project (USAPP), Mexican War Pronunciamientos; The Pronunciamiento in Independent Mexico 1821–1876. Santa Anna submitted his own manifesto calling for unity 'from its internal and external enemies'.'Manifesto of General Santa Anna', Veracruz, 16 August 1846. See: Swenson, 'Measures of Conciliation', JMH 86, no. 4 (Oct. 2022), pp. 868–71.
14. Fowler, Santa Anna of Mexico, pp. 66–7.
15. 'Plan of the Citadel', Mexico City, 4 Aug. 1846; 'Declaration of the garrison of San Luis Potosí', 9 Aug. 1846. (USAPP).
16. 'Manifesto of General Santa Anna,' Veracruz, 16 Aug. 1846. (USAPP).
17. Ulysses S. Grant, Personal Memoirs of U.S. Grant, vol. 1, pp. 133–4.
18. Weekly National Intelligencer, Washington DC, 15 May 1847. Excerpt from New Orleans Delta quoting from El Monitor, Mexico City, 6 April 1847.
19. HED No. 60, 951. (LOC). Extracts from El Monitor, 21 April 1827.
20. Irving W. Levinson, Wars within War: Mexican Guerrillas, Domestic Elites, and the United States of American, 1846–1848 (Fort Worth: TCU Press, 2005), pp. 34–5; Levinson cites: Reglamento para el servicio de secciones ligera de la guardia nacional de los estados y territoris de la republica, foja XI, 481.3/2586. p. 60, Archivo de la Defensa Nacional, Mexico, D.F.; Louisville Morning Courier, 14 May 1847 (2).'Late from General Scott's Army'.
21. Diario del Gobierno, 2 May 1847 (No. 51), BNE. Quoting: Regenerador Republicano (Puebla), 24 April 1847.
22. Diario del Gobierno, 2 May 1847 (No. 51), BNE.
23. Ibid. BNE.
24. Manuel Muro,Historia de San Luis Potosi, vol. 2 (San Luis Potosi: M. Esquivel y Cía, 1910), p. 419. Letter from Adame to Santa Anna, 23 Jan. 1847.
25. Ramón Adame,'Considerando, que en consecuencia de los últimos acontecimientos de la campaña, puede ser invadido el territorio del Estado por las fuerzas de los Estados-Unidos al mando del general Taylor' (1847). Dupee Mexican History Collection Broadsides. Brown Digital Repository, Providence, Road Island: Brown University Library). Articles 3, 4, 5. See also: Levinson: Wars within War, pp. 34–5.
26. Ibid. Articles 9, 10, 11, 14, 13, 17.
27. Ibid.Articles 18, 33 20, 22, 24, 23.
28. Muro, Historia de San Luis Potosi, vol. 2, p. 535.
29. Muro, Historia de San Luis Potosi, vol. 2, p. 537; Scott, Memoirs, pp. 574–5.
30. Muro, Historia de San Luis Potosí, vol. 2, p. 537.
31. Levinson,Wars within War, p. 100.
32. Michoacan's citizens later renamed the state 'Michoacán de Ocampo,' in honour of Ocampo's service.
33. Melchor Ocampo, Obras Completas de Melchor Ocampo, vol. 2 (Mexico City: F. Vazquez, 1901), p. 262. Circular: 'La Guerra entre Mexico y Norteamérica', 29 April 1847, pp. 263–8.
34. Ibid. p. 267–70 pp.

35. Ibid. pp. 271, 274–5.

36. Baltimore Sun, Maryland, 11 May 1847.

37. Buffalo Commercial, 27 May 1847.

38. Washington Telegraph, Washington, Arkansas, 26 May 1847.

39. Iris Español excerpt via Daily Delta, New Orleans, 27 May 1847. Soult's execution of prisoners, rather than Reille's, was commonly referred to as the general policy of executing guerrillas implemented by Napoleon.

40. Ibid.

41. HED No. 60, pp. 1171–2. LOC. Scott (at Jalapa) to Taylor (near Monterrey) 24 April 1847.

42. Scott, Memoirs, p. 452.

43. HED No. 60, pp. 972–4. LOC. Scott Proclamation at Jalapa, 11 May 1847.

44. Ramón Gamboa, Impugnación al informe del señor General Antonio López de Santa-Anna, y constancias en que se apoyan las ampliaciones de la acusación del señor diputado Don Ramon Gamboa (Mexico City: Vicente García Torres, 1849), p. 33. See also: HED No. 60, p. 959. LOC. Scott (Jalapa) Nicolas Trist (Veracruz) 7 May 1847.

45. HED No. 60, p. 968. LOC. Worth (Puebla) to Scott (Jalapa), 19 May 1847. See: Louisville Morning Courier, 29 June 1847.

46. Diario del Gobierno, 26 May 1847 (No. 75), BNE.

47. The Times, London, 15 June 1847; American Star – No. 2, Puebla, 8 July 1847. BLAC.

48. HED No. 60, pp. 1178–80. LOC. Taylor (Monterrey) to Adjutant General (Washington DC), 16, 23, 30 June 1847.

49. Louisville Morning Courier, Kentucky, 16 June 1847. El Arco Iris (Veracruz) articles cited 30 and 31 May 1847. Infante Don Carlos (1788–1855) was the second surviving son of King Charles IV and claimed the throne after Ferdinand VII's death in 1833. Another group supported the dead king's infant daughter.

50. Weekly National Intelligencer, Washington DC, 31 July 1847. Report from Jalapa 17 June 1847.

51. Liverpool Mercury, 31 Aug. 1847; Leeds Mercury, 26 Sept. 1847.

52. Star of Freedom, Leeds, 10 Oct., 14 Nov. 1846. See: Morning Post, London, 18 Oct. 1848.

53. William R. Manning (ed.), Diplomatic Correspondence of the United States: Inter-American Affairs, 1831–1860, vol. 6 (Dominican Republic, Ecuador, France) (Washington DC: Carnegie Endowment for International Peace, 1935), p. 580. Jacob L. Martin, American Chargé d'Affaires in Paris, to US Secretary of State James Buchanan, 15 May 1847.

54. Congressional Globe, 30th Congress, pp. 252–3. LOC. Senator John Dix (NY), 26 Jan. 1848.

55. Ibid.

56. Frederick Merk, The Monroe Doctrine and American Expansionism, 1843–1849 (New York: Alfred A. Knopf, 1966), pp. 50–4; Quoting: Le Moniteur 11 June 1846; Guizot, Histoire Parlementaire de France, IV (Paris, 1864), pp. 127, 559–73; Washington Union 5 July 1845. Merk notes that in Polk's annual message to Congress in the fall of 1845 the President used the term 'balance of power' three times. 'Thereafter, it was used by Democrats incessantly to suggest that European monarchs were intent on keeping the American world divided.'

57. Weekly National Intelligencer, Washington DC, 4 November 1848. In 1867, the same year the French-installed Mexican emperor Maximilian von Habsburg was executed in Querétaro City, Guizot published a defiant eulogy of his tenure as the architect of French foreign policy in the 1840s – absolving himself and France of much of the wrongdoing regarding the Carlists by blaming the British, the Spanish and Prince Klemens von Metternich, who was Chancellor and Foreign Minister of the Austrian Empire until he too was ousted in the 1848 revolutions that swept Europe. See: François Guizot, The Last Days of the Reign of Louis Philippe (London: R. Bentley, 1867), pp. 125–6.

58. Louisville Morning Courier, Kentucky, 29 June 1847. (Report relayed from the New Orleans Commercial Times).

59. HED No. 60, 1192. LOC. Sec. of War Marcy (Washington DC) to Gen. Taylor (Monterrey), 26 June 1847.

60. American Star – No. 2, Puebla, 1 July 1847. BLAC.

61. St Johnsbury Caledonian, Vermont, 12 June 1847.

62. Times-Picayune, New Orleans, 10 July 1847; Carlos María Bustamante, El Nuevo Bernal Díaz del Castillo, ó sea, Historia de la invasión de los Anglo-Americanos en México (Mexico City: Vicente García Torres, 1847), p. 16.

63. Bustamante, El Nuevo Bernal Díaz del Castillo, p. 138.

64. Diario del Gobierno, 7 July 1847 (No. 116), BNE. The Queretaro article is dated 27 June 1847.

65. Ibid. 23 July 1847 (No. 132), BNE. Michaocán article dated 15 July.

66. Ibid. 21 July 1847. (No. 130), BNE.

67. Ibid. BNE.

68. Ibid. BNE.

69. Ibid.23 July 1847 (No. 132), BNE.

70. Ibid.25 July 1847 (No. 134); 31 July 1847 (No. 140), BNE.

71. Ibid. 7 August 1847 (No. 147), BNE.

72. Ibid. 8 August 1847 (No. 148), BNE. San Luis Potosi, 31 July 1847.

73. Ibid. 9 August 1847 (No. 149), BNE. Morelia, State of Michoacan, 29 July 1847.

74. Public Ledger, Philadelphia, 30 Aug. 1847. Report from New Orleans Picayune (Veracruz) dated 14 Aug.

75. John Bassett Moore, ed. The works of James Buchanan, comprising his speeches, state papers, and private correspondence; vol. 7 (Philadelphia, London, J.B. Lippincott Company, 1909), p. 411. Buchanan to Bancroft, 14 Sept. 1847; HED No. 60, pp. 791–2; Colonel Henry Wilson (Veracruz) to Marcy (Washington DC), 15 Aug. 1847; Morning Chronicle, London, 15 Sept. 1847. Various European royal figures lived on the Rue de Courcelles, including Marie Christine Ferdinande de Bourbon (1806–1878), former Queen and Regent of Spain and mother of Queen Isabella II of Spain. Her uncle was King Louis Philippe. 'Christina had some time ago, and perhaps has still, the notion that it would be possible to establish the Munoz dynasty on the throne of Mexico.'

76. Public Ledger, Philadelphia, 30 Aug. 1847.

77. Diario del Gobierno, 10 Aug. 1847 (No. 150), BNE.

78. Ibid.

79. Ibid. See: Tantoyuca Plan, 7 Jan. 1848. (USAPP) In early January the authorities of Tamaulipas (Tampico) believed the US was attempting 'to conquer our territory', and issued a pronunciamiento. Article 6 of the Tantoyuca Plan rescinded the alcabala.

80. Ibid. 12 Aug. (No. 152), BNE. See also: El Diario, 11 Aug. 1847 (No. 151)

81. Ibid. 15 Aug. 1847 (No. 155), BNE.

82. Ibid. 20 Aug. 1847 (No. 160), BNE.

83. Daily American Star, Mexico City, 14 Oct. 1847. (BLAC). 'Intercepted Letters'.

84. Ibid. 14, 15 Oct. 1847. (BLAC)

85. Fayetteville Weekly Observer, North Carolina, 14 Sept. 1847.

Chapter 5: *Los Diablos Tejanos*

1.   American Star No. 2, Puebla, 8 July 1847. (BLAC).

2.   HED No. 60, pp. 1171–2. LOC. Scott (at Jalapa) to Taylor (near Monterrey) 24 April 1847; Major Ian B Lyles, Mixed Blessing: The Role of The Texas Rangers in The Mexican War, 1846–1848, (Normanby Press, 2015).

3.   American Star, Mexico City, 23 Sept. 1847. (BLAC).

4.   See: Nathan A. Jennings, Riding for the Lone Star: Frontier Cavalry and the Texas Way of War (Denton: University of North Texas Press, 2016). Jennings' term 'cavalry-centric' warfare has been adopted by this author.

5.   Lyles, Mixed Blessing, p. 15.

6.   Ibid.

7.   Grant, Personal Memoirs of U.S. Grant, vol. 1, pp. 69–70.

8.   Ibid. p. 70.

9.   Ibid. pp. 79–80.

10. John Borneman, 'Race, Ethnicity, Species, and Breed: Totemism and Horse-Breed Classification in America'. Comparative Studies and History 30, no. 1 (Jan. 1988), p. 33.

11. Albert M. Gilliam, Travels over the table lands and cordilleras of Mexico. During the years 1843 and 44 (Philadelphia: John W. Moore, 1846), pp. 226–7.

12. Capt. William Seaton Henry, Campaign Sketches of the War with Mexico (New York: Harper and Brothers, 1847), pp. 24–5, 54, 218.

13. Quoted in: Nathan C. Brooks, A Complete History of the Mexican War: Its Causes, Conduct, and Consequences, p. 57. Bancroft (Washington DC) to Taylor (Fort Jesup, LA) 15 June 1846.

14. Stephen B. Oates (ed.), John S. Ford, Rip Ford's Texas (Personal Narratives of the West), p. 89.

15. HED No. 60, p. 955. LOC. Scott (at Jalapa) to Marcy (Washington DC) 6 May 1847.

16. Ibid. p. 959. LOC. Scott (Jalapa) Nicolas Trist (Veracruz) 7 May 1847.

17. Ibid. pp. 1175–8. LOC. Taylor (Monterrey) to Adjutant General (Washington DC) 8, 16 June 1847. See: HED No. 60, pp. 1178–80. LOC. Taylor (Monterrey) to Adjutant General (Washington DC), 23, 30 June 1847.

18. Hartford Courant, Connecticut, 14 Aug. 1847.

19. American Star No. 2, Puebla, 8 July 1847. (BLAC).

20. Daily American Star, Mexico City, 3 Nov. 1847 (BLAC).

21. Lyles, Mixed Blessing, p.5.

22. HED No. 60, 1194. LOC. Marcy (Washington DC) to Taylor (Monterrey), 17 July 1847. Taylor acknowledged receipt of the instructions on 16 Aug..

23. Ibid. pp. 1003–4. LOC. Marcy (Washington DC) to Scott 19 July 1847.

24. New Albany Democrat, 23 Sept. 1847. 'A Letter from the Army'. Quoted in: Oran Perry (ed.), Indiana in the Mexican War (Indianapolis: WM. B. Burford, 1908), p. 226.

25. Washington Union, 10 Sept.1847.

26. Louisville Morning Courier, 28 Oct. 1847. See: F. Cabello, et al, Historia de la guerra últimas en Aragón y Valencia (Zaragoza: IFC, 2006), p. 211. The Guides of Aragon were based in Morella (northern Valencia) during the First Carlist War (1833–1839) under Catalan guerrilla General Ramón Cabrera.
27. Buffalo Commercial, 9 Oct. 1847; Daily American Star, Mexico City, 12 Oct. 1847. (BLAC).
28. Brooklyn Daily Eagle, New York City, 1 Nov. 1847.
29. Times-Picayune, New Orleans, 22 Nov. 1847. See: Evening Post, New York, 29 Nov. 1847.
30. HED No. 60, p. 1007. LOC. Marcy (Washington DC) to Scott, 6 Oct. 1847.
31. Santoni, Mexicans at Arms: Puro Federalists and the Politics of War, 1845–1848 (Fort Worth: Texas Christian University Press, 1996), pp. 215–16; Hitchcock: Fifty Years in Camp and Field, p. 309.
32. Hitchcock, Fifty Years in Camp and Field, p. 309. 26 Nov. 1847. See: Manning, Diplomatic Correspondence, vol. 8 (Mexico), p. 962. Nicholas Trist to James Buchanan, Mexico City, 25 Oct. 1847.
33. Scott, Memoirs, pp. 580–2. Scott declined the 'highly seductive' offer of dictatorship.
34. Weekly National Intelligencer, Washington DC, 11 Dec. 1847.
35. Ford, Rip Ford's Texas, p. 66; The Washington Union, 5 Nov. 1847.
36. Ford, Rip Ford's Texas, pp. 66–9; Washington Union, 5 1847.
37. Washington Union, Washington DC, 18 Nov. 1847; Louisville Morning Courier, 20 Nov.
38. Times-Picayune, New Orleans, 22 Nov. 1847.
39. Times-Picayune, New Orleans, 11 Nov. 1847; Independent Monitor, Tuscaloosa, Alabama, 23 Nov. 1847.
40. Hitchcock, Fifty Years in Camp and Field, p. 335. Lambo was a merchant turned pirate in Byron's satiric poem Don Juan (1819).
41. Ibid. pp. 263–5. Diary entry 20 June 1847. New Orleans, 6 Jan. 1849. Santa Anna offered to pardon Dominguez, which he turned down. (Ibid. pp. 340, 344). For Texan interaction with the smuggling network prior to the war, see Thomas J. Green, Journal of the Texian expedition against Mier; subsequent imprisonment of the author; his sufferings, and the final escape from castle of Perote (New York: Harpers, 1845), pp. 347–57.
42. Smith, The War with Mexico, vol. 2, p. 89.
43. Hitchcock, Fifty Years in Camp and Field, pp. 343–4.
44. Ford, Rip Ford's Texas, p. 76; Louisville Morning Courier, Kentucky, 23 Dec. 1847. (via the El Arco Iris)
45. Abbeville Press and Banner, South Carolina, 24 Nov. 1847. Quoting a letter from a father to son; Wilcox, History of the Mexican War, p. 515. See: Brooklyn Daily Eagle, New York, 17 Jan. 1848. Lane's account. See also: Times-Picayune, New Orleans, 25 Jan. 1848.
46. Baltimore Sun, 6 Jan. 1848. (via The Picayune)
47. Ford, Rip Ford's Texas, pp. 81–2.
48. Fayetteville Weekly Observer, North Carolina, 4 Jan. 1848. News from Times-Picayune, 22 Dec. 1847.
49. Ford, Rip Ford's Texas, pp. 87–8.
50. Celedonio Dómeco Jarauta, 'Viva la republica Mexicana', 19 January 1848 (San Francisco: Sutro Library: California State University, Mexican Pamphlet Collection). Tula is in the state of Hidalgo created in 1869.

51. Ibid. The Sabina River composes the border between Texas and Louisiana.
52. Times-Picayune, New Orleans, 15 Jan. 1848; New Orleans Weekly Delta, 31 Jan. 1848.
53. Washington Union, 17 April 1848. General Joseph Lane report dated 2 March 1848.
54. Daily American Star, Mexico City, 9 Dec. 1848. (BLAC). Wallace L. Ohrt, Defiant Peacemaker: Nicholas Trist and the Mexican War (College Station: Texas A&M University Press, 1997).

Chapter 6: The Allure of Napoleonic Empire

1. Congressional Globe, 30th Congress, Library of Congress (LOC), Washington DC, p. 176. James A. Pearce, 13 Jan. 1848.
2. President Polk's 3rd Annual Message to Congress, 7 Dec. 1847. Congressional Globe, 30th Congress, LOC, Washington DC, p. 6. Polk's message was received by the US Army in Mexico City in late December. See: Daily American Star, Mexico City, 26 Dec. 1847. (BLAC).
3. Ibid. pp. 7–8.
4. Ibid. p. 7.
5. Ibid. See: David M. Pletcher, The Diplomacy of Annexation: Texas, Oregon, and the Mexican War (Columbia: University of Missouri Press, 1973).
6. Ibid. p. 8.
7. HED No. 60. LOC, p. 1005. Marcy to Scott, 1 Sept. 1847.
8. Ibid. p. 994. Scott to Marcy, 4 June 1847, Puebla.
9. Scott, Memoirs, pp. 552–3.
10. President Polk's 3rd Annual Message to Congress, 7 Dec. 1847. Congressional Globe, LOC, p. 8.
11. Edgefield Advertiser, South Carolina, 14 Oct. 1846.
12. Times-Picayune, New Orleans, 14 Oct. 1847. 'Eight More Regiments to be Called.'
13. Flag of Freedom, Puebla, 1 July 1847. (BLAC)
14. Weekly National Intelligencer, Washington DC, 4 Dec. 1847. The article was quoting the Williamsburg Gazette.
15. Buffalo Courier, New York, 28 Jan. 1848.
16. John Franklin Jameson (ed.), Correspondence of John C. Calhoun, vol. 2 (Washington DC: American Historical Society, 1900), p. 737. John C. Calhoun to Thomas G. Clemson, 24 Oct. 1847.
17. Weekly National Intelligencer, Washington DC, 4 Dec. 1847.
18. Ibid.
19. Congressional Globe, LOC, p. 80. Calhoun, 30 Dec. 1847. See Richard R. Stenberg, 'The Failure of Polk's Mexican War Intrigue', Pacific Historical Review 4, no. 1 (Mar. 1935): pp. 39–68; John Douglas Pitts Fuller, The Movement for the Acquisition of All Mexico, 1846–1848 (Baltimore: Johns Hopkins Press, 1936).
20. Franklin, Correspondence of Calhoun, vol. 2, pp. 740–1; Congressional Globe, LOC, pp. 26, 53–6. 339. Calhoun, 20 Dec. 1847. See: Calhoun to Andrew Pickens Calhoun (Correspondence), 4 Dec 1847: The war 'may, indeed, have a different termination … that is, to be held by the Army and Volunteers as an independent country. Keep this to yourself.'
21. Brooklyn Daily Eagle, New York, 22 Nov.; New York Herald, 3, 22 Jan.(1848).
22. Eisenhower, Agent of Destiny, p. 313; Quaife, The Diary of James J. Polk during his Presidency, 1845–1849, vol. 3, p. 271. 31 December 1847. The recall letter was sent on

13 Jan. Like Trist's recall, Congress learned about it later. See: Congressional Globe, LOC, p. 242. 25 Jan. 1848.

23. Congressional Globe, LOC, pp. 87–8. Lewis Cass, 3 Jan. 1848.

24. Ibid. pp. 88–90. See also: Senator James D. Wescott Jr. (Florida), 3 Jan. 1848, pp. 89–90.

25. Ibid. pp. 96–8. John C. Calhoun, 4 Jan. 1848.

26. Ibid. pp. 98–100.

27. Ibid. pp. 111–13. Cass, Crittenden, 5 Jan1848.

28. Ibid. pp. 114–15. Jefferson Davis, 5 Jan. 1848.

29. The Baltimore Sun, 6 Jan. 1848. (via Times-Picayune). Report from Mexico City dated 8 Dec. 1847. See: The Washington Union, 6 Jan. 1848.

30. Quaife, The Diary of James J. Polk, vol. 3, pp. 283, 300–1, (4, 15 Jan. 1848). Scott pushed for Trist to complete the treaty. See: Scott: Memoirs, p. 576. Despite being recalled, 'I encouraged him, nevertheless, the finish the good work he had begun. The Mexican commissioners, knowing of the recall, hesitated. On application, I encouraged them also.'

31. Congressional Globe, LOC, pp. 181–4. William P. Mangum, 17 Jan. 1848. See: Daily American Star, Mexico City, 17 Dec. 1847. (BLAC).

32. Ibid. pp. 184–5. Andrew P. Butler, 17 Jan. 1848.

33. Ibid. p. 204. Patrick W. Tompkins, 19 Jan. 1848.

34. Ibid. p. 242. John C. Clarke (Rhode Island), 25 Jan. 1848.

35. Ibid. p. 296. Caleb B. Smith, 3 Feb 1848.

36. Ibid. pp. 320–2. Jacob Miller, 8 Feb. 1848; Middlebury Register, Vermont, 18 Jan. 1848; Washington Union, Washington DC, 22 Jan. 1848; New York Herald, New York City, 6 Jan. 1848.

37. Congressional Globe, LOC, pp. 328–9. John Milton Niles, 9 Feb. 1848.

38. Natchez Weekly Courier (Mississippi), 29 March 1848 (Quoting El Monitor); New York Herald, 12 July 1848 (excerpt from New Orleans Picayune, 12 July, citing El Monitor); Washington Union, 12 July 1848.

39. New Orleans Crescent, 7 Aug. 1848; Charleston Courier, 12 Aug. 1848.

40. See: Levinson, Wars within War, pp. 85–9.

Bibliography

Abbreviations
AHN: Archivo Histórico Nacional (Madrid)
BLAC: Nettie Lee Benson Latin American Collection, University of Texas, Austin
BNE: Biblioteca Nacional de España (Madrid)
IFC: Institución Fernando el Católico (Zaragoza)
JMH: The Journal of Military History
LOC: Library of Congress, Washington DC
USAPP: University of St Andrews Pronunciamiento Project

Newspapers
American (in Mexico)
American Star – No. 2 (Puebla)
Flag of Freedom (Puebla)
The (Daily) American Star (Mexico City)

American (in USA)
Baltimore Commercial
Green-Mountain Freeman (Montpelier, Vermont)
Fayetteville Weekly Observer (North Carolina)
Hartford Courant (Connecticut)
Middlebury Register (Vermont)
New Orleans Weekly Delta
New York Tribune
Niles' National Register (Baltimore)
Poughkeepsie Journal (New York)
Richmond Enquirer (Virginia)
State Indiana Sentinel (Indianapolis)
The Abbeville Press and Banner (South Carolina)
The American Citizen (Canton, Mississippi)
The Brooklyn Daily Eagle (New York)
The Buffalo Commercial
The Buffalo Courier
The Buffalo Journal
The Charleston Courier (South Carolina)
The Evening Post (New York)
The Fayetteville Weekly Observer (North Carolina)
The Free Soil Courier and Liberty Gazette (Burlington, Vermont)
The Gettysburg Compiler
The Liberator (Boston)
The Louisville Morning Courier (Kentucky)

The Mississippi Free Trader (Natchez)
The Natchez Weekly Courier (Mississippi)
The New Orleans Crescent
The New York Herald
The Pennsylvania Gazette (Philadelphia)
The Pennsylvania Packet (Philadelphia)
The Somerset Herald (Pennsylvania)
The St. Johnsbury Caledonion (Vermont)
The Sunbury Gazette (Pennsylvania)
The Tennessean (Nashville)
The Virginia Gazette, Williamsburg
The Washington Union (DC)
Times-Picayune (New Orleans)
Vermont Aurora (Vergennes)
Vicksburg (Daily) Whig (Mississippi)
Washington Telegraph (Washington, Arkansas)
Weekly National Intelligencer (DC)
Wilmington Journal (North Carolina)

British
Evening Mail (London)
Newcastle Weekly Courant
The Bath Chronicle
The Caledonian Mercury (Edinburgh)
The Derby Mercury
The Liverpool Mercury
The Morning Chronicle (London)
The Morning Post (London)
The Observer (London)
The Times (London)
The Star of Freedom (Leeds)

French (in Spain)
Gazeta de Madrid

Irish
The Freeman's Journal (Dublin)

Mexican
Diario del Gobierno (Mexico City)
El Arco Iris (Veracruz)
El Boletín (Jalapa)
El Monitor Republicano (Mexico City)
Regenerador Republicano (Puebla)

Spanish
Gazeta del Gobierno de México (Mexico City)
Gazeta de Zaragoza
Iris Español (Mexico City)

Primary Sources

Adams, Charles Francis (ed.). *Memoirs of John Quincy Adams, Comprising Portions of His Diary from 1795 to 1848*, Vol. 2. Philadelphia: J.B. Lippincott & Co., 1874.

Annals of Congress, 9th Congress (1805–1807), 1st Session, Appendix: 'Public Acts of Congress', Washington DC: Library of Congress (LOC).

Archivo Histórico Nacional (AHN), Madrid. Accessed: 20 Sept. 2018–1 Nov. 2019. http://pares.culturaydeporte.gob.es/inicio.html.

Ballentine, George. *The Mexican War, By an English Soldier. Comprising incidents and adventures in the United States and Mexico with the American army.* New York: W.A. Townsend & Company, 1860.

Biblioteca Nacional de España: Hemeroteca Digital (BNE). Accessed: 25 Sept. 2018–5 Oct 2019. http://www.bne.es/es/Catalogos/HemerotecaDigital/

Bonaparte, Napoleon. *The Confidential Correspondence of Napoleon Bonaparte with His Brother Joseph, Sometime King of Spain*, 2 Vols. New York: D. Appleton and Company, 1856.

Bourke, Thomas. *A Concise History of the Moors in Spain, From the Invasion of that Kingdom to the Final Expulsion from it.* London: J. Rivington, 1811.

Brooks, Nathan C. *A Complete History of the Mexican War: Its Causes, Conduct, and Consequences: Comprising an Account of the Various Military and Naval Operations, from Commencement to the Treaty of Peace.* Philadelphia: Grigg, Elliot & Co., 1851.

—— *El Nuevo Bernal Diaz del Castillo, ó sea, Historia de la invasión de los Anglo-Americanos en México.* Mexico City: Vicente García Torres, 1847.

Clausewitz, Carl von. *On War (Vom Kriege)*. Berlin, 1832.

Cohen, Myer M. *Notices of Florida and the Campaigns.* Charleston, SC: Burger & Honour, Charleston, 1836.

Congressional Globe, Library of Congress (LOC), 21st–30th Congress, Washington DC, 1829–1849.

Covert-Spring, Andrés de la. *Napoleón lo Manda, drama historico-novelesco, en dos actos.* Barcelona: D. Francisco Oliva, 1843.

D'Aguilar, Sir George Charles, (ed./transl.). *The Officer's Manual: Military Maxims of Napoleon.* Dublin: Richard Milliken and Son, 1831.

Denon, Vivant. *Travels in Upper and Lower Egypt in Company with Several Divisions of the French Army, During the Campaigns of General Napoleon in that Country*, Vol. 1. London: T.N. Longman and O. Rees, 1803.

Espoz y Mina, Francisco.*Memorias del general Don Francisco Espoz y Mina, escritas por el mismo*, 5 Vols. Madrid: M. Rivadeneyra, 1851.

Jameson, John Franklin (ed.). *Correspondence of John C. Calhoun*, Vol. 2. Washington DC: American Historical Society, 1900.

Gamboa, Ramón. *Impugnación al informe del señor General Antonio Lopez de Santa-Anna, y constancias en que se apoyan las ampliaciones de la acusación del señor diputado Don Ramón Gamboa.* Mexico City: Vicente García Torres, 1849.

Gazeta de Madrid. Biblioteca Virtual Miguel de Cervantes. Accessed: 2 Nov. 2018–2 June 2019.www.cervantesvirtual.com

Gilliam, Albert M. *Travels over the table lands and cordilleras of Mexico During the years 1843 and 44.* Philadelphia: John W. Moore, 1846.

Glover, Michael. *The Peninsular War, 1807–1814.* London: Penguin Books, 1974.

Graham, Colonel J.J. *On War: By General Carl von Clausewitz.* London: N. Trübner & Co., 1873.

Grant, Ulysses S. *Personal Memoirs of U.S. Grant*, Vol. 1. New York: Charles L. Webster & Company, 1885.

Green, Thomas J. *Journal of the Texian expedition against Mier; subsequent imprisonment of the author; his sufferings, and the final escape from castle of Perote*. New York: Harpers, 1845.

Grotius, Hugo. *On the Law of War and Peace (De jure belli ac pacis libri tres)*, 1625. Cambridge University Press, 1852.

Guizot, François. *The Last Days of the Reign of Louis Philippe*. London: R. Bentley, 1867.

Halleck, Henry. *Military Art and Science; or Course of Instruction in Strategy, Fortification, Tactics of Battles, &c; Embracing the Duties of Staff Infantry, Cavalry, Artillery, and Engineers, Adapted to the Use of Volunteers and Militia*. New York: D. Appleton & Company, 1846.

Hanoteau, Jean (ed.). *Memoirs of General de Caulaincourt, Duke of Vicenza, 1812–1813*. London: Cassell and Company Limited, 1935.

Hansard's Parliamentary Debates, First Series, Vols. 17, 21, 25. London: UK, 1970.

Headley, Joel Tyler. *The Life of Winfield Scott*. New York: Charles Scribner, 1861.

Henry, Capt. William Seaton. *Campaign Sketches of the War with Mexico*. New York: Harper and Brothers, 1847.

Hitchcock, Ethan Allen. *Fifty Years in Camp and Field*. New York: Ed. W.A. Croffut. G.P. Putnam's Sons, 1909.

Institut d'Égypte. *Memoirs Relative to Egypt, Written in that Country During the Campaigns of General Bonaparte, In the Years 1798 and 1799*. London: T. Gillet, 1800.

Jarauta, Celedonio Dómeco. 'Viva la republica Mexicana'. (19 January 1848). San Francisco: Sutro Library: California State University. Mexican Pamphlet Collection.

Jomini, Antoine-Henri. *Traité des Grandes Opérations Militaire*. Paris: Giguet et Michaud, 1805.

——— *The Art of War*. (1838) Reprint: Philadelphia: J.B. Lippincott & Co., 1862.

——— *Précis de l'Art de la Guerre: Des Principales Combinaisons de la Stratégie, de la Grande Tactique et de la Politique Militaire [The Art of War]*. Brussels: Meline, Cans et Copagnie, 1838.

——— *Life of Napoleon, with Notes by H.W. Halleck*, 4 Vols. New York: D. Van Nostrand, 1864.

——— *Vie politique et militaire de Napoléon*. Paris: Chez Anselin, 1827.

Lejeune, Louise François. *Memorias del general Lejeune, 1792–1813*. Zaragoza: Institución Fernando el Católico (IFC), 2015.

Manning, William R. *Diplomatic Correspondence of the United States Concerning the Independence of Latin American Nations, Vol. 3 (Spain)*. New York: Oxford University Press, 1925.

——— *Diplomatic Correspondence of the United States: Inter-American Affairs, 1831–1860*, Vol. 6 (France), Vol. 7 (Great Britain), Vol. 8 (Mexico). Washington DC: Carnegie Endowment for International Peace, 1935, 1936, 1937 (respectively).

Margaret, Duchess of Newcastle (Charles Harding Firth, ed.). *The Life of William Cavendish, Duke of Newcastle, to which is added the true relation of my birth, breeding, and life*. London: G. Routledge & Sons, 1890.

Meade, George. *The Life and Letters of George Gordon Meade*, Vol. 1. New York: Charles Scribner's Sons, 1913.

Michaud, Joseph (ed.). *The Saracen, Or Matilda and Malek Adhel, A Crusade Romance from the French of Madame Cottin*. New York: Isaac Riley, 1810.

Oates, Stephen B (ed.), Ford, John S. *Rip Ford's Texas (Personal Narratives of the West)*. Austin: University of Texas, 1963.

Ocampo, Melchor. *Obras Completas de Melchor Ocampo*, Vol. 2. Mexico City: F. Vazquez, 1901.

O'Meara, Barry Edward. *Napoleon at St. Helena, 2 Vols*. New York: Scribner and Welford, 1889.

Perry, Oran (ed.). *Indiana in the Mexican War*. Indianapolis: WM. B. Burford, 1908.

Pierce, Darrow and Winfield Scott. *Scott's Militia Tactics; Comprising the Duty of the Infantry, Light-Infantry, and Riflemen*. (Second Edition) Hartford: Oliver D. Cooke, 1821.

Prescott, William H. *The History of the Conquest of Mexico*. New York: The Modern Library, 1843.

Quaife, Milo (ed.). *The Diary of James J. Polk during his Presidency, 1845–1849*. 4 Vols. Chicago: A.C. McClurg & Co., 1910.

'Reviewed Work(s): *Life of Napoleon by Baron Jomini and H. W. Halleck*' The North American Review 99, no. 205 (1864): pp. 573–80.

Rocca, Albert-Jean Michel. *Memoirs of the War of the French in Spain*. London: John Murray, 1815.

Sage, Evan T. *Livy with an English Translation in Fourteen Volumes*, Vol. 9. London: William Heinemann, 1935), p. 445.

San Luis Potosí (State), and Adame, Ramón. 'Considerando, que en consecuencia de los últimos acontecimientos de la campaña, puede ser invadido el territorio del Estado por las fuerzas de los Estados-Unidos al mando del general Taylor' (1847). *Dupee Mexican History Collection Broadsides*. Brown Digital Repository (BDR). Providence, Rhode Island: Brown University Library. Accessed: 1 Nov. 2018–15 Dec. 2018. https://repository.library.brown.edu/studio/item/bdr:602937/.

Scott, Winfield et al. *Abstract of Infantry Tactics; Including Exercises and Manoeuvres of Light Infantry and Riflemen; for the Use of the Militia of the United States*. Boston: Hilliard, Gray, Little, and Wilkens, 1830.

Scott, Lieutenant General Winfield. *Memoirs*. New York: Sheldon, 1864.

Sherer, Moyle (ed.). *The Duke of Wellington: Military Memoirs of Field Marshal*, 2 Vols. (Reprint of 1803) Philadelphia: Robert Desilver, 1836.

Suchet, Louis-Gabriel. *Memoirs of the War in Spain, from 1808 to 1814*, 2 Vols. London: Henry Colburn, 1829.

The Advocate of Peace (1837–1845) 2, no. 14 (Mar. 1839): pp. 232–7.

The Constitution of the Aztec Club of 1847 and the List of Members, 1893. Washington DC: Judd & Detweiler Printers, 1893.

University of St. Andrews Pronunciamiento Project (USAPP), Mexican War Pronunciamientos. Arts and Humanities Council (AHRC), 2007-2010. Accessed 1 Dec. 2018–15 June 2019. https://arts.st-andrews.ac.uk/pronunciamientos.

Vattel, Emer de. *The Law of Nations, or, Principles of the Law of Nature, Applied to the Conduct and Affairs of Nations and Sovereigns* (1758). Philadelphia: T. & J.W. Johnson, Law Booksellers, 1852.

Vernon, Gay de, John Michael O'Conner. *A Treatise on the Science of War and Fortification Composed for the use of the Imperial Polytechnick School, and Military Schools; and Translated for the War Department, for the use of the United States*, vol. 2. New York: J. Seymour, 1817.

Wilcox, Gen. Cadmus M. *History of the Mexican War*. Washington DC: The Church News Publishing Co., 1892.

Secondary Sources

Allaben, Frank. *John Watts de Peyster*, Vol. 2. New York: Frank Allaben Genealogical Society, 1908.

Alonso, Manuel Moreno. *La batalla de Bailén: el surgimiento de una nación*. Madrid: Silex, 2008.

Bassford, Christopher. *Clausewitz in English: The Reception of Clausewitz in Britain and America, 1815–1945*. New York: Oxford University Press, 1994.

Becerra de Becerra, Emilio. *Las hazañas de unos lanceros: Historia del Regimiento de Caballería I de Lanceros de Castilla, según los papeles de Don Julián Sánchez García, 'El Charro'*. (Reprint) Diputación Provincial de Salamanca, 1999.

Bell, David A. *The First Total War: Napoleon's Europe and the Birth of Warfare as We Know It*. Boston: Houghton Mifflin, 2007.

Berouche, Alain. *Pirates, flibustiers et corsaires de René Duguay-Troüin à Robert Surcouf; Le droit et les réalités de la guerre de Course*. Saint-Malo: Éditions Pascal Galodé, 2010.

Birtle, Andrew James. *U.S. Army Counterinsurgency and Contingency Operations, 1860–1941*. Washington DC: United States Army Center of Military History, 1998.

Bonura, Michael A. *Under the Shadow of Napoleon: French Influence on the American Way of Warfare from Independence to the Eve of World War II*. New York: New York University Press, 2012.

Braisted, Todd W. *Grand Forage 1778: The Battleground around New York City*. Yardley, PA: Westholme Publishing, 2016.

Brown, Howard G. *Ending the French Revolution: Violence, Justice, Terror, and Repression from the Terror to Napoleon*. Charlottesville: University of Virginia Press, 2006.

Cabello, F. et al. *Historia de la guerra últimas en Aragón y Valencia*. Zaragoza: Institución Fernando el Católico, 2006.

Edgar, Walter. *Partisans & Redcoats: The Southern Conflict that Turned the Tide of the American Revolution*. New York: Harper Collins, 2001.

Eisenhower, John S.D. *Agent of Destiny: The Life and Times of General Winfield Scott*. New York: The Free Press, 1997.

Elting, John. *Swords around the Throne: Napoleon's Grande Armée*. London: Phoenix Giant, (1989) Reprint, 1997.

Esdaile, Charles. *Fighting Napoleon: Guerrillas, Bandits, and Adventurers in Spain, 1808–1814*. New Haven: Yale University Press, 2004.

Fowler, Will. *Santa Anna of Mexico*. Lincoln: University of Nebraska Press, 2007.

Fuller, John Douglas Pitts. *The Movement for the Acquisition of All Mexico, 1846–1848*. Baltimore: Johns Hopkins Press, 1936.

Gates, David. *The Spanish Ulcer: A History of the Peninsular War*. London: George Allen & Unwin, 1986.

—— *The Napoleonic Wars, 1803–1815*. London: Arnold, 1997.

Girbal, Florentino Hernández. *Juan Martín, El Empecinado: Terror de los franceses*. Madrid: Ediciones Lira, 1985.

Glover, Michael. *The Peninsular War, 1807–1814*. London: Penguin Books, 1974.

Grenier, John. *The First Way of War: American War Making on the Frontier, 1607–1814*. Cambridge University Press, 2005.

Guardino, Peter. *The Dead March: A History of the Mexican-American War*. Harvard University Press, 2017.

Heebøll-Holm, Thomask. *Ports, Piracy, and Maritime War: Piracy in the English Channel and the Atlantic, c. 1280–c. 1330*. Amsterdam: Brill, 2013.

Hillmann, Henning. *The Corsairs of Saint-Malo: Network Organization of a Merchant Elite under the Ancien Régime*. New York: Columbia University Press, 2021.

Jennings, Nathan A. *Riding for the Lone Star: Frontier Cavalry and the Texas Way of War*. Denton: University of North Texas Press, 2016.

Johannsen, Robert A. *To the Halls of the Montezumas: The Mexican War in the American Imagination*. New York: Oxford University Press, 1985.

Johnson, Timothy D. *Winfield Scott: The Quest for Military Glory*. Lawrence: University Press of Kansas, 1998.

—— A Gallant Little Army: The Mexico City Campaign. Lawrence: University Press of Kansas, 2007.

Larrañaga, Ramon Guirao. Guerrilleros y Patriotas en el Alto Aragón (1808–1814). Huesca: Editorial Pirineo, 2000.

Levinson, Irving W. Wars within War: Mexican Guerrillas, Domestic Elites, and the United States of America, 1846–1848. Fort Worth: TCU Press, 2005.

Lyles, Major Ian B: Mixed Blessing: The Role of The Texas Rangers In The Mexican War, 1846–1848. Normanby Press, 2015.

Matysak, Philip. Sertorius and the Struggle for Spain. Barnsley, UK: Pen and Sword, 2013.

Merk, Frederick. The Monroe Doctrine and American Expansionism, 1843–1849. New York: Alfred A. Knopf, 1966.

Ohrt, Wallace L. Defiant Peacemaker: Nicholas Trist and the Mexican War. College Station: Texas A&M University Press, 1997.

Oman, Charles. A History of the Peninsular War, 5 Vols. Oxford: Clarendon Press, 1908.

Pérez, Andrés Cassinello. Juan Martín, 'El Empecinado', o el amor a la libertad. Madrid: Editorial San Martín, 1995.

Pletcher, David M. The Diplomacy of Annexation: Texas, Oregon, and the Mexican War. Columbia: University of Missouri Press, 1973.

Ross, Michael. The Reluctant King: Joseph Bonaparte: King of the Two Sicilies and Spain. London: Sidgwick & Jackson, 1976.

Santoni, Pedro. Mexicans at Arms: Puro Federalists and the Politics of War, 1845–1848. Fort Worth: Texas Christian University Press, 1996.

Smith, George Winston and Charles Judah (ed.). Chronicles of the Gringos: The U.S. Army in the Mexican War, 1846–1848. Albuquerque: University of New Mexico Press, 1968.

Smith, Justin. The War with Mexico, 2 Vols. New York: Macmillan, 1919.

Spahr, Thomas W. 'Occupying for Peace: The U.S. Army in Mexico, 1846–1848'. PhD diss., The Ohio State University, 2011.

Syse, Henry and Gregory M. Reichburg. Ethics, Nationalism, and Just War: Medieval and Contemporary Perspectives. Washington DC: Catholic University of America Press, 2007.

Tone, John Lawrence. The Fatal Knot: The Guerrilla War in Navarre and the Defeat of Napoleon in Spain. Chapel Hill: The University of North Carolina, Press, 1995.

Varga, Daniel. The Roman Wars in Spain: The Military Confrontation with Guerrilla Warfare. Barnsley, UK: Pen and Sword, 2015.

Weigley, Russel. The Partisan War: The South Carolina Campaign of 1780–1782. Columbia: University of South Carolina Press, 1975.

Articles

Alexander, Don. W. 'French Replacement Methods during the Peninsular War, 1808-1814'. Military Affairs 44, no. 4 (Dec. 1980): pp. 192–7. [The Journal of Military History]

—— 'French Military Problems in Counterinsurgent Warfare in Northeastern Spain, 1808–1813'. Military Affairs 40, no. 3 (Oct. 1976): pp. 117–22. [The Journal of Military History]

Arnold, Linda. 'The U.S. Intervention in Mexico, 1846–1848'. (pp. 262–72) A Companion to Mexican History and Culture. Oxford: William H. Breezley, ed. Blackwell Publishing, 2011.

Denis E. Berge. 'A Mexican Dilemma: The Mexico City Ayuntamiento and the Question of Loyalty, 1846–1848'. The Hispanic American Historical Review 50, no. 2 (May 1970): pp. 229–56.

Bonura, Michael A. 'A French-Inspired Way of War: French Influence on the U.S. Army from 1812 to the Mexican War'. *Army History*, no. 90 (Winter 2014): pp. 6–22.

Borneman, John. 'Race, Ethnicity, Species, and Breed: Totemism and Horse-Breed Classification in America'. *Comparative Studies and History* 30, no. 1 (Jan. 1988): pp. 25–51.

Díaz Terrejón, Francisco Luis. 'El movimiento guerrillero en España durante la ocupación napoleónica (1808-1814)'. *Iberoamericana (2001–) Nueva época*, Año 8, No. 31 (Sept. 2008): pp. 129–35.

Elliot, Maj. Charles W. (ed.). 'Some Unpublished Letters of a Roving Soldier-Diplomat: General Winfield Scott's Reports to Secretary of State James Monroe, on conditions in France and England in 1815–1816'. *The Journal of the American Military Foundation*1, no. 4 (Winter 1937/8): pp. 165–73.

Fabel, Robin F.A. 'The Laws of War in the 1812 Conflict'. *Journal of American Studies* 14, no. 2 (Aug. 1980): pp. 199–218.

Hamill Jr., Hugh M. 'Royalist Counterinsurgency in the Mexican War for Independence: The Lessons of 1811'. *The Hispanic American Historical Review* 53, no. 3 (Aug. 1973): pp. 470–89.

Hendrix, W.S. 'Military Tactics in the 'Poem of the Cid'. *Modern Philology* 20, no. 1 (Aug. 1922): pp. 45–8.

Jensen, Geoffrey. 'Military consequences of cultural perceptions: The Spanish army in Morocco, 1912–1927'. *The Journal of the Middle East and Africa*8, no. 2 (2017): pp. 135–50.

Johnson, James Turner. 'Maintaining the Protection of Non-combatants' in (Syse and Reichburg) *Ethics, Nationalism, and Just War: Medieval and Contemporary Perspectives*. Washington DC: Catholic University of America Press, 2007.

Kagan, Richard L. 'Prescott's Paradigm: American Historical Scholarship and Decline of Spain'. *The American Historical Review* 101, no. 2 (Apr. 1996): pp. 423–46.

Knobler, Adam. 'Holy Wars, Empires, and the Portability of the Past: The Modern Uses of Medieval Crusades'. *Comparative Studies in Society and History* 48, no. 2 (April 2006): pp. 293–325.

Laqueur, Walter. 'The Origins of Guerrilla Doctrine'. *Journal of Contemporary History* 10, no. 3 (July 1975): pp. 341–82.

Mahon, John K. 'Anglo-American Methods of Indian Warfare, 1676–1794'. *The Mississippi Valley Historical Review*45, no. 2 (Sept. 1958): pp. 254–75.

North, Jonathan. 'General Hoche and Counterinsurgency'. *The Journal of Military History* 67, no. 2 (April 2003): pp. 529–40.

Saglia, Diego. 'O My Mother Spain!: The Peninsular War, Family Matters, and the Practice of Romantic Writing'. *ELH*65, no. 2 (Summer 1998): pp. 363–93.

Schmidt-Nowara, Christopher. 'The Broken Image: The Spanish Empire in the United States after 1898'. *Endless Empire: Spain's Retreat, Europe's Eclipse, America's Decline* (Alfred W. McCoy, Josep M. Fradera, Stephen Jacobson, ed.) University of Wisconsin Press, Madison, 2012: pp. 160–6.

Skelton, William B. 'Army Officers Attitudes toward Indians, 1830–1860'. *The Pacific Northwest Quarterly* 67, no. 3 (July 1976): pp. 113–24.

Smith, Justin. 'La Republica de Rio Grande'. *The American Historical Review* 25, no. 4 (July 1920): pp. 660–75.

—— 'The Mexican Recognition of Texas'. *The American Historical Review* 16, no. 1 (Oct. 1910): pp. 36–55.

Stenberg, Richard R. 'The Failure of Polk's Mexican War Intrigue'. *Pacific Historical Review* 4, no. 1 (Mar. 1935): pp. 39–68.

Swenson, Benjamin J. ' "Measures of Conciliation": Winfield Scott, Henry Halleck, and the Origins of US Army Counterinsurgency Doctrine'. *The Journal of Military History* 86, no. 4 (Oct. 2022): pp. 859–81.

Tenenbaum, Barbara A. 'Merchants, Money, and Mischief. The British in Mexico, 1821– 1862'. *The Americas* 35, no. 3 (Jan. 1979): pp. 317–39

Warren, Harris Gaylord. 'The Origin of General Mina's Invasion of Mexico'. *The Southwestern Historical Quarterly* 42, no. 1 (July 1938): pp. 1–20.

Yates, John D., and Henry Halleck. 'Insurgents on the Baja Peninsula: Henry Halleck's Journal of the War in Lower California, 1847–1848'. *California Historical Quarterly* 54, no. 3 (1975): pp. 221–44.

Index